Using
Social Theory

Using Social Theory: Thinking Through Research
This book provides some of the core teaching for a 16-week course (D834 *Human Geography, Philosophy and Social Theory*) which is offered by The Open University Master's Programme in the Social Sciences.

The Open University Master's Programme in the Social Sciences
The MA/MSc programme enables students to select from a range of modules to create a programme to suit their own professional or personal development. Students can choose from a range of social science modules to obtain an MA in the Social Sciences or specialize in one subject area; or may choose to follow an MS in Research Methods in a specific discipline area. The course *Human Geography, Philosophy and Social Theory* (D834) is part of the MSc in Human Geography Research Methods.

OU-supported learning
The Open University's unique, supported ('distance') learning Master's Programme in the Social Sciences is designed to facilitate engagement at an advanced level with the concepts, approaches, theories and techniques associated with a number of academic areas of study. The Social Sciences Master's programme provides great flexibility. Students study in their own environments, in their own time, anywhere in the European Union. They receive specially prepared course materials, benefit from structured tutorial support throughout all the coursework and assessment assignments, and have the chance to work with other students.

How to apply
If you would like to register for this programme, or simply find out more information, please write for the Master's Programme in the Social Sciences prospectus to the Course Information and Advice Centre, PO Box 724, The Open University, Milton Keynes, MK7 6ZS, UK (telephone +44 (0)1908 653231) (e-mail: general-enquiries@open.ac.uk). Alternatively, you may wish to visit the Open University website at www.open.ac.uk where you can learn more about a wide range of courses and packs offered at all levels by The Open University.

Using
Social Theory

Thinking Through
Research

Edited by
**Michael Pryke, Gillian Rose
and Sarah Whatmore**

SAGE Publications
London • Thousand Oaks • New Delhi

in association with

The Open
University

SAGE Publications Ltd
6 Bonhill Street
London EC2A 4PU

SAGE Publications Inc
2455 Teller Road
Thousand Oaks, California 91320

SAGE Publications India Pvt Ltd
B-42, Panchsheel Enclave
Post Box 4109
New Delhi – 100 017

British Library Cataloguing in Publication data

A catalogue record for this book is available from the British Library

ISBN 0 7619 4376 5
ISBN 0 7619 4377 3 (pbk)

Library of Congress Control Number available

Typeset by Mayhew Typesetting, Rhayader, Powys
Printed and bound in Great Britain by The Cromwell Press, Trowbridge, Wiltshire

Contents

Notes on Contributors

John Allen is Professor of Economic Geography, Department of Geography, The Open University. His recent publications include *Lost Geographies of Power* (Blackwell, 2003) and *Rethinking the Region: Spaces of Neoliberalism* (Routledge, 1988) with Doreen Massey and Allan Cochrane.

Nick Bingham is lecturer, Department of Geography, The Open University. He has edited *Contested Environments* (Wiley, 2003) with Andrew Blowers and Chris Belshaw, and published work on the challenging geographies of electronic and bio-technologies. Current research focuses on the contestation of innovation.

Nigel Clark is lecturer, Department of Geography, The Open University. He is the editor of Environmental Changes: Global Challenges (Open University, 2003) with Mark Brandon, and is currently researching geopolitics, ethics and non-human agency.

Mike Crang is a lecturer in the Department of Geography, University of Durham. His recent books are *Tourism: Between Place and Performance* (Berghahn, 2002) edited with Simon Coleman, *Thinking Space* (Routledge, 2000) edited with Nigel Thrift, *Virtual Geographies* (Routledge, 1999) edited with Phil Crang and Jon May. His current work is on electronic communication and urbanity.

Doreen Massey is Professor of Geography, Department of Geography, The Open University. Her books include *Spatial Divisions of Labour* (Macmillan, 2nd Edition, 1995), *Space, Place and Gender* (Polity, 1994) and *Power Geometries and the Politics of Space-Time* (Heidelberg, 1999). She is co-founder and co-editor of *Soundings: a Journal of Politics and Culture* (Lawrence and Wishart).

Michael Pryke is lecturer, Department of Geography, The Open University. He has edited *Cultural Economy* (Sage, 2002) with Paul du Gay, and *Unsettling Cities: Movement and Settlement* (Routledge, 1999) with John Allen and Doreen Massey. His most recent research is on cultures of money and finance.

Gillian Rose is senior lecturer, Department of Geography, The Open University. She has taught feminist and cultural geographies at the Universities of London and Edinburgh, and her publications include *Feminism and Geography* (Polity, 1993) and *Visual Methodologies* (Sage, 2001).

Nigel Thrift is a Professor in the School of Geographical Sciences at the University of Bristol. His main research interests are in international finance, the history of clock time, the intersections between biology and information technology, management knowledges and non-representational theory. Recent publications include *Cities* (Polity, 2002) with Ash Amin, *The Handbook of Cultural Geography* (Sage, 2003) co-edited with Kay Anderson, Mona Domosh and Steve Pile and *Patterned Ground* (Reaktion, 2003) co-edited with Stephan Harrison and Steve Pile.

Sarah Whatmore is Professor of Geography, Department of Geography, The Open University. Her most recent book is *Hybrid Geographies: Natures, Cultures, Spaces* (Sage, 2002).

Preface

This book forms the core of *Human Geography, Philosophy and Social Theory*, one course in the MSc in Human Geography Research Methods at The Open University. The book began life several years ago. It is the outcome of many conversations and is very much the product of a collective enterprise. At the end of this journey, needless to say, debts of gratitude are owed to a number of people. Thanks should be extended to the Course Manager, Caitlin Harvey, who successfully guided the book and its related materials through an administrative obstacle field and kept us on course. Professor Chris Philo of the Department of Geography, University of Glasgow, offered excellent advice and suggestions as part of his role as external assessor. A number of his postgraduate students – Kate Briggs, Allan Lafferty, Richard Kyle – responded superbly to our request to read and comment on drafts of all chapters; they provided full and helpful comments. Thanks are also due to Susie Hooley for secretarial and administrative support, and to the OU editor Melanie Bayley, and to Chris Williams of the Masters Programme Board, Faculty of Social Sciences. Lastly, thanks to Robert Rojek of Sage for his enthusiasm for the project.

Michael Pryke, Gillian Rose, Sarah Whatmore
on behalf of The Open University Course Team

Introduction

Michael Pryke, Gillian Rose and Sarah Whatmore

Many of you may have read or be about to read an impressive-sounding list of books and journal articles that fall within a category often referred to as 'social theory' or 'philosophy'. You may well be familiar with names such as Michel Foucault, Jacques Derrida, Elisabeth Grosz, Bruno Latour, Richard Rorty . . . and this is just the beginning of what could easily become a lengthy list, one happily recited with the encouragement of those who say they 'do theory'. To work with the materials that such social theorists and philosophers offer is to engage in abstract knowledge and ideas. If we follow any one of these theorists, we are theorizing or philosophizing – speculating, playing with ideas, contentions, opinions and beliefs – about the world, but according to the particular sets of procedures and assumptions that each standpoint contains. Hence those who are quite often unfairly referred to as 'theory junkies' may be heard describing themselves say as 'Foucauldians', as adopting a 'Foucauldian approach' to a particular issue; those following Latour may well say that they are adopting an 'Actor Network Theory' approach, and so on. Yet what is less clear is how the move is made between talking the theory talk and walking the theory walk: that is, between reading the social theory and philosophy, and actually putting it to use in research. What does it mean, in other words, to engage in research and to follow a particular social theorist or philosopher? The question is asked because some may argue that, while philosophizing or theorizing may seem intellectually attractive, it is quite another matter figuring out how abstract ideas are to be deployed when doing research. Put more bluntly, some may ask what difference is social theory or philosophy supposed to make to the conduct and outcome of research?

Thinking through research

In many ways we gave the book its subtitle 'thinking through research' in the anticipation of such issues. Admittedly, as a subtitle it may seem a little odd, for it implies that there is such a process as unthinking research. And in a way there is. To some people, it's tempting to say, research and thinking – or, more accurately, thinking with the aid of theoretical materials – are almost two separate activities. Maybe this provocation needs some qualification. If thinking is associated with social theory and philosophy, then thinking in this sense is not felt to be the stuff of sound and rigorous research. In the mind's eye of this approach, research is something that is simply done: it's a practical thing – you just get out there and do it. It is not something to be contemplated or subjected to speculation or indeed scrutinized for its often implicit assumptions. What is more, as each stage of the research process is already clearly labelled – you get the question, you do the empirical work, you analyse and write up – such is the clarity of the signposting that the whole matter of research should be quite straightforward, or so it would seem.

In this book, in contrast, we argue that research and thinking *should* run alongside one another. As the chapters develop, it becomes clearer that research is not a straightforward process. In the messiness of research, the concerns of theory and research already run together, even for those who see themselves as free from such supposedly dispassionate pursuits. After all, the idea of rigour and rigorous research, the easy division between inside and outside ('going out and doing research'), all betray a certain philosophical position about the world, about the researcher and the objects (humans and non-humans) to be encountered in the research process. Even something seemingly as innocuous as 'writing up' is not a theory-free zone, in so far as the process of writing is itself not free from conjecture and issues such as representation and reflexivity, forms of analysis, and writer–audience relationships. Equally, philosophical stand-points, as ways of understanding the world, contribute significantly to the formulation of a research question, in that they draw attention to issues of creativity, originality and, indeed, the limits of what it is possible to ask.

As a *guide* to these kinds of issues, this book offers suggestions as to what they mean for *doing* research and the consequences, intellectual or otherwise, they entail. This is not so much a 'how to do' book in the conventional methods sense, as one that sets out to give you the tools, skills and dexterity to think your way through the research process. As such, you will find little in the way of rules, techniques or prescriptions in the text, but you will find a series of prompts designed to hone your thinking skills and crafts.

Thinking skills and crafts

In this book, we consider philosophy and social theory as something of a *resource* in the research process. The philosophical materials that it has to offer are not 'add-on', but rather are introduced as sets of ideas, values, and assumptions appropriate to the different stages of the research process. The result, we hope, is a series of philosophically informed crafts and a range of craft-informed philosophies. Thinking through research, we would argue, can make a difference to how you set about the task of doing research: how you recognize the implicit assumptions in your research, the consequences of following one line of inquiry and the implications of choosing between different approaches and theoretical positions. Indeed, the crafts that are the active outcomes of such an engagement frequently include the often taken-for-granted skills such as reading and writing, as well as more abstract-sounding practices like conceptualizing and analysing.

In this sense, philosophy acts as an aid to reflect upon but not resolve debates between contrasting views, alternative positions and diverse accounts of the world that forms the focus of our research.

Understood as a resource, with a variety of views, beliefs and speculations, this book guides you in the thinking appropriate to different stages of the research process. To take an example from Part I of the book, 'Asking Questions', if we follow the pragmatism of Richard Rorty in generating a research question, we flag the importance of language, of the development of new vocabularies and the seductive power of metaphorical redescription. The skill or craft is to select a research question that works better for certain descriptive purposes than does any previous tool. Should this line be followed, the research question generated becomes a tool for doing something that could not have been done under a previous set of descriptions. To follow another route, say that of realism, means that the research question is the outcome of different concerns and emphases, such as the rigour of conceptualization which determines the quality of access to a world 'out there'. The prompts that emerge from following this line of thinking mean that research questions may be judged by their deemed usefulness in terms of how well they approximate to the way the world is. In this way philosophies and theoretical standpoints are thought of as sets of resources to be worked with and alongside the research process. Philosophy and social theory as resources become sets of tools for engaging in research.

Thinking through approaches

There are, of course, many ways to approach philosophy. In your research career thus far, you may have opted to pursue a theoretical line different from the ones explored in this book. Alternatively, you may have little or no experience of abstract ideas as such. Another likely possibility is that you have already broached some of the issues addressed in this book through the prism of social theory – through various '-isms' and '-ologies'. Because our route has been different we have not spent time with the '-isms' you may read about should you have come to philosophy via this path. So, in the chapters that follow, you will not come across references to the linguistic turn, or lengthy introductions to the crisis of representation, or to realism, and so on. The main reason for the absence of in-depth discussions of each of these – admittedly significant – moments in the recent history of the social sciences is that this book is not about philosophy as such but about the differences that it makes to the skills, processes and outcomes of engaging in research. This is a book that deals with the contemplative part of a methods course and so, for us, the way we have thought about philosophizing or theorizing and its influences is with an engagement in research in mind. And given the similarities between the research process and philosophizing and theorizing, as we have noted, each stage of the research – reflected in the book's three main parts – in many ways chose their philosophical and theoretical figures.

The selection thus includes only those figures whose ideas and assumptions have some purchase on the research process. To take an example from Part II of the book, 'Investigating the Field', the figures chosen – Bruno Latour and Isabelle Stengers – are considered together because their concerns speak to and inform an exploration of the task of generating research materials in the field. Stengers' notion of 'mapping into knowledge' is used to elaborate the ways in which the task of knowledge production (because, some may say, that's exactly what is going on through empirical work) might be approached as a co-fabrication between the researcher and the diverse others engaged in the research process. This notion emphasizes how an approach (made through a certain philosophical position), which considers the researcher 'going out and doing empirical work', masks how this stage of the research process jointly produces 'data'. It is a reminder of the limitations of thinking that the researcher alone produces knowledge or 'facts'.

Moreover, the choice of philosophers and theorists, and philosophies and theories, has also been made in relation to what certain approaches have to say about each stage of the research process, such as the production of a research question, the generation of data, and so on. For example, in Part III, the 'just do it' approach to writing up is quizzed with the aid of Jacques Derrida and Bruno Latour. Both – in their own distinct ways – are critical of the 'fantasy of an unproblematic mode' of writing up social science. Their concerns speak to our reflections on what might be involved and what it might mean to write in other ways. Yet this is not to suggest that any one figure referred to at a certain stage of the research process is *the* figure to be used in, say, writing or embarking on fieldwork. Rather, the dialogue struck emerges from issues relevant to that particular stage of the research process. The choice of Latour and Stengers in Part II or of Rorty and Luce Irigaray in Part I reflects current thoughtful possibilities relating to field*work* and the asking of questions respectively, but they do not exhaust what can be said about such matters, nor are they restricted merely to these practices. What all of the chapters help to do is to develop skills that you may use to approach your research materials and hence to equip you to work with any particular intellectual influence that you may wish to employ in your research. In this way, a productive, almost circular process is encouraged: to research through reflecting, mulling over, speculating, is to practise the continual honing of thinking crafts to be employed and shaped further through research. What this also means is that you may use the conversational styles presented in the various chapters to help you to address the range of materials and so help to direct their concerns to the concerns of your research. Such a skill – and it is a skill to have learnt the confidence to converse theoretically, to ask questions of philosophers and social theorists – should allow you to take any one approach, whether it's from this book or elsewhere does not matter, and to follow it throughout the research process.

Thinking through histories

A word of caution: the chapters and the book are not about any one figure or philosophy or theory. This means that you will not come away from the book with an exhaustive knowledge of, say, Latour or Derrida, Gilles Deleuze or Michel Foucault. We hope, however, that you will learn to be comfortable among the writings of such figures, will feel able to ask questions of their work, and will appreciate why embarking on such a task brings research and the skills of thinking together to produce 'better research'.

As you will soon realize, if you have not guessed it already, very few, if any, of the issues introduced in this book are entirely 'new'. The figures you will come across, the questions and issues they address, form part of long, entwined histories. For example, Rorty's position can be traced back to a critique of the seventeenth-century figure, René Descartes. Rorty's sense of what makes a question, for instance, comes out of that particular critique and the way his thinking has been shaped by the likes of Dewey, Peirce, Heidegger and Wittgenstein. Writers and intellectual figures such as Stengers, Deleuze, Derrida, and others in the book, form part of what is often referred to as 'continental philosophy', a set of conversations that has been ongoing since the publication of Kant's critical philosophy in the late eighteenth century. And while the traces of many of the convictions, values and intellectual concerns have been around for a long time, the materials we have chosen broadly reflect current ways of posing research issues.

By current, we mean, for example, that in certain chapters you will come across figures, such as Rorty, Deleuze and Derrida, whose approach highlights language, because for them language is all-important. When they were writing their key texts it was the time of crisis of representation, the linguistic and the cultural turn, and so these events naturally embody some form of engagement for them. In turn, such events served to shape how we may understand and perceive the research process and its different components. At the time we came to write this book, the intellectual moment was slightly different. This does not mean that the importance of language as an approach has diminished, far from it, but it does mean that other approaches, such as materiality – most strongly represented in this book by the writings of Bruno Latour and Isabelle Stengers – are introduced into the conversation.

There is a contextuality to events and ideas, and although current ways of asking questions, investigating and writing owe much to past practices, they also bear the hallmark of present debates and flights of thought. What this contextuality also makes clear is that there is a need to display a degree of humility simply because what we think we 'know' now, may well be undermined in the not too distant future. 'Newness' does not necessarily equate with best. Nevertheless, whether 'old' or 'new', the point is that philosophical materials can enhance our grasp of just what it is that we do when we practise research; that we need to stand back and reflect rather than getting 'out there' and 'just doing it'.

Thinking through the consequences

What is the value of working with philosophical and theoretical approaches and themes? Pause and reflect for a moment on how we can be sure about the way the world is. How might we think about our relationship to the people or objects we are about to investigate? To reflect in this way is itself a philosophical act and it is more than halfway to recognizing that there are philosophical assumptions we act and think with everyday. It's just that they make up our common sense and so are not recognizable as 'philo-sophies' because philosophies, particularly those with a big 'P', are seen as external to us, as it were. Perhaps the chief value of contemplating and reflecting alongside abstract influences is to recognize that this is not so. Even claims we make about the daily run of the world bear the traces of (quite often long-dead) beliefs.

The variety of such influences means that in this book the chapters do not collectively present a single 'take' on philosophy or social theory. We do not present one set of implications for the research process as a whole, but rather a plurality of views and thoughts. And because of this variety, a whole series of tensions, albeit productive tensions, understandably emerge between the philosophies discussed. Derrida and Latour, to take two key figures from 'continental philosophy' discussed in a number of chapters, have their differences (expressed occasionally in quite scathing terms); Deleuze, Rorty and Irigaray at times sit uncomfortably together. The point, however, is that the discussions of their influences and what each can tell us about moments in the research process, are not meant to produce harmony. This is an occasion where discord is productive and it is achieved through a continual engagement with philoso*phies*. The whole text thus does not add up to a single method for thinking philoso*phy* – and here we could add ideas or theoretical approaches – through research. What it does add up to, however, is the accumulation of skills acquired by using philosophy to think through research.

Although the book follows the usual research sequence from begin-ning to ask questions to the task of writing up the findings, it is hoped that the book will be used in a number of ways as the reader revisits chapters for what they can offer at different moments in the research process. There is a point to be made here about the non-linearity of doing research and this reflects our wish to convey the importance of returning to the text, dipping in where appropriate, as an issue grabs you – but not for the first (or indeed possibly the last) time.

In the tentative guidance that follows, we hope that the tone of the various conversations set, where authors frequently draw on their own experiences and their tussles with often quite abstract ideas, invites optimism about doing research. Overall, the chapters present an invitation to act upon the materials of this book by employing them iteratively, where the continuous shaping and reshaping of research as a process mirrors your own doubts, as well as passions. In this way we hope that they allow you to work your own experiences and interests – and, yes, enthusiasms – through the text. After all, what's the point of research if you cannot do it passionately, as well as, of course, philosophically?

PART I
Asking questions

INTRODUCTION
Gillian Rose

Much of the excitement and the trepidation of starting a new research project depends on the development of a question that can generate an answer and the excitement often lies in asking new questions which invite equally clear and specific answers. However, not all kinds of questioning need be of this type, and demonstrating this diversity is in a way the main purpose of Part I. Different kinds of question exist. There are different modes of questioning, and these different modes also often have rather different senses of what might constitute 'an answer'. Chapter 1 offers one version of questioning where the posing of a question is to anticipate the kind of answer that we might offer, whereas Chapter 2 adopts a more experimental version that highlights the 'not yet fully worked through' question as a formative moment of the research process. Chapter 3 offers another: it looks at the work of a writer who sprinkled questions liberally throughout her work, especially her early work, but who very rarely offered a direct answer to any of them. It is with the possibility of asking questions differently, of adopting a questioning stance to questions, that the relevance of philosophy to the process of generating a research question lies. If, as the book Introduction has just suggested, the task of philosophy is to think about the basic assumptions that underlie our understandings and practices, then it is important to give some thought to the assumptions you are making when you think about 'a question'. The three chapters in Part I try to show how philosophy does indeed matter to thinking about, and creating, research questions.

Questions, after all, raise some profound issues about what kind of knowledge is possible and desirable, and how it is to be achieved. For example, do all questions have to be made in words? What constitutes an answer? Who or what is able to answer back? What is a solution? What is truth, or credibility? How important is doubt to all this? What is a subject and how is it made? Each of the three chapters here take some philosophical work that does, in its own way, broach some of these themes, and each chapter pulls out the implications of those philosophies for the kinds of question a research project might ask.

Each chapter starts off, at least, with that notion of a question being a form of words. The first chapter, which brings parts of Rorty's and Foucault's work into conversation, suggests that questions, and answers, do indeed have to be framed in words, in language, in human systems of understanding. Questions are produced through language; they have to be formulated through words and can only be answered by words. The second chapter, however, explores the work of two philosophers who challenge the assumption that, as Rorty claims, 'language goes all the way down'. Deleuze and Derrida suggest, in contrast, that the most productive questioning might happen as a consequence of events that have little to do with language. Inspiration and creativity, they suggest, depend more on the contingency and play of everyday life, a life which far exceeds the limits of language. As a consequence, their take on questions suggests that they are less forms of words and more a mode of living, a mode which is open and receptive to the richness and unpredictability of living in the world. Chapter 3 looks at how just one aspect of this richness might also affect the practice of questioning. Working with Irigaray and Grosz, it explores how human bodies may force certain kinds of questioning on us. Again, this questioning is not confined entirely to the linguistic; and it also problematizes the kinds of answer it invites.

All of this philosophical work, different as it is in so many ways, displaces the idea that the research question is a simple starting point. In its demand that we need to think about our questions – their structure, their medium, their origin – these philosophies suggest that research questions are made and not found; they are generated and not discovered. The formulation of a research question is itself a process in which philosophical considerations must play a part. Part I demonstrates how philosophies entail a range of consequences for the process of doing research and how we ask research questions.

A question of language

John Allen

Introduction

At an early stage of your research project, at a welcome moment or not, someone is likely to ask you what your research is all about. What exactly, you hear them say, is the question (or questions) that you hope to answer through your work? Now, even if your plans are still rather vague, you will be expected to give an answer of sorts. You will have had some thoughts on this anyway, so at least you will be able to offer a tentative answer or provide a first stab at a research question. But that does not always suppress the doubt – well not for me at least – that last week's question, which seemed so apt at the time, is now beginning to look a little unfocused, woolly even, as new angles emerge and fresh questions take shape in your mind. Perhaps that is just the way things are: getting to grips with a research question, questioning the question, playing with words are simply part of the *process of doing* research. Or rather, that is what it feels like at the beginning.

Much of this chapter is given over to this moment in the research process: what does it mean, or what does it take, to formulate a research question? For my part, the formulation of a research question is perhaps best thought about as a *task* to be achieved, something that you have to work at which, like anything that you have to craft or fashion, takes more than one attempt. Looked at in this way, the effort that you put in is one of reflection, revision and iteration, as you attempt to refine a research question which conveys all that you hope to achieve or rather all that you hope to say. I stress this process of crafting a question because, like it or not, others will judge your research efforts both by the questions that you pose and by the answers that you give.

In the next section, I shall explore what it means to come up with a research question, not in the 'how to do it' mould, but rather to reflect upon the process of generating a question and what we take the beginning point to be. For, at the very start, it sometimes seems that there is little 'out there' in the world that helps us to choose between different formulations and so we are thrown back upon our own linguistic devices, almost as if the whole process were some kind of elaborate word game. Well, in fact, some philosophers would tell us that this is hardly surprising, given that language is all that we have to work with, in so far as we cannot step outside it to 'know' the world 'as it really is'. We are, it would seem, caught up in language and the very process of arriving at a research question obviously takes place within language. In a later section ('Questions are produced, not found'), I outline two philosophical standpoints which, in rather different ways, force you to address this possibility: that you cannot get in between language and the world to come up with a better research question.

The first position draws upon the work of Richard Rorty, a contemporary North American philosophical pragmatist, and the second draws upon the early writings of Michel Foucault, a French philosopher and historian writing in the late twentieth century. Where Rorty remains ever hopeful about the prospect of generating new questions, new vocabularies that allow us to describe things in ways which enable us to do things we could not do before, Foucault wants to remind us that our discourses, what has been already said, limit what it is possible to ask and blind us from asking new kinds of question. Both accounts, in their own way, oblige us to think through what is involved in the formulation of a research question where there is no means apparent other than language to access the world.

Finally, I draw out the consequences of this philosophical position for the process of research, before linking forward to ways other than language through which you as researchers encounter the world. First, though, I want to start from what is hopefully a familiar position: a state of curiosity.

A research question: what is it? where to begin?

Curiosity can take you in any number of directions, often inspired by the wide reading that you have done in a particular area or perhaps by a deep-seated belief in the importance of a particular topic. How you hit upon a question or an intriguing hypothesis sometimes feels more like guesswork, however, than any philosophical process of deduction or induction. The sorts of influence that lead you to come up with a plausible question often involve having to anticipate likely answers, rather than apply a deductive 'it follows that' kind of logic or arrive at a more general insight through inductive reasoning. Trial and error, conjecture, informed guesswork, may not sound that philosophical, but they do convey the *speculative* element that lies at the heart of what it means to generate new ideas and questions. As curiosity opens up the scope of your inquiry, so one question begs another and, at the very moment that you try to tie a lead down, others proliferate.

Anticipating answers, posing questions

If, as I have suggested, we have to anticipate the kinds of answer that our research might offer, in one sense we have already started to fashion a possible series of questions. By this, I do not mean that through a blinding flash of insight or inspiration we suddenly arrive at a well-formed question. Rather I mean something far less dramatic and, in fact, something far more haphazard. Let me try to elaborate.

Say, for instance, that your chosen area of interest involves the investigation of a series of new economic changes at the workplace or, alternatively, a recent shift in the broad spectrum of political activism and dissent. In relation to the former, something, for example, about the new insecurities of employment at the workplace caught your imagination as a topic or, in respect of the latter, your keen interest in the Internet led you to be curious about the development of online activism and e-protest. Whatever the case, you want to know more about the extent of these interesting new developments. Where are they taking place? How far have they progressed? Why are they happening? And what implications do they hold for the future of work or for the future of political protest?

The questions themselves are quite unremarkable until, that is, you actively wish to *research* them, and then they *open* up in all kinds of ways. A simple question like *where* the new economic insecurities have taken hold, for instance, invites a further set of questions beyond that of straightforward location: such as which groups of workers and industries have borne the brunt of employment change? Our curiosity may lead us to plunge straight into the data on the growing part-time workforce in services, but a hunch may suggest otherwise and turn us towards the full-time workforce in the old manufacturing industries. Either lead may prove fruitful. Thus from a straightforward location question, a host of further issues presents itself for consideration and exerts pressure on us to think about the detail of the investigation, the extent of its empirical coverage, and the kinds of evidence sought. Already there are a lot of things going on and any one of the above issues will have some bearing on the kinds of answer anticipated.

In much the same way, to ask *why* new forms of precarious employment have come about is to raise questions about what we understand by causality and connection. What kinds of association do we assume hold between actors, firms, events or political ideas that could bring about such a risky state of affairs at the workplace? When we assume that one thing follows another, do we have in mind a contingent set of factors or something more rigid? Or are we talking about a much looser and heterogeneous set of ties and associations altogether? And just to add a further twist to this, to ask where something like the shift towards precarious employment has taken place may require that we already know, or have a good idea at least, why it has happened. Questions spin out into other questions and certain questions require a particular response.

But this, I should stress, is all part of the process of *beginning*.

Beginning and beginning-again

Edward Said, a philosopher, literacy critic and political writer all rolled into one, in his book, *Beginnings* (1978), set himself the task of reflecting philosophically about what it means *to begin* a project, be it a novel, philosophical tract, historical exercise or research endeavour. What particularly interested him was what sort of project tends to insist upon the importance of **beginnings** and what sort of work is involved in beginning something or in even contemplating the start of a project. Rather than take the beginning of something for granted, as the first stage of a linear process that moves on relentlessly from one stage to the next, Said looked more closely at many of the taken-for-granted assumptions about what it means to begin something. Only now it is not just any beginning that concerns us, but the activity of beginning a research project and of formulating a research question.

beginnings

In thinking about beginning as an *activity* with its own peculiar characteristics and ambiguities, rather than merely the first stage of a much longer project, Said was keen to problematize the very idea that beginning something is a philosophically innocent exercise. More than that, he was keen to show that the process of beginning is bound up with all kinds of thoughts, relationships and practices that are rarely acknowledged, let alone reflected upon. For him, the richness and complexity of beginning as an activity implied:

1   that whatever it is that you have had thoughts on is already a project under way; that you have *already begun* to reflect upon what it is that you wish to investigate;
2   that beginning, in Said's words, 'implies return and repetition rather than, say, simple linear accomplishment' (1978, p.viii); that *beginning allows for beginning-again* where the work of reflection and iteration are part of the sustained activity;
3   that any starting point *places* the project in relation to all that has gone before; that beginning something establishes a relationship of continuity or antagonism (or both) to an existing body of thought;
4   that beginning implies *intention*, in the sense that there is a purposeful engagement with a subject area; that how we begin gives *direction* to what follows.

Let me expand upon each of these points in the context of what it means to begin to formulate a research question.

Of the four points, perhaps the first is almost intuitive in the sense that you have probably read in your field and mulled over the possibilities before reaching the stage, albeit very preliminary, of 'fixing' a research question. The idea that, from the very first moment, a project is already under way, however, draws attention to the *experimental* nature of beginnings, where we may stumble across all kinds of ideas and developments, some of which may serve only as a distraction. Or rather that is what it may seem like. To sort out which leads add something to our thinking by opening up new questions from those that seem to take us off at a complete tangent is precisely the *work* of beginning.

Consider an earlier example – that of the growth of new forms of political dissent through online activism and e-protest. Because it is a relatively new development, it is a field of study that could open up in all kinds of unforeseen ways. Much of our time is likely to be spent tracking down incidents of online activism and trying to understand them (posing questions of the 'where', 'how', 'why' and 'what' variety). As we begin to feel confident about the scope of the subject, new connections may suggest themselves, some of which elude our grasp and indeed comprehension. What few 'solid' leads that we have to go on no longer feel quite so certain, but then again . . . In this way, doubt and reflection, as positive qualities, characterize a process that has already begun.

This takes us to Said's second point, that the work of reflection and iteration is part of the sustained activity of beginning. To reach the point where you are able to elaborate confidently the research question that you are trying to answer entails a journey that is rarely, if ever, linear. Once the process of experimentation is under way, it involves, as we have seen, following leads wherever they may take us. The more that you find out about something like online activism and e-protest, the more possibilities there seem to be to work with that you had not quite anticipated before. You may, even at this early stage, decide to change your mind; you may revise your initial thoughts and in so doing revise a still somewhat nebulous research question. You may even abandon one question for another because something does not quite fit anymore. In other words, in some fashion or other, you *begin-again*. This, to follow Said's reasoning, is all part of the work of beginning.

Said's third point is of a rather different order from the previous two and draws attention to the fact that no beginning starts from scratch. Whatever the area that we choose to research there are *antecedents* of one type or another, be it a body of previous thought or a set of empirical shifts, which we can neither ignore nor dispense with at will. Of course, there may be echoes of previous ideas and approaches in our thinking that we may not be entirely aware of, but it is precisely part of the beginning work to find out whether or not this is in fact the case. There is, in academic work, an intellectual responsibility at the beginning of any research to find out what has gone before and to engage such materials with an open mind or at least one that is not entirely made up (the issue of intellectual responsibility is a theme that runs throughout this book).

It is this process of engagement which places a new project in relation to all previous work, existing trends and prior thinking. Such an engagement represents both the beginning of a project and its point of *departure*, in so far as the choice of beginning sets out the lines of difference and

similarity from what has gone before. The very question that you ten-
tatively set for yourself at the start of a project shows where you intend to
depart from previous insights and how far your thinking overlaps with
existing attitudes, concerns and conceptions. There is an element of risk
involved at this precise moment as, on the basis of experimentation, you
set out your claim to originality.

If we continue with the example of online activism and e-protest,
having perhaps revised your initial thoughts about the scope of the inquiry,
you still nevertheless want to say something different about political
protest from what has gone before. Although the subject matter of online
activism is a relatively recent one, you may want to press a claim for
cyberactivism, for instance, as a distinctly new form of political mobilization, one that has not been witnessed before and which marks out a new
chapter in the history of political struggle. So your provisional research
question (which, note incidentally, anticipates the answer to some extent)
might seek to place itself in relation to existing accounts of political
struggle by asking: 'How far is online activism a new form of political
protest?'

Now, this may appear straightforward enough as a point of departure,
yet the question is not without risk. Suppose e-protest turns out to be just
another way of mobilizing people that is little different from before, aside
that is from the use of the Internet? Instead of paper-based petitions we
now have electronic petitions; in place of glossy pamphlets and leaflets
we have accessible websites, and so forth. What if online campaigning
amounts to little more than a new technique of political collaboration?
Such concerns and dilemmas form part of the beginning engagement with
what has gone before and anything learnt feeds back into a reformulation
of your research question.

Finally, and following on from the previous point, there is Said's
assertion that the beginning of a project represents an engagement with a
particular purpose in mind. Thus to pose something like a research question reveals an intellectual intention to investigate an event or phenomenon
in a particular way; it gives *direction* to what follows by suggesting certain
avenues of inquiry and not others. While the process of experimentation
may open up a field of research in all kinds of ways, many of which may be
unforeseen, the intended direction of the study interestingly has the
opposite effect: it closes down research possibilities.

This may seem odd at first sight, but in the process of anticipating the
kinds of answer that might be given to the question in hand, we are pressed
to leave out all sorts of material evidence and (what look like) promising
leads. Right at the very beginning we find ourselves stumbling in one
direction rather than another because our intention, for instance to
investigate cyberactivism with a loose question in mind, narrows the focus
of inquiry. As you work your question, as you try to run to ground its
possibilities, so you limit the number of things you can reasonably say
about political protest and social movements in general.

Much, clearly, is at stake at the beginning of a research project, in terms of the manner of experimentation, the revision of our ideas, the engagement with what has gone before and the commitment to a certain line of inquiry that a particular research question suggests. But, in pointing this out, there is also the broader philosophical issue of what it *means* to begin that underpins these observations. If to begin a research project is a more complex, ambiguous affair than appears at first glance, then that is because much relies upon *how* you begin: the questions that you pose, the leads that you open up, the links that you explore and the literatures that you choose to interrogate, all make a difference. Put another way, the beginning has ramifications far beyond that of being merely the initial stage of your research.

How you begin also forces you to consider a bigger philosophical issue: namely, whether or not your ideas correspond to or adequately 'fit' the world 'out there'. In so far as much of what you do at the beginning – posing questions, writing down your ideas, reading literatures, talking through research possibilities, and picturing alternatives – takes place within language, is there some way of getting between the 'word' and the 'world' to tell what is 'our' construction and what is 'really out there'? Are any of our claims detached from our language and our beliefs? Can we know the way the world is apart from language, by somehow stepping outside it?

These questions move us on to a broad philosophical plane that takes us initially into the realm of language, discourse and epistemology.

Questions are produced, not found

knowledge-claims

For some philosophers, language and its conventions are the main if not the sole way in which we can express our **knowledge-claims**. On this view, in order to arrive at a new angle on something or to give a different twist to a received understanding, language, narrative and discourse are the only possible means through which such claims may be aired. New leads, new ideas, new questions, and the particular knowledges bound up within them, do not mirror a world 'out there'. There is no separate realm of 'facts' which, if we work at it, our accounts somehow move closer to or provide a better representation. True enough, the world is 'out there', but for many that is beside the point as our beliefs about the world are not.

Finding one's feet in a new research area is tricky if we accept this view, however. There is, after all, something comforting about the notion that if we mess around in the real world long enough, some leads will turn up. In fact they may well do so, but rather than such leads and questions suggesting themselves to the researcher from the mass of evidence 'out there', the two philosophical figures that we are about to consider would want you to see things differently. On their understanding, leads and questions do not 'jump out' at us from the real world, they are *produced*.

The first position (outlined in the next subsection) is one adopted by Richard Rorty, a philosopher working in the North American pragmatist tradition of John Dewey and William James. In contrast to the views of these earlier nineteenth- and twentieth-century pragmatists, however, Rorty insists that we cannot connect with a world of experience outside

language   language. **Language,** as a set of tools for dealing with the world rather than a medium of representation, is for him all that we have to work with. As

vocabularies   such, we judge our descriptions of things, the **vocabularies** that we use, by how well they best suit our current purposes. In research terms, on this view, there is nothing 'out there' to discover, no frontiers of knowledge to

redescription   break through, only language as a tool for **redescription** that allows us to do things we could not do before and to think in other, more useful ways. If we accept this line of reasoning, the fruits of our research efforts become 'true', according to Rorty, because they are useful; they are not useful because they are true.

The second position (outlined in the subsection that follows) stems from the earlier work of Michel Foucault, a philosopher writing in France in the latter half of last century, whose critical histories of the practices of modern medicine, the penal system and attitudes towards sexuality, centred

discourses   on their discursive construction. **Discourses,** for Foucault, comprise groups
statements   of related **statements** which govern the variety of ways in which it is possible to talk about something and which thus make it difficult, if not impossible, to think and act outside them. What can be said about a particular subject matter, how it is said and by whom stem from a specific discursive practice. Thus in research terms, knowledge-claims are seen as moves in a kind of power-game, where only certain kinds of question are possible to ask. So, if we go down this philosophical route, knowledge and power reinforce one another and set out the grounds by which truth is claimed.

One of the interesting things that we will see about Rorty and Foucault is that despite their differences they seem to share an assumption that our existing vocabularies, our current ways of thinking about things, have become somewhat entrenched. If anything, they act as a barrier to fresh thinking, almost a nuisance that needs to be overcome if we are to imagine things differently and to pose new questions. It is this, the sense in which we can imagine things differently, to provide answers to questions not yet adequately posed, that I want to keep in focus. Neither account speaks directly to how you produce a research question, but both provide a *philosophical* understanding of the process involved which rules out the possibility that it is the world 'out there' which decides which question 'fits' better or is the most appropriate.

Rorty's pragmatist moves

One of the claims that Richard Rorty is fond of repeating, almost like a mantra, is that language 'goes all the way down' (1982, p.xxx; 1991a, p.100). Because the social world 'out there' does not present itself to us in any simple fashion, or 'throw up' clues for us to find, we can only apprehend it through language. And because we cannot step outside language, we have little choice other than to produce our descriptions of the world in line with what use they might serve. This is the first **pragmatist** move. Knowing things and using them are indistinguishable practices. On this understanding, language is not some aimless exchange, it is performed with some given purpose in mind. For Rorty, all our knowledge is known to us under some description or other which best suits our current purposes. Knowledge as such is useful to us, it gives us the power to do things that we want to do. Or in Rorty's words:

> Pragmatists hope to make it impossible for the sceptic to raise the question, 'Is our knowledge of things adequate to the way things really are?' They substitute for this traditional question the *practical* question, 'Are our ways of describing things, of relating them to other things so as to make them fulfil our needs more adequately, as good as possible? Or can we do better?' (Rorty, 1999, p.72)

So, if your research is driven by a particular purpose and your aim is to add something to the existing stock of knowledge, then, realistically, you should put to one side any worries that you may have about facing a world of 'hard' facts and work away at producing an innovative research question from the linguistic tools available. In other words, you should set about the task of refining a question that best suits your given research interests and needs.

Now, as far as I can make out, Rorty does not believe that this process of linguistic construction is something that is best left to idle contemplation. There is work involved, the sustained activity of the kind described by Said in the previous section. In Rorty's hands, however, this work has a distinctly pragmatic edge where the notion of what 'best suits' holds the key to any inquiry. For the issue is not about constructing a question which directs us towards a better, more accurate picture of what is 'out there', but rather one that works better for certain purposes than any previous tool. A research question in this line of thought becomes a tool for doing something that could not have been done under a previous set of descriptions. The question opens up possibilities, but only for as long as it allows people *to do things that they could not do before* – to see things in a different light, to put things together that were previously held apart, to examine something differently, and so forth.

If you think back to the example of the new insecurities of employment at the workplace as a potential research topic, on this account, we should simply drop the idea that our thoughts about the topic somehow mirror what is actually going on in the world of work and busy ourselves trying to come up with a question that enables us to go about researching the topic in a more productive manner. The permanent edginess around jobs, work and pensions that currently seems to surround matters of lifestyle and employment, where risk is routine, may be a more productive entry point compared to what has gone before, for instance. We can only give it a try, to see where it might lead in terms of anticipating answers to potential questions. What we cannot do, according to Rorty, is hold this belief up to the world as if it were a mirror that we can polish to progressively achieve a more adequate reflection.

Rorty first spelt out a number of these ideas in *Philosophy and the Mirror of Nature*, which was published in 1980, and followed this up with a collection of essays in 1982 entitled *Consequences of Pragmatism*. It was the publication of *Contingency, Irony and Solidarity* in 1989 which proved to be the most controversial and widely read of his writings, however, not only because novelists and poets received preferential billing over philosophers, but also because it lauded 'ironists'; that is, those individuals who are 'never quite able to take themselves seriously because [they are] always aware of the contingency and fragility of their final vocabularies, and thus of their selves' (1989, pp.73–4). This was intended less as an expression of humility, however, and more as a statement concerning the contingent status of all that we know, and thus an injunction to try things differently. In the first essay of the 1989 volume, 'The contingency of language', he set out a way in which he thought we could do just that and move beyond entrenched vocabularies to embrace the possibility of new thinking. In broad terms, he argued:

1   that there is no 'method' to any of this, all that anyone can really do is 'redescribe lots and lots of things in new ways', to develop *new vocabularies* that tempt others to adopt descriptions that make previous ones appear limited;
2   that inquiry is akin to a process of *recontextualization*, where metaphorical redescription provides a jolt to the imagination by shaking up previous thinking, for example where familiar words are used in unfamiliar ways to pose a novel question.

On the former, Rorty is suggesting that all that we can do is produce more *telling redescriptions* in the hope of inciting others to work with and even extend them. An ironist, he argues 'hopes that by the time she has finished using old words in new senses, not to mention introducing brand-new words, people will no longer ask questions phrased in the old words' (1989, p.78). Redescribing things again and again thus becomes part of what it means to experiment, to seek a more productive entry point compared to what has gone before. For Rorty, there is no in-built faculty that allows us to recognize the 'truth' in some description when we first stumble across it. Rather, all that is available to us is a sense of what best suits a given purpose. A description that 'best suits', not one that 'best fits', a world beyond us is probably the sum of it. While this position does not mean that we have a licence to say whatever we like about anything, it does seem to suggest, to me at least, that all questions are possible so long as they are practicable and potentially convincing. Our redescriptions should work better for certain purposes and provoke others into using them. As Rorty puts it:

> This sort of philosophy does not work piece by piece, analysing concept after concept, or testing thesis after thesis. Rather, it works holistically and pragmatically. It says things like 'try thinking of it this way' – or more specifically, 'try to ignore the apparently futile traditional questions by substituting the following new and possibly interesting questions'. It does not pretend to have a better candidate for doing the same old things which we did when we spoke in the old way. Rather, it suggests that we might want to stop doing those things and do something else. (Rorty, 1989, p.9)

Even if we were to go along with this, however, how do you then arrive at a provocative vocabulary of some event, experience or recent development which itself is suggestive of new questions, new lines of inquiry? For Rorty, the answer seems principally to lie with the process of *metaphorical redescription*.

metaphorical redescription
What does Rorty mean by this? The nub of it for him, it seems, is that **metaphorical redescription** allows us, as he puts it, to 'use familiar words in unfamiliar ways' (1989, p.18), not for the sake of novelty, but to enable us to see something differently for the first time, to cast something familiar in a new light. Tossing a metaphor into something that we write, he says, 'is like using italics, or illustrations, or odd punctuation or formats' (1989, p.18); it represents 'a voice from outside' (1991b, p.13) that alerts us to something different, something new. In short, thinking metaphorically for Rorty is a kind of tool for jolting our imaginations, where a new, metaphorical use of old words (e.g. 'flexible firms'), neologisms (e.g. 'genes') or novel associations (e.g. cyberactivism) may prompt us to think about things in a different way. Of course, there is no guarantee that the kind of recontextualization that he has in mind will provoke the type of reaction he envisages, but what he is trying to suggest is that metaphor is the means by which we *produce* new descriptions, new vocabularies, that enable us to go about things differently.

metaphor
Rorty draws upon the work of two philosophers to present his case, Donald Davidson (a philosopher of language) and Mary Hesse (a philosopher of science). Through them, he is at pains to stress that **metaphor** does not lead to the production of new meaning as such. Rather it provides a new language for exploration that perhaps stops us from going down familiar avenues of inquiry. The construction of a new description of something, the ability to pose the question differently, does not in this respect enable us to carry on as before with our studies, albeit with some modifications to our vocabulary (for example, a 'new' politics of resistance or a 'new' cultural geography, yet cast in a distinctly familiar mould).

Rather, a new vocabulary shifts the ground irrevocably and enables us to do something else entirely.

For my part, I am not sure that we have to make quite this leap, as it is not entirely evident from the examples that Rorty offers that it is 'something else entirely' that is at issue. The juxtaposing of previously unrelated texts or ideas, the deployment of terms from one context to another in which they were previously absent or the use of an 'old' term in a new metaphorical guise, all seem to me to be the kinds of skill that Rorty has in mind. If it were otherwise then every new piece of redescription would have to be 'ground-breaking' or equivalent to a paradigm shift, and most, it seems, are not.

At a practical level, much of our language is dead metaphor anyway (the 'mouth' of a river, the 'leg' of a chair), and its extension when we are trying to think about things in new ways may have little in terms of shock value. Rorty seems to understand this when he argues that:

> To think of metaphorical sentences as the forerunners of new uses of language, uses which may eclipse and erase old uses, is to think of metaphor as on a par with perception and inference, rather than thinking of it as having a merely 'heuristic' or 'ornamental' function. (Rorty, 1991b, p.14)

In drawing attention to the heuristic or ornamental function of metaphor, Rorty wants to reserve the role of metaphor for the imaginative jolt, not the exercise that passes for a simple model of what is out there or some decorative function. The latter 'ornamental' use of metaphor, in particular, has a long history of use in literature and poetry where a feeling may be evoked to great effect through an imaginative use of words, but in general the ornamental use of metaphor has often tended to be just that: mere decoration. The uses of geographic metaphor, for example in cultural studies, where meanings are 'mapped' and subjectivities are 'cartographically' represented, neither of which owes anything to the techniques of mapping, are ornamental in form. That is, they do not offer new ways of thinking about their subject matter. Where metaphorical redescription acts as a precursor to a new vocabulary, however, it is more likely to generate questions that surprise, that for Rorty change the conversation.

Perhaps an example of such a conversation stopper is the vocabulary of risk which sprang on to the social science academic scene in the late 1980s/early 1990s. For some, risk rapidly became the central dynamic around which a range of institutional settings from science, class and politics to the workplace, the family and the environment, are organized. At the time, many wondered aloud about just how novel or indeed plausible such a claim was, but nonetheless found themselves busy engaging it. Others found the mix of uncertainties and anxieties expressed through a vocabulary of risk a useful tool to explore familiar topics; these, in turn, allowed them to do things they could not do before as they sought out new leads and explored patterns of behaviour previously overlooked. The point is that, although not all were convinced by the new vocabulary, once a number were tempted by what could be done with it, they expressed little interest in what had been said before about these institutional matters.

So, from Rorty's point of view, it is precisely the appearance of partially formed yet promising vocabularies that *produces* new leads and new questions. For him, 'fresh thinking' is something that is adopted by others once they have become convinced of its usefulness for one purpose or another. In privileging language and distrusting experience, however, the adoption of a particular vocabulary seems to rely upon rhetorical persuasion above all else. There is no room in Rorty's 'liberal' world for the possibility that some vocabularies may be repressed or sidelined, or indeed that language itself may be wrapped up with power and politics in ways that limit the questions that we pose.

Foucault's discursive practices

If language, for Rorty 'goes all the way down', where all our knowledge amounts to descriptions to suit our current purposes, probably the equivalent uncompromising claim for Foucault is that all knowledge presupposes power. The production of knowledge through language and convention is mixed up with power in ways that implicate the latter in all that we take to be 'true', as well as the circumstances under which something becomes 'true'. To be fair, language is not really the issue for **discursive practices** Foucault; rather it is the **discursive practices** – the statements which provide a language for talking about something – which hold his attention and which, he claims, serve to restrict the number of things it is possible to say about different topics and areas of study. Discursive practices are, in his words, characterized by 'a delimitation of a field of objects, the definition of a legitimate perspective for the agent of knowledge, and the fixing of norms for the elaboration of concepts and theories' (Foucault, 1977, p.199).

If this sounds a little high-handed, then that is far from Foucault's intention. For him, there is an everyday sense to the way in which the 'obviousness' of a discourse works its way through our thinking and sets the norms for discussion and debate. The emphasis placed by Foucault upon power's relationship to knowledge is a productive one, where we are able to engage in all kinds of practice, but only in so far as we can make sense of them. However, it is how we are able to articulate and make sense of something that is far from open-ended and which, according to Foucault, is systematically governed in both its formulation and understanding. There are limits to the questions that we may ask of things if we want to appear meaningful and intelligible.

As researchers, we are likely to find ourselves caught up in the thinking that circulates around a particular topic and which predisposes us to 'know' it in a certain way. When it becomes difficult to think about a topic in any other way, then, according to Foucault, we are not only **regime of truth**   subject to a particular '**regime of truth**', in so far as we are unable to think outside it, we also sustain and extend that arrangement. In short, we are positioned by discursive practices and, in turn, serve to ground them.

On this understanding, our research interests and topics are framed by what has already been said about them and, as a consequence, limit what we can say about them. So if we wish to engage through our research in a debate about new forms of political activism and dissent, for instance, we have little choice but to position ourselves within its existing knowledge-claims. To do otherwise would be to risk misunderstanding and, quite simply, to appear unintelligible. For Foucault, the point is not that we are stuck within fixed, 'trammel' lines of knowing, but rather that for all the possible questions that we may ask about a particular topic, they remain systematically governed in both style and understanding. On this basis, it would seem that *only certain answers are allowed for* – those which fall **discursive**   within the rules and conventions of a particular **discursive formation**. Or in **formation**   his words:

> By system of formation, then, I mean a complex group of relations that function as a rule: it lays down what must be related, in a particular discursive practice, for such and such an enunciation to be made, for such and such a concept to be used, for such and such a strategy to be organized. To define a system of formation in its specific individuality is therefore to characterize a discourse or a group of statements by the regularity of a practice. (Foucault, 1972/1969, p.74)

Thus any potential research topic, such as the exploration of new forms of political struggle, is likely to come with its own conceptual baggage which, in various ways, governs what is 'sayable' about, for example, dissent, protest and political mobilization. If we follow Rorty, we are still able to give all possible leads a try, but now we should also reflect upon the predispositions which make it possible even to contemplate new forms of political struggle at this particular moment. In this way, we might get a handle on what Foucault meant by the assertion that 'discourses produce the objects of knowledge' and that none of our questions makes sense outside discourse.

Together with 'The order of discourse' (1981/1970), Foucault's inaugural lecture given in 1970 at the Collège de France, *The Archaeology of Knowledge* (1972/1969), published in 1969, represents his most explicit attempt to outline the rules and categories which underpin the formation of discourses and thus of knowledge itself. The latter text, in many respects, is a kind of methodological postscript to an earlier work published in 1966, *The Order of Things* (1970/1966), written, it would seem, with the explicit intention of distancing himself from a chronological interpretation of the 'history of ideas'. In trying to expose the almost 'unvoiced' rules by which our objects of study are given to us, Foucault sets out to describe the discontinuous and delimiting nature of discourse. At a general level, he considers discursive formations to be:

1   a group of statements (the archive) which may differ in substance or even contradict one another, yet possess a certain *regularity* in the *relations* between statements that provides an unproblematic way of talking about a topic;
2   discontinuous practices, which may cross over one another, exclude one another, even work along new lines, yet remain *governed* by what it is possible to say and think about a particular topic.

This is a rather terse formulation, but in many ways all that it really means is that certain ground rules *enable* us to make all kinds of descriptions and opposing characterizations about, say, the politics of struggle or the politics of development as one example of struggle, yet those self-same rules *limit* what it is possible to say about economic development without appearing odd or beyond comprehension. As with Rorty, there are no 'truths' about development 'out there' waiting to be discovered, but in contrast our ideas do not become true because they are useful; rather, for Foucault, the 'truth' about something is historically

> . . . constituted by all that was said in all the statements that named it, divided it up, described it, explained it, traced its developments, indicated its various correlations, judged it, and possibly gave it speech by articulating, in its name, discourses that were to be taken as its own. (Foucault, 1972/1969, p.32)

It is not, I should stress, that we cannot stand outside a universalizing discourse of development, with its consistent statements about growth, self-reliance and sustainability for instance, or take a step back from any discourse masquerading as knowledge for that matter. In your research endeavours, the ability to cast off, say, the predispositions of your discipline which currently frame your field of study is an important milestone *en route* to asking new questions, but that does not necessarily make it any easier to think outside such constitutive discourses, or to dismiss their practical consequences.

So how should one position oneself in relation to such distracting and preoccupying discourses? Perhaps by following Said's lead in recognizing that our starting point places us in relation to all that has gone before and that the process of engagement involves dealing with the discourses which have shaped our field of inquiry – as scattered and as dispersed through any number of observations, statements and findings as they may be. By tracing the positions that various researchers and commentators have taken up within a particular field of study and the sets of questions which define it, it may be possible to take on the role of archaeologist and to analyse the 'archive' for the discursive regularities which compose it.

As I see it, though, the lessons of archaeology are not the only ones that we can draw from Foucault's description of discourses. At a more modest level, in terms of the possible range of questions that we can ask about our subject matter and remain plausible, Foucault's work high-lights the restricted nature of what can be said, on what terms and, invariably, by whom. The role of chance in all this is likewise dimin-ished, as the possibility is always there that what remains 'unthought' is, strictly speaking, unavailable to us as a resource from which potential research questions may be drawn. If knowledge-claims are moves in a kind of language power-game, as Foucault seems to suggest, then the production of unlimited new leads and new questions is effectively ruled out. There are only so many 'subject-positions' that we, as researchers, can occupy.

If we turn this on its head, however, on a more positive note, what Foucault's archaeological analysis has to offer is precisely a way to arrive at 'fresh thinking' by recognizing the discursive constraints that we operate under and how we may conduct ourselves differently in relation to our chosen topic. The temptation to adopt a new vocabulary, on this under-standing, overlooks the fact that we have first to grasp where we are speaking from and how it is that we think we have something to say.

The question, then . . .

The purpose of the chapter, as stated at the outset, has been to introduce you to a particular way of thinking about what it means to produce a research question. As the first of three chapters with this aim in mind, the decision to start with Richard Rorty and Michel Foucault, as you may have guessed, was far from accidental in so far as they represent a distinctive philosophical approach to the relationship between, on the one hand, our words and our language, and, on the other hand, the world 'out there' as it really is. For when it comes to the formulation of new knowledges, ideas and questions, both side with the 'word' rather than with the 'world', because for them there is no way of getting between language and its object. In short, there is no way of telling what is 'our' construction and what is really 'out there', and thus little point in claiming that some ideas 'fit' reality better than others.

This is not an issue that, for you as a researcher, is going to go away, nor indeed is it one that you can resolve after a moment's thought. **epistemological** Essentially, the issue is an **epistemological** one, by which I mean that it revolves around how 'we know what we know' – the conditions and practices that make knowledge possible. If you come down on the side that our knowledge of the world is possible only through the mediation of language, that there is no independent way to know the world other than through the words, marks and noises that construct it for us, then you occupy a position not dissimilar to Rorty and Foucault.

Such a position, however, is not without its consequences. For one thing, you cannot side with the 'word' rather than the 'world' and then proceed to talk *as if* your ideas and questions somehow refer to or represent more accurately what is really going on in, say, the economy or in the community at large. For Rorty at least, our ideas do not refer to or represent anything; as a form of linguistic description they are the only tools that we have at our disposal to make a difference – in particular, to ask the kinds of question that we could not ask before. Indeed, some old questions may become unaskable simply because new questions bring about an entirely different way of thinking about something.

There is more than just a hint of consistency involved in what I have just said. The implication is that philosophical positions, although far from hermetically sealed, provide a set of resources which, if you choose to adopt one rather than another, entail consequences throughout the process of doing research. At the beginning (a moment replete with its own ambiguities, as we have had cause to note), when you find yourself trying to provide answers to questions not yet adequately posed, your engagement with philosophical ideas is likely to influence what it is that you hope to say through your research. Someone like Rorty or Foucault will not provide you with a guidebook as to what questions you should ask, but they do alert us to what is at stake in the production of new ideas and questions – in terms of what questions it is *possible* to ask and what it is *possible* to know.

But, as the next chapter will argue, that is almost certainly too simple.

Further reading

For those interested in an exposition and sympathetic critique of the ideas of Rorty and Foucault, Richard Bernstein's *The New Constellation* (Polity Press, 1991) remains one of the most insightful treatments of their thinking, especially in relation to politics and ethics. Richard Rorty's *Philosophy and Social Hope* (Penguin, 1999) outlines his more recent thinking on these issues. For an engaging and wide-ranging account of the relationship between the 'real' and the 'constructed' nature of the world, see Ian Hacking's *The Social Construction of What?* (Harvard University Press, 1999).

2
The play of the world

Nigel Clark

> What are these fiery imperatives, these questions which are the beginning
> of the world? (Gilles Deleuze, 1994, p.200)

Introduction

Coming face to face with something strange and new, looking afresh at the
familiar, making a connection between things or ideas that were previously
apart – these are some of the pleasures of doing research. What makes
research enticing, however, can also come across as daunting and intimidating. That is because finding ourselves in the presence of the 'new' or
feeling ourselves to be engaged in something 'original' are not simply
felicitous moments that we might one day hope to experience as we go
about our research. They are also, in a sense, *demands*. Some degree of
'originality' in research is called for by funding bodies, doctoral pro-
grammes, journal editors and just about everyone else who minds the gates
of the social science establishment. And that requirement can seem very
demanding indeed when you are taking your first steps into the field of
independent or self-generated research.

   In this chapter, we dwell further on the process of generating a
research question, with particular attention to the demand for originality.
What is originality, I will be asking, and where is it to be found? Are
there ways to make the requirement for 'originality' or 'newness' seem
less threatening and more promising? As you will have gleaned from the
last chapter, good research questions require effort on your part. They
have to be crafted out of the materials or resources at hand, rather than
conjured out of the ether. But just what are the materials out of which
this work of generating questions takes place? As we have seen, both
Rorty and Foucault point to certain constraints on the resources which
are available at any time or place to think with or think through. What
they suggest, in their respective ways, is that the particular arrangement
of words and things that we inherit from our social milieu tends to
channel our thinking. In this way, what we end up thinking and doing
may be only a fraction of the possibilities that could conceivably be open
to us.

Rorty, more obviously than the early Foucault, suggests a way out of these strictures. As we saw, he proposes a playful, experimental use of language as a way to generate fresh perspectives on a familiar world. Rather than assuming that the world 'out there' should dictate our descriptions, Rorty affirms that there is play or contingency in language. Language is not obligated to the world. It is a medium in which we have a certain liberty to create and invent, and this includes using language metaphorically to craft original research questions – questions which offer a new angle or fresh purchase on the objects of our inquiry.

This idea that there is 'contingency' in language – or in culture more generally – is one of the predominant intellectual themes of recent decades. Especially in the social sciences and humanities, fewer and fewer theorists adhere to the notion that human thought is determined or constrained by an objective world – a world outside or independent of thinking beings. We need to be mindful, however, that there are different ways in which the contingency of language or culture can be understood, and that each of these ways has its own effects and implications. In this chapter, I want to address the work of two French philosophers, Jacques Derrida and Gilles Deleuze, who, like Rorty and Foucault, challenge the assumption that the prime task of thought is to mirror an external world. Derrida and Deleuze both seem to affirm the free play of language in a manner resonant with Rorty. But on closer inspection, I will be arguing, their respective writings suggest something quite different from the prioritizing of human language that is at the core of Rorty's philosophical stance.

Deleuze and Derrida are part of the same generation and general intellectual milieu as Foucault. Though there are significant differences in the philosophical backgrounds, intentions and writing styles of Deleuze and Derrida, there are also some crucial points at which their writings converge. Deleuze makes a strong claim that thought should be inventive rather than merely descriptive. But this is far from a privileging of language, because for him the play of words is intimately tied up with the broader play of the world. Language has the capacity to be creative and inventive, Deleuze seems to be saying, only because it is open to a wider world which is equally generative and experimental.

Derrida, on the other hand, initially seems closer to Rorty, in that a great deal of his work engages primarily with language and draws out the unpredictable and contingent nature of writing. However, while Derrida may deny that 'word' and 'world' can ever attain a pure and seamless fusion, this is not the same thing as saying that they are utterly and inevitably separated. While it may be expressed in more subtle and 'textual' fashion than in the writings of Deleuze, there are nevertheless numerous indications in Derrida's work that the idea of the closure of language to the world around it is something he deeply resists.

Both Derrida and Deleuze, then, set about opening the play of words to the play of the world. But what might this mean for the question of originality in research? What are the implications of a philosophical position which refuses to separate language from the rest of reality for the 'work' of crafting a research question? We have seen that neither Rorty nor Foucault provides us with a blueprint for posing questions, or indeed, for thinking and acting in general. This is no less the case for Deleuze and Derrida, whose philosophical writings, if anything, are even more of a challenge for those in search of guidelines for thought and research. For all the talk of 'play', it must be said, there is nothing leisurely about reading Derrida or Deleuze. Their books are hard going: complex, convoluted and frequently mystifying – even for the well-initiated. But there are ways of reading their respective works, if we accept the help of some of their many commentators, that can have real and direct consequences for our 'questioning' of the world around us.

From language to life

We have already encountered Rorty's particular take on the idea of thought as a kind of invention. Well before Rorty, Deleuze had taken up this theme. Deleuze, in turn, was deeply indebted to the French philosopher, Henri Bergson. The following lines, penned by Bergson in the 1940s, are cited by Deleuze in an early work, and thereafter play a pivotal role in his writings:

> Discovery, or uncovering, has to do with what already exists . . .; it was therefore certain to happen sooner or later. Invention gives being to what did not exist; it might never have happened. (Bergson, cited in Deleuze, 1988/1966, p.15)

This distinction between revealing a world 'out there' and actively participating in the coming into existence of new things or new worlds is at the heart of *Difference and Repetition* (1994/1968), Deleuze's first major outlining of his own philosophical position. In this book, he argues that if our intention is to depict the world, then no matter how rich and diverse this world appears to us, and no matter how accurately we represent it, our thought remains in the thrall of what already exists, or what has already taken place. Drawing from a wide range of sources, including contemporary science, avant-garde art and earlier philosophers such as Spinoza, Nietzsche and Bergson, Deleuze explores another option, which is for thought to concern itself with the conditions under which new things come into existence.

In this sense, rather than looking for the something previously undiscovered, thinkers or researchers should aim 'to bring into being that which does not yet exist' (Deleuze, 1994/1968, p.147). For Deleuze, as for those philosophers who prioritize language, '[t]o think is to create' (1994/1968, p.147). Deleuze, too, encourages a rich and stylish use of language, but he is quite clear that the ultimate aim of this is to unleash the potentials of

life 'life' in general and not simply of language or culture. In a later interview, in which he reflects on *Difference and Repetition* and subsequent work, Deleuze puts it like this:

> One's always writing to bring something to life, to free life from where it's trapped. . . . The language for doing that can't be a homogeneous system, it's something unstable, always heterogeneous, in which style carves differences of potential between which things can pass, come to pass, a spark can flash and break out of language itself, to make us see and think what was lying in the shadow around the words, things we were hardly aware existed. (Deleuze, 1995, p.141)

The idea that thought or experience can break out of the enclosure of language and make contact with other elements or forces in the world is a theme which runs through much of Deleuze's work. It is one he returns to and develops further in *A Thousand Plateaus* (1987/1980), a book co-written with psychoanalyst Felix Guattari, and perhaps Deleuze's best-known work. Here, in typically poetic fashion, Deleuze and Guattari give examples of the sort of meetings of apparently unconnected classes of objects that happen constantly in the real world: 'a semiotic fragment rubs shoulders with a chemical interaction, an electron crashes into a language, a black hole captures a genetic message' (1987/1980, p.69). And they are quite explicit: this is the play of the world, *not* the play of metaphor: 'we are not saying "like an electron", "like an interaction"' (1987/1980, p.69). Indeed, as Deleuze and Guattari intimate, the whole structure of *A Thousand Plateaus*, with all its complex array of ideas and examples, can be seen as putting into practice the idea of disparate elements coming together in a multitude of different ways (see 1987/1980, p.6).

Now, it may not be immediately apparent what the practical implications are that we might draw from such eventualities as an 'electron crashing into language' (though it may have something to do with the word-processing malfunctions I experience from time to time!). Before going on to tease out the consequences of such ideas for the question of originality – or the origination of questions – I want to introduce Derrida's rather more subdued and meticulous version of the opening of language to the world.

Derrida's impact on contemporary philosophy first stemmed from a series of books roughly contemporaneous with Deleuze's *Difference and Repetition*, including *Of Grammatology* (1976/1967) and *Writing and Difference* (1978/1968). These works introduce Derrida's 'deconstructive'

deconstruction approach to philosophy. **Deconstruction**, at this stage of Derrida's work, entails close readings of well-known texts by philosophers, social scientists and literary figures, which attempt to demonstrate how such writings have even more potential than their own authors recognized. In particular, Derrida seeks out the 'small but tell-tale moment' when a text seems to over-reach its own premises or intentions (Spivak, 1976, p.xxxv). In this way, he tries to show that writing – or language – does not simply describe the world, but is itself productive and generative – with effects that can neither be anticipated nor controlled (Derrida, 1978/1968, p.11). As Derrida explained in a 1968 interview, this has implications for our understanding of the operations of language *vis-à-vis* the world: 'for the notion of translation', he suggests, 'we would have to substitute a notion of *transformation*' (1981a/1972, p.20, emphasis in original).

Thus far, it might seem as though we are back with Rorty's claim of the inescapability of language. And indeed, many of Derrida's readers have interpreted his work precisely as a sophisticated argument for the impossibility of breaking out of the 'textuality' of language and culture to an outside world. But there are other ways to read Derrida's work. Just as Derrida argues that each written text opens out into the wider world of its intellectual or cultural 'context', so too does he seem to be saying that writing and culture in general also open into a broader context, which is to say that there is always a hinge, a point of contact or connection between language and the wider world. Such a perspective on 'word and world' is suggested at numerous points in Derrida's work, including the opening pages of *Of Grammatology* where he proposes that the relationships between the elements of language or writing with which he is concerned might also apply to the arts, to cybernetics, and even to biology, including the 'most elementary processes of information within the living cell' (1976/1967, p.9).

Provocations and openings

So while Derrida may be much more cautious than Deleuze in drawing connections between disparate categories of objects, and much less willing to stray from the philosophical and literary fields he knows best, what the two writers share is an interest in the creative potential of any opening to an outside – any play that occurs *between* different entities or systems. In Derrida's later work, such as *Politics of Friendship* (1997), in which his focus partially shifts from written texts to political and social issues, the theme of encounters with difference or strangeness receive sustained attention. These works, as John Caputo notes, concern themselves with how we might 'make way' for whatever is 'forth-coming' or 'in-coming' from beyond our circle of experience and familiarity (Caputo, 1997, pp.70, 103). This in-coming or coming-forth is what Derrida refers to as an

event   'event'. 'Event' and 'invent' have similar derivations: invention comes from the Latin *invenire* – to come upon – and event from *evenire* – to come forth or happen. One way of looking at deconstruction, then, is to see it as an exploration of the 'singularity' of the event, as an inquiry into how we might come to terms with the event's uniqueness and unpredictability. As Caputo sums up: 'For Derrida, deconstruction is set in motion by something that calls upon and addresses us, overtakes (sur-prises) and even overwhelms us, to which we must respond, and so be responsive and responsible' (1997, p.51).

But what are the implications of this concern with the 'event' of an opening, a connection or a meeting for the posing of new questions or the beginning of projects? Derrida himself has drawn attention to the part this 'openness' plays in the generating of a project. When asked by an interviewer where he got the idea for a book or article, he replied:

> A sort of animal movement seeks to appropriate what always comes, always, from an *external* provocation. By responding to some request, invitation, or commission, an invention must nevertheless seek itself out, an invention that defies both a given program, a system of expectations, and finally surprises me myself – surprises me by suddenly becoming for me imperious, imperative, inflexible even, like a very tough law. (Derrida, 1995, p.352, emphasis in original)

From the broader context of Derrida's work, it can be inferred that a 'request' may be more than just a formal invitation to write a piece: it can be any sort of solicitation, any kind of prompting, jolting or imploring that comes from the world around. What happens first, Derrida seems to suggest, is an intuitive or visceral opening up to whatever it is he finds provocative. Only later, as the project takes off, does it seem to impose its own demands for rigour and focus.

For Deleuze, no less than for Derrida, it is an 'external provocation' which triggers a new idea or a new project. Again this involves something outside ourselves taking hold of us: 'a fiery imperative', an incitement which is as unpredictable as it is irresistible. As Deleuze puts it in *Difference and Repetition*:

> . . . there is only involuntary thought. . . . Something in the world forces us to think. This something is an object not of recognition but of a fundamental *encounter*. . . . It may be grasped in a range of affective tones; wonder, love, hatred, suffering. (Deleuze, 1994/1968, p.139)

Not surprisingly, the term Deleuze gives to this thought-provoking encounter is an 'event'. And the event is at least as central to his writings as it is to Derrida. As Deleuze recounted during an interview late in his life, 'I've tried in all my books to discover the nature of events' (1995, p.141). As with Derrida, Deleuze's foregrounding of the event reflects his own belief that the subject of thought or action is inevitably 'in the world'. The thinker, for Deleuze, is thus entangled in the goings-on or happenings that concern him or her. It is not a case of the thinker trying to get a handle on the world from the outside, as it were. When Deleuze and Guattari write that the aim of philosophy 'is to become worthy of the event' (1994, p.160), what they mean is that thought should attempt to make sense out of things that occur in order to release or realize their potential. For mere goings-on to become proper 'events', however, thinkers or researchers have not only to try to comprehend what is happening, but at the same time to open themselves to the transformative effects of these happenings. As in the case of Derrida's deconstructions, it is this affirmation of openness, this notion that the thinker must be moved by whatever is forth-coming or going-on that seems to set Deleuze at odds with more conventional models of thought and research.

Hostage to events

But how can being 'moved' by happenings, goings-on or encounters generate a research project? I want to turn now to an example: one of those rare cases where the researcher tells us exactly where they were, what they were doing, and how they felt as the idea for a project came upon them. This will help give us a sense of how, in practice, originality or inventiveness is linked to a certain openness or willingness to be 'called upon' or 'overwhelmed'.

My example comes from the book *Virtual Geography* (1994) by the Australian cultural theorist McKenzie Wark. His story features an incident from the television coverage of the Iraq hostage crisis that was screened on 23 August 1990, some months prior to the first Gulf War. This is the moment when Iraqi president Saddam Hussein pats the head of seven-year-old Stuart Lockwood as he makes a remark about hostages playing a role as 'heroes of peace'. As Wark recounts:

> I'm lying in bed with my lover and the cat, watching TV, when this hostage things spews out of the TV at me. By a strange accident of geography, the NBC morning news program is shown in Sydney, Australia, around midnight. So here we are, a cozy domestic scene, lapping up the sweet with the bland, suddenly invaded by hostages and threats and urgency and Bryant Gumble. Neither of us is really watching the set at the time. It just happens to be on, a boring interzone of banal happenings, vectoring into our private space. I think it is the word 'hostage' that trips me into actually paying attention. I watch with an unwilling fascination, trying not to let myself submit to this distasteful but canny image. That's when I see something curious; the medium close-up where Saddam Hussein touches that boy. A dictator caresses his hostage in our bedroom. The report gives the impression that the hostage show-and-tell talk show was a long one, but it's those few seconds of the dictator and the boy that made it into the vision mix. The tape is many generations old, blurred and pixelated, but so too is the Orientalist story it revives from the dead. Curiouser and curiouser. At the next commercial break, I pull on an old track suit and head out the bedroom door. 'Where are you going?' my lover asks. 'To work,' I say. 'To work.' (Wark, 1994, p.6)

The 'Orientalist story' is a reference to the work of Edward Said, whom you encountered in the last chapter. It's the term Said uses to describe a certain way of imagining the east – associated with the colonial era, in which Europeans stereotyped Middle Eastern people, among other things, as sexually repressed but also sensual and perverse. Wark is reminded of this story by the way the Iraqi president's gesture is presented and framed by the news coverage. But what also strikes him is the new twist that global TV coverage has given the Orientalist narrative by projecting it into the intimate space of his bedroom. For our purposes here, however, there is no need to get engrossed in the details of the Orientalist thesis, or with Wark's particular take on global media. The important thing is to get a feel for Wark's own sensitivity to the way in which a quite specific convergence of factors sparks his interest. As he continues his account:

> I turn on the heater in the study – it gets cold in Sydney in August. I could smell trouble. I could sense an event coming on. Months later, I could close the door to this study, with its mountains of old newspapers, videotapes, photocopies with coffee-cup rings all over them. By then this private zone of disorder would look like a pathetic tribute to the carnage in Baghdad. This little room would become a monument made out of trashed information, jerrybuilt concepts, and emergency rations of toxic espresso and vodka, neat. (Wark, 1994, p.7)

Now, this is no absolute beginning, for Wark informs us that he has already had a long interest in global media events, and he also clearly has a background in cultural theory and philosophy, including a grasp of what Deleuze means by an 'event'. But there is a sense here of a fresh start, a moment of inspiration that has clearly played a major role in the genesis of the book *Virtual Geography*. What we should take note of is the way that the 'researcher' allows an incident – something 'in-coming' – to act as provocation. Though it may not be a recipe for domestic bliss, Wark lets the situation enter his world and set him on a new course. What happens is not so much that he sees a TV representation of something happening in the real world and decides he can offer a better explanation. Nor is it simply that a section of the unknown – something hitherto 'unresearched' – is suddenly discovered in the airwaves or in the corner of the bedroom. Rather, a whole set of factors converge, a coincidence which is made up of a fragment of media coverage, the technologies that convey it, the background knowledge and half-formed theories of the researcher, his geographical location, the time of the day, his domestic arrangements, his emotional state, and so on. Or as Derrida once put it: 'Let's just say the event of the coincidence is a place where the innumerable threads of causality fall together, coincide, begin to cross and reconfigure' (cited in Ulmer, 1994, p.201). What Derrida or Deleuze, or Wark himself, calls 'an event' has to be extracted out of all this. The event, in other words, is not lying in wait: it has to be 'invented' by the researcher or, rather, co-produced by the intersection of researcher and goings-on.

The logic of invention

In the case of a project such as the one Wark sets out on, the 'event' is the problem, or the question he sets out to answer, which in this case might simply be: 'how do we make sense of these strange images which present themselves in my bedroom?' The important thing for us to take out of this is that many of the usual guidelines for doing research are unlikely to help us to generate this sort of question-event, even though they may later be very useful in making sense of it. That is because many approaches to research still work on the assumption that the researcher's prime task is to identify phenomena that already exist 'out there' in the world. This becomes apparent when research guides speak of finding 'gaps in the existing literature' or call for a focused literature search to ascertain that a chosen topic or project hasn't already been 'covered' by another researcher.

But we should not assume that a simple contrast exists between seeing research in terms of events, in which the researcher *makes* connections, and viewing research in terms of a logic of discovery, in which the researcher *finds* gaps to be filled, for the field of research theory and practice is rich and diverse. There is a long history of questioning the notion of uncovering a world 'out there', and even Henri Bergson, writing more than sixty years ago, was not the first to challenge the 'logic of discovery'. There are all kinds of ways in which social science research methodologies pick up on this 'problematizing' of the separation of researchers from world, and draw attention to the implication of researchers in the world in which they working. And yet, as I suggested above, there is also evidence that aspects of the logic of discovery persist in social research advice, and in particular in the way that the originality or moments of inspiration are addressed.

Or, as the case may be, not addressed. It is worth recalling Bergson's claim that a logic of discovery assumes that each of its constitutive moments of discovering or uncovering 'was . . . certain to happen sooner or later' (cited in Deleuze, 1988/1966, p.15). Could it be that this sense of expectation of the new, this confidence in the pre-existence of novelty in the world, explains the rather slender attention devoted to inspiration or originality in most guides to social research? For it seems to be the case that research training in the social sciences or humanities does not dwell on the processes by which areas of interest have initially taken shape, or the moments at which concerns or curiosities have been sparked. Instead, the usual assumption is that the potential researcher arrives with such interests already at hand, and simply in need of development or refinement.

The implication of an approach which hinges on events, one which **a logic of invention** follows '**a logic of invention**' (to use Gregory Ulmer's term), is that by identifying a particular configuration that would otherwise go unnoticed the researcher actually brings the field or the problem into existence (Ulmer, 1994, pp.47–8). And this means the originary or creative process becomes much more prominent, much more difficult to by-pass or take for granted. Without attentiveness and work on the part of the researcher, the particular moment at which the constitutive elements of a 'problem' coincide would be of no consequence, a non-event, a potentiality left unrealized. In this sense, a general reading around an existing topic or a more focused literature search may contribute a strand to the co-incidence that constitutes a problem or a field of concern, but other more 'extraneous' and less 'disciplined' inputs may also be required to bring a new field 'to life'.

Indeed, the majority of methods texts construct the research process as an essentially orderly one, in which surprises are accommodated, anomalies are accounted for and catastrophes are averted. But as Derrida suggests, something important may be lost by the sort of methodological rigour which 'masters every surprise in advance' (1978/1968, p.172). We have seen from both Wark's example and the work of Derrida and Deleuze that a moment of invention involves a certain abandonment to what is happening, and we have also seen that what it is we are opening up to is a weave of circumstances in which our own particular positioning is just one element. In this sense, as Deleuze argues at length in *Difference and Repetition*, the emergence of a problem or question is always at least in part a gamble, a dice throw, a surrender to chance: 'Ideas are problematic combinations that result from (dice) throws', he suggests. 'The most difficult thing is to make chance an object of affirmation' (1994/1968, p.198).

Ontologies of becoming

But how do we know 'something unforeseeable' is going to show up? How can we have any confidence that there will be happenings or goings-on out of which we might generate the event of a question? To ponder these sorts of question is to be drawn more deeply into the way in which Derrida or Deleuze, or any other philosopher, actually thinks the world works. For if we are to delve into the issue of how and why there are 'goings-on' or 'happenings' in the first place, then we are not just dealing with 'epistemological' issues about the generation of knowledge, or the judgement of what counts as valid knowledge. We find ourselves moving into issues of **ontology**: the philosophical term for the question of what reality is actually like.

ontology

For both Derrida and Deleuze the issue of how we engage with the world – and how we generate new problems – is inseparable from a vision of the generativity or creativity of the world itself. Derrida and Deleuze, and many other philosophers of their generation, are part of a tradition of philosophy that sees 'reality' as constantly in motion and ceaselessly self-transforming. This is a tradition which is less interested in what the stuff of the world *is*, and more interested in what the stuff of the world *does*, less concerned with the 'essence' of the forms that comprise the world, and more concerned with the geneses or transmutations that make for a rich variety of forms. Or to put it in the language of philosophy, they see the world in terms of 'becoming' rather than 'being'.

Deleuze and Derrida offer two related but distinguishable versions of an **ontology of becoming**. There is a tendency in Deleuze to focus more strongly on the way in which transformations come about through an outward movement, by way of a kind of eruption or overflowing. Derrida, on the other hand, tends to place more emphasis on changes that are triggered by incoming elements, movements that are disruptive rather than eruptive (Caputo, 1993, pp.57–9). But both types of movement involve 'openings' of selves or systems to an outside, both entail generative encounters between diverse elements, as we have seen. In this way, Derrida and Deleuze share a view of the world as a groundless and unending weave of likenesses and differences. And in this regard, it is accidents, intersections and contaminations rather than 'pure' forms which are considered 'essential' – because they are the unavoidable and utterly necessary processes that make and remake the worlds we inhabit (see Derrida, 1988, p.118; Deleuze, 1994/1968, p.191).

Such an elevation of the 'essential possibility' of chance and contingency distinguishes a Derridean or Deleuzean 'logic of invention' from the more conventional guides to research – with their marginalization of the incidental and accidental. But it is important also to distinguish such an approach from research hinging on a 'Rortyian' play of language. For, as long as play or contingency is confined to language, there are likely to be limitations imposed on the degree to which we allow ourselves to be 'moved' by happenings outside ourselves and/or our spheres of shared language and culture – or outside the range of the human in general.

The flash of lightning, for example, has often been taken as a metaphor for sudden illuminations or connections made in the realms of human thought and deed. But what might happen if we were to move beyond metaphor – with its inference of merely symbolic association – and actually consider the literal implications of the phenomenon of electrical discharges for thinking about connectivity and communication? Consider, then, the following engagement with electrical phenomena by sociologist and feminist theorist, Vicki Kirby:

> As I live in something of an eyrie whose panorama includes a significant sweep of the Sydney skyline, I've often watched electrical storms arcing across the city. As I've waited for the next flash, trying to anticipate where it might strike, I've wondered about the erratic logic of this fiery charge whose intent seems as capricious as it is determined. . . . Reading about electricity's predilection for tall buildings, lone trees on golf

ontology of
becoming

courses, tractors and bodies of open water, I . . . learned that these electrical encounters are preceded by quite curious initiation rights. An intriguing communication, a sort of stuttering chatter between ground and sky, appears to precede the actual stroke. A quite spectacular example is the phenomenon of St Elmo's Fire, a visible light show that can sometimes be seen to enliven an object in the moment, just before the moment, of the strike. (Kirby, 2001, pp.59–60)

Kirby goes on to ponder how it is that lightning seems to know in advance how to find the tallest objects to strike:

. . . if we begin by considering a lightning stroke, any old lightning stroke, we will probably assume that it originates in a cloud and is then discharged in the direction of the ground. However, if this directional causality were true, it would be reasonable to ask how lightning can be appraised of its most economical route to the earth before it has been tested. (Kirby, 2001, p.60)

Now you might be wondering what a *social* scientist is doing getting caught up in a purely physical phenomenon such as lightning. And it is not how lightning is represented, or its power as a figure of speech that interests Kirby: it is the whole complex and mysterious network of 'communication' involved in the electrical storm. Much of Kirby's prior work draws on Derrida to explore the way in which systems of language or communication operate, including the question of whether the messages that animate living bodies can be considered as a kind of language. With the lightning example, Kirby pushes this possibility still further, as she begins to ponder what the paradoxes of electronic interconnectivity at a distance might mean for understanding 'communication' in all its other manifestations.

Where is Kirby's inquiry into lightning leading? It seems too early to tell, for here is an 'external provocation' still in its formative moments, a thought-event not yet fully worked through. As in the case of McKenzie Wark's account, the details of what lightning can or can't do are less important to us than the ability of the 'researcher' to recognize a coincidence or convergence of disparate 'goings-on'. What the story suggests is that Kirby's receptiveness to information that first appears to belong to a field utterly alien to her own is tied up with the particular ontology she embraces. Because Kirby, like Derrida, views the world in terms of complex interweavings rather than discrete objects or categories, there is always a potential opening to make strange and unpredictable connections. Moreover, there appears to be no limit, no final cut-off point as to the source of these concurrences.

In other words, the philosophical position we hold has very important implications for our receptiveness and ability to process novel experiences and information. And this in turn plays a big part in the shaping of the field of potential research topics and questions. According to a Deleuzean or a Derridean logic of invention I have been suggesting, new questions are generated when something draws us out of ourselves, out of our usual circle of thought, ideas and concerns. A philosophy which sees such openings and interconnectivities as constitutive of the world in general – as an 'essential possibility' – is going to find it easier to embrace this sort of occurrence than a philosophy which privileges given forms or appearances, or a philosophy that privileges the contingency of language, as against a more generalized play of differences and similarities.

Events and non-events

A sociologist being inspired by lightning is an extreme case, even more so perhaps than a cultural theorist being galvanized by an encounter with a dictator in his bedroom. The convergences and overlappings that might draw research in new directions, however, need not be as dramatic as either of these cases. What we have to remember – a point made by Derrida, Deleuze and all the other philosophers of becoming – is that coincidence and juxtaposition, chance and novelty, are quite normal and often mundane. We do not have to go far to find them, and they do not have to be earth-shattering or mind-blowing. They may draw us only a degree or two from our normal course, and they may transform our thought processes in only the subtlest ways. But whether they are mild or momentous, we need to be attuned to goings-on – ready and willing to extract an event from the flow of mere happenings. As Derrida puts it: 'Not just any relationships can produce a work, an event. Coincidence must be loved, received, treated in a certain way. The question is, in which way?' (cited in Ulmer, 1994, pp.226–7).

In which way indeed? It's a good question, but I'm afraid its one for which Derrida has no final or absolute answers. And neither, it seems, do any other philosophers with similar leanings. Working out rules, laws or principles for dealing with contingencies, as we will see, is just too much of a contradiction in terms. Let me try to ease us into this issue by way of one more example, this time a tale from my own research history.

I had been doing a lot of work on cyberculture, concentrating on the ways in which new electronic technologies affect our experience of the world in general and nature in particular. At the same time, but on a different tack, I had also been thinking about a much earlier technological 'medium' – the medium of the sailing ship – and how linking the world by sea affected the way the world was experienced. Opening up the world through cybernetic and nautical 'media' had a particular significance to me because I was living at Europe's antipodes in the South West Pacific – which sometimes seems like a long way from where the most important things happen.

Like many cyberculture enthusiasts, I took inspiration from the 1982 film *Blade Runner*, with its striking depictions of a post-human future. So, partly for work, partly for pleasure, I decided to read the novel on which

Blade Runner was based – Philip K. Dick's 1968 science fiction classic *Do Androids Dream of Electric Sheep?* (1993/1968). To my surprise, at the front of the novel was the following Reuters news release, dated 1966:

> A turtle which explorer Captain Cook gave to the King of Tonga in 1777 died yesterday. It was nearly 200 years old. The animal, called Tu'imalila, died at the Royal Palace ground in the Tongan capital of Nuku, Alofa. The people of Tonga regarded the animal as a chief and special keepers were appointed to look after it. It was blinded in a bush fire a few years ago, Tonga Radio said Tu'imalila's carcass would be sent to the Auckland Museum in New Zealand.

Well, I can't remember exactly my domestic arrangements or even where I was at the time, but I do remember that it felt like an originary moment. Auckland is my home town, the Auckland Museum a place where I had both played and worked. I could even picture the turtle in its tableau in the natural history hall. Suddenly, all the disparate trails of my favourite topics converged on a single point: cyberculture, maritime exploration, and representations of nature all collided on my own doorstep. A research project beckoned.

To cut a short story even shorter, I pursued as many of the leads as I could, but the particular and irreducible moment of their convergence in that book's epigraph, in my hands, there in Auckland, somehow failed to ignite. In the form of that specific intersection, there was simply not enough to grasp me or draw me in further. I did bundle all these themes into a conference paper which seemed to keep a small roomful of people mildly amused for twenty minutes, but it never got written up. All was not lost, however. I went on to make reference to *Blade Runner* in an article about rethinking the body in the era of digital communication. I also wrote a piece about the 'imagining' of cyberspace and how this linked up with accounts and memories of early European exploration of the Pacific. Somewhat to my surprise, this article generated an online art exhibition about digital culture and its relationship to islands and oceans. But neither androids nor turtles played any part whatsoever.

In effect, what I did was to backtrack and unravel some of the strands that made for Tu'imalila 'convergence', strands that I was then able to weave together in alternative ways, to produce quite different 'events'; the point being that not all conjunctions or encounters carry the same
non-events   potential. There are events, but there are also, for our intents, '**non-events**'. And, indeed, a philosophy of becoming that depicts reality as a restless mesh of cross-cutting forces and materials by definition offers the researcher or thinker more 'goings-on' than can ever be on-going. A world of almost limitless potential is, unavoidably, a world in which only certain possibilities can be acted upon. But it is also a world in which dropped strands can be picked up again; one in which threads or tangents or lines of interest are always capable of being woven together in more than one way.

Decision time

If we are consistently subjected to contingent goings-on, if the threads of our lives are forever entangling themselves with other strands of existence, you might be wondering how are we to decide which encounters and coincidences to take seriously. How do we judge which lines to pursue, which solicitings we will allow to lead us astray? Amidst all the uncertainties we have entertained throughout this chapter, there *are* some 'irreducibles', at least a couple of 'points of order' which follow, inevitably, from the sort of ontology of becoming we have been exploring. And the first of these is simply that there is no escaping the need for judgement on our part. This goes for theorists and for researchers as it goes for everyone else caught up in the becomings of everyday life. 'Events press hard upon us and demand a decision, a finite cut in the flow of events, a response . . .' as Caputo puts it (1993, p.106). Such decisions may be minor or momentous, subtle or seismic in their implications, but the simple fact of being part of a world of endless possibilities means that we must choose some paths at the expense of others.

The second point that proceeds, no less ineluctably, from viewing the world as a weave of differences and similarities, is the impossibility of disentangling ourselves. One thing we cannot do, one trick we cannot perform, is to extract ourselves entirely from the mesh of worldly goings-on – and view them from a distance. To put it simply, there is no place above, outside or beyond that is not itself tied up with the rest of the world, that is not itself always already made up of comings and goings, meetings and mixtures. Having nowhere to stand outside the fray also means that there is no ground from which to couch laws or principles of judgement that are beyond circumstances, or applicable to every eventuality. And where does this leave us, as Caputo asks? 'If judgement is unable to start out from the principle, unable to proceed from on high, then how are we to judge, how are we to ride out and absorb the shocks and jolts of factical life?' (Caputo, 1993, p.97). Or, more pertinently, how are we going to spend our inevitably limited research time or money wisely?

Where we are left – without universal laws – is to make our judgements on the spot, in the thick of it, from within the tangle of goings-on. In other words, we have to improvise, to make our decisions out of the resources we have at hand. What is most obviously and immediately at hand is our own experience of past events. After all, we have ourselves been forged, shaped and reshaped out of a lifetime of encounters and engagements: to lesser or greater levels we have all been 'seasoned by events' (Caputo, 1993, p.100). For all that each new configuration of forces and elements that we enter into has some degree of novelty, it will also have aspects of familiarity: characteristics or contours recognizable from prior experience.

Our previous 'experience' may be 'at hand' in more ways than one, however. What is suggested by Derrida's 'animal movement', or by

Deleuze's reference to the 'affective tones' in which we might experience an encounter, is that tussling with a world excessively rich in possibility may involve more than just the 'consciousness' we tend to equate with 'thought'. Deleuze is quite explicit about this: 'body, passions, sensuous interests', he argues, 'are not diversions', they are 'real forces that *form* thought' (1983/1962, p.103). Indeed, for those philosophers of becoming who do not limit the interwoven forces and agencies that interest them to the realms of language or culture, there is no particular barrier to the idea of a dispersal of thought through bodies or different sensory modes; nor to drawing on strands of research outside the conventional range of the social sciences. In this regard, some social scientists have begun to tap into evidence from the life sciences which suggests that human beings and other organisms record experiences and knowledge in ways that include much of the body besides the brain (see Thrift, 2001). New understandings of the way that viscera, skin, posture and gesture are all implicated in the processing of information is giving renewed credence to the idea that emotion, instinct or gut-feeling deserve a role in human judgement.

But just as there are no ultimate guidelines lying *outside* the messy world of circumstances and eventualities to guarantee our judgements, neither should we expect to find certainty *within*. 'Hearing out' the deep recesses of our bodies may have a previously undervalued contribution to add, but turning inward is ultimately no more of a foolproof register for sifting and sorting out promising insights than looking outward. If gut-feelings were infallible, my *Blade Runner*-exploration/turtle-android con-figuration would have burgeoned into something rich and bountiful. And there would probably be a lot fewer tragic love songs in the world.

There is another way of helping judge 'event-worthy' goings-on and in-comings from within the thick of it, however, and it is one that is almost banal in its familiarity. Just as contemporary philosophies of becoming conceive of a distribution of sensation and thought across interconnected body parts, so too is agency and thought dispersed across networks of thinking beings. It is hardly necessary to remind social scientists that any thinker or researcher is always already implicated in social or cultural networks. If we need assistance in judging the potentiality of 'whatever gives', in distilling events from a sea of goings-on, then the obvious place to turn is those who have been through similar processes: those who are 'matured by events' (Caputo, 1993, p.100). These others may be colleagues we encounter 'in the flesh', or they may be conversants we engage with in more dispersed ways, by tapping into experience and knowledge that is distributed through networks of bibliographic or electronic texts. What the complexity of 'happenings' implies is that no single perspective is likely to provide all the input we need, and once more we might consider the importance of redundancy, of coming at the same question from a multi-tude of angles. What this might mean, in the case of sifting one research question from many, is tapping into a range of opinions: voices and eyes (and other senses) that are positioned at various points in the problem-field we are composing; people with different angles, different interests, different takes on 'what gives'.

But, as is the case with our more 'visceral' leads, a network of 'informed others' can offer assistance but not guarantees to the decision-making process. Given the absence of infallibility, the process of judgement is inevitably permeated by risk as well as promise – by the hazard, at very least, of pursuing a less fulfilling and productive research path over a potentially richer vein. And it is in this regard that the timing of our most playful and experimental phases is important. While there is no stage of a research project in which we would wish to close ourselves completely to goings-on around us, or to stop asking questions, there are clearly times when the consequences of vacillations, 'wrong turns' or 'dead-ends' are much less of a threat than they are at others.

intuitive
judgement

Indeed, experimental evidence suggests that **intuitive judgement** – decision-making that uses the full range of senses – is at its most acute under conditions when stress or pressure is minimal. Such judgement, it has been said, 'is founded on a kind of combinatorial playfulness that is only possible when the consequences of error are not overpowering' (J.S. Bruner, cited in Bastick, 1982, p.350). A certain passivity, a state of relaxation, even dispersed attention, it appears, is most conducive to the moment of 'insight' (recall McKenzie Wark in his cosy domicile, Vicki Kirby watching a storm . . .). By this logic, we would expect the early stages of the research project – perhaps even before the research is a project in any formal sense – to be most conducive to such moments, at least more so than the times when deadlines are pressing or funds running low. But as you will see from later chapters, there are other junctures when possibilities open out again, when judgements between competing possibilities are again called for.

What should not be passed over lightly – even in the most relaxed moments of the research project – is the risk of coming adrift, of losing our bearings entirely. Gayatri Spivak once pointed out, in a rather marvellous introduction to Derrida's work, that deconstruction's groundlessness, its 'prospect of never hitting bottom' is itself intoxicating (1976, p.xxvii). It is a pleasure, a temptation that deconstruction has to attend to, has to deconstruct further, as Spivak puts it. This is also an important issue for those who are influenced by Deleuze, for there are some readings of his work that seem to assert such a proliferation of life-affirming possibilities that we are left wondering if there is ever a time to settle down. After declaring his enthusiasm for the work of Deleuze, John Caputo eventually confesses: 'I find it too exhausting, all the outpouring and overflowing, all the firing away of forces night and day' (1993, p.53). Even Deleuze, however, concedes that there is one way of doing science or doing research that is good for 'inventing problems', but quite another way of going about things that is necessary for actually solving these problems. There is a time, he argues, when an 'organization of work' is needed, a task for which we need much more formalized procedures than intuition and open-ended experimentation (Deleuze and Guattari, 1987/1980, p.374).

Derrida, as we have seen, also draws attention to the time in a project when the wave of inventiveness congeals into something 'imperious, imperative, inflexible even'. Indeed, he argues, there are compelling reasons for settling on a project – and this is one of the areas where Derrida's approach diverges most markedly from that of Deleuze. For Derrida, it is not simply that we need to organize the field of problems in order to realize the potentiality of our project. It is more that some of what we encounter in the world draws us in, in a special and irresistible way: it obligates us or ties us down. That is why, as we have seen, deconstruction is also about being responsive and responsible. If we are genuinely interested in 'otherness', in the difference in the world, and if we allow ourselves to be held in thrall by things that break into our lives and draw us out of our own circle, then a kind of obligation emerges. In the world of deconstruction, as Caputo puts it: 'there is no squeamishness about responsiveness. . . . There is no squinting here over obligation, no anxiety about gravity and heavy weights, no hand-wringing about being tied down' (1993, pp.59–60). To recall McKenzie Wark's example, it is ultimately we, the researchers, the ones who are drawn into goings-on, who become hostage to what fascinates us.

Conclusion

sense of obligation

This **sense of obligation** or responsiveness is one of the implications that can be drawn from a philosophy of becoming. For, if the world is depicted as generative and generous, then the subjects who are caught up in this world, constituted by this world, may take it upon themselves to behave 'generously'. It is interesting to note how Derrida's own writing over the course of his working life has shifted from engagements with important philosophical and literary texts to a more direct focus on pressing political and ethical concerns. He offers us clues about this turn, when he suggests that 'the political and historical urgency of what is befalling us should, one will say, tolerate less patience, fewer detours and less bibliophilic discretion. Less esoteric rarity. This is no longer the time to take one's time . . .' (1997, p.79).

It is this urgency, Derrida continues, that obliges us to make decisions, to make choices about the work we are going to do – even though we are likely to experience these judgements as 'cutting, conclusive, decisive, heart-rending' (1997, p.79). In our own, perhaps more modest, way, as researchers caught up in a project of our own invention, there will also undoubtedly be a sense of urgency, sometimes because of logistical demands and sometimes because of the nature of our concerns. Here, too, a little heart-rending might be also be required, for there is unavoidably a time when several possibilities must give way to a single problem, when a question must learn to enjoy some solitude.

As we have seen, the philosophical opening of word to world has important implications for what might count as 'available resources and materials' for posing problems and composing questions. This does not discount Rorty's play of language as a source of fresh perspectives. What it does, rather, is to try to extend this play – and all its generative potentials – into the widest sphere imaginable. But as you will have gathered, a radical opening of possibilities for posing questions does not necessarily make the task of the researcher easier or simpler, for our immersion in the play of the world presents demands of its own. The necessity of decision-making is a reminder that neither the foregrounding of chance, nor the acknowledgement of our bodily implication in the issues and problems that appeal to us relieves us of the need for rigour and attentiveness. Indeed, one of most challenging aspects of the call for inventiveness that might be distilled from the work of Derrida and Deleuze is that it calls for playfulness *and* vigilance, a kind of relaxed receptivity *and* a willingness to pursue what takes a hold of us with unrelenting effort and stringency.

There are, however, further challenges that arise from seeing the world as a weave of differences and similarities that we have scarcely touched upon. We have seen that a dispersed or distributed view of thought and agency draws physical bodies into the event of posing problems and generating questions. But 'bodies' too are differentiated, and have their own particular characteristics. While the work of both Derrida and Deleuze seems to offer some intriguing possibilities for exploring the differentiation of bodies and its consequences for generating ideas and problems, it is debatable whether either of these theorists has pursued these possibilities as far as they might. There are other philosophers, however, who have taken the question of our embodiment and the embodiment of our questioning much further, and it is these theorists to whom we turn in the following chapter.

Further reading

There is a great deal of writing about both Deleuze and Derrida, though there is surprisingly little work that talks about them together. John Caputo's *Against Ethics* (Indiana University Press, 1993) is one exception, and a lively and heartfelt one at that. Chapter 5, 'The epoch of judgement' is particularly useful for thinking about events. Deleuze's concern with the dynamic and playful nature of the world is explored in a number of the essays in *Becomings: Explorations in Time, Memory and Futures*, edited by Elizabeth Grosz (Cornell University Press, 1999b), especially Chapter 2 by Manuel De Landa: 'Deleuze, diagrams, and the open-ended becoming of the world'. Though it is a demanding read, Christopher Johnson's *System and Writing in the Philosophy of Jacques Derrida* (Cambridge University Press, 1993) makes a strong case that Derrida, too, is interested in the play of the world, and not just the play of language.

3
A body of questions
Gillian Rose

Introduction

The previous two chapters have considered the work of a range of contemporary, mainly European, philosophers and have explored the consequences of their thought for the process of asking questions. The chapters suggested that their work can be distinguished according to how they rate the possibility of a radically new question producing unthinkably new answers. For Rorty and for Foucault, if for rather different reasons, this possibility is limited. Rorty's central claim is that, since 'language goes all the way down', questions can only be a form of redescription; and, while redescription allows for new kinds of understanding to develop, it is always caught in already existing language. Foucault, certainly in his earlier work, also saw language – or at least, discourse – as powerfully all-enveloping. He argued that what it was possible to say outside discourse was inevitably restricted. The philosophers explored in Chapter 2, however, have a rather different emphasis. Both Derrida and Deleuze – again, despite their differences – choose to think more about the instabilities of language and the world. Although not denying the centrality of language, discourse and meaning to human life, they suggest that certain sorts of play and experimentation can be inventive of the new, not just a metaphorical redescription of it. Some risky encounters can really step outside language and in their newness break out of the prison house of what is already said and done.

This chapter will pursue this discussion of language, knowledge, questions and newness. It will explore how questions can be at once intelligible and open to the unfamiliar. It will do so in a particular context though. What I want to do is work with the philosophies of Elizabeth Grosz and particularly of Luce Irigaray, both of whom have thought long and hard about the relationship between language and what lies beyond its limits. (In this chapter, I assume that language and knowledge are so inextricably bound together as to be the same thing.) Grosz and Irigaray are concerned about how we can think things radically new, but also about how our existing understandings constrain that process. So I'll examine how they negotiate that relation between what is known and what is new. Their philosophy lies at the juncture between longstanding feminist concerns and some of the philosophy that this book has already touched upon, because what they focus on is the bodily.

embodied   It is obvious that we are all, of course, **embodied**. We all have bodies. We all live through our bodies: we think, touch, feel, breathe, smell, dream and sleep with our body, and we constantly encounter other bodies. But the implications of how we live our body in everyday life are by no means obvious or straightforward. Some of the ways in which women's bodies are treated have long been subject to various kinds of feminist protest: for example, reproductive technologies, pornography, rape laws. Nor is it clear how embodiment should be treated by philosophy. Much philosophy simply ignores the fact that human life is corporeal through and through; or, if it acknowledges the fact, assumes a male body (Lloyd, 1984). Some more recent philosophers – and Deleuze, as we have seen from Chapter 2, is an example – have started to think about the bodily, but not in particularly sustained kinds of ways. But I'm running ahead of myself here. To wonder what would happen if philosophy did start to philosophize through the body is to assume that we already know what 'the body' is and what difference admitting it into philosophy would make. And we don't. Or, at least, different philosophers have different arguments to make about that.

Many feminist philosophers are deeply indebted to Foucault for their discussions of the bodily (although many also criticize his lack of interest in the ways in which bodies are gendered). They turn to his notion of **discourse**   **discourse** and argue that what bodies mean in human affairs is not deter-mined by their anatomy, or their genetic or hormonal or chromosomal make-up. Rather, bodies are made to mean by discourses: discourses of femininity and masculinity, discourses that racialize bodies into black or white, discourses that make some bodies able and others not, discourses that mark bodies as classed. Bodies mean nothing in and of themselves. They become meaningful only when they are produced by discourse. In this kind of work, bodies are understood as sort of blank pages, to be written on by systems of meaning and signification, language and knowledge. Such an approach therefore understands bodies as the product of discourse and language. Bodies are constructed by understandings of them. I shall look more closely at this position in the next section of this chapter. It bears some scrutiny, I think, because researchers in the social sciences take many of its assumptions for granted. It is, though, very different from the other feminist philosophy I want to spend rather more time on in this chapter, and those differences need to be explored carefully. Although both posi-tions have been very productive for feminists, each has rather different consequences for thinking about asking research questions. And formu-lating research questions is, once again, the focus of this chapter.

In his later work, Foucault began to move away from the claim that bodies were entirely discursively produced. He began to think a little differently about the body. He started, in his last books on sexuality, to suggest that the body might exist outside discourse, and from that outside have some kind of effect on discourse: bodies could thus have some kind of agency, some sort of potentiality, with which they could make their own mark. Might, then, bodily weight and boundaries, rhythms and flows, the process of ageing and the progress of disease, for example, have some effect on how we understand not only bodies, but our ways of thinking?

corporeality What if philosophy took this **corporeality** seriously? For feminists, this is a crucial question, and a difficult one. There are huge debates among feminists about just how philosophy may deal with the bodily, especially with what is familiarly known as the female body, and there is not space in this chapter to talk about any but a very few feminist philosophers. I have chosen to work with just some of those who insist that philosophy must engage with the corporeal. For these feminists, language and discourse – as they are usually understood – are not the be-all and end-all of human experience. According to them, the body is a site of all sorts of things that are not wholly within language, that are not fully knowable, that are on the edge of being articulable. For these feminists, then, it is the body that can offer some kind of interruption to the familiarities of language, and the body that can and should make us think anew. According to Grosz (1994, p.xi), bodies 'generate what is new, surprising, unpredictable'. I shall focus on the work of Irigaray in particular because, for her, a fundamental tactic for encouraging that bodily intervention is a certain kind of questioning. Her questions hover on the edge between the known and unknown, which is also where she places the bodily. Her particular kind of questions aims to tell us something about how newness might come into our understanding.

This chapter thus addresses the process of formulating a research question in rather a different way from the previous two chapters. While Chapter 1 focused on the limits to language and the role of metaphorical redescription in asking new questions and obtaining new answers, Chapter 2 emphasized the possibility of creating something new, innovating through experimental events. This chapter thinks mostly about questions that can balance on the cusp between the known and the unknown. I want to explore how Grosz's and Irigaray's interrogations of the body are both rooted in discursive understanding but are also open to what is outside it. And I want to consider how being open in our questioning is formulated, looking at Irigaray in particular. How can our questions be open to newness? Following Irigaray through these arguments is especially instructive for understanding how a particular philosophical position leads to a particular kind of questioning.

Constructed bodies, knowing questions

In this section I shall take a little time to characterize a kind of understanding of the bodily that is very common in the social sciences: the claim that bodies are constructed through discourses (hence the label often attached to this kind of work, 'constructionist'). I shall explore in particular the kinds of question invited by this approach. I want to attempt this characterization because the feminist work I am going on to consider later in this chapter is very different, and I want to be able to specify the ways in which it differs. I should say immediately, though, that I am not implying that the feminists I discuss later are somehow better or more advanced or more critical than the feminists I discuss here. My – perhaps rather naive – view is that the more feminisms we have the better: each has its strengths which show most effectively in particular situations. My aim here is simply to start thinking about questions, not so much in terms of the substantive issues they address, but in terms of their philosophy. In particular, I'll concentrate on the balance they assume between what is known and what is not.

culturally constructed

As I noted above, one of the most productive ways in which feminists have thought about the bodily is by arguing that it is '**culturally constructed**': that is, bodies have no particular meaning or effect in and of themselves. Rather, their significance is built by culturally specific meanings given to them. This is evident in one of the most basic distinctions with which many feminists still continue to work, in one form or another: that between 'sex' and 'gender'. 'Sex' is understood as the biological difference between men and women. It is seen by many feminists as a natural given, but also as something that is in itself inert. According to this argument, sex makes no difference to how men and women should be seen. Instead, what defines the difference between men and women is gender: the ideas, ideologies, meanings and fantasies that together make up culture and together define masculinity and femininity. Gender, then, is cultural, while sex and the body remain in the realm of nature. This distinction between sex and gender was taken for granted in much of the feminist literature I encountered when I first started reading it in the mid-1980s. It seemed then an obvious and easy distinction. In particular, it had the major advantage of refusing to suggest that anything about femininity was rooted in biology or physiology or anatomy, and thus that everything about femininity was open to change. The bodily was seen as stable and unchanging, while gender was up for grabs. This was an exciting, indeed exhilarating claim, and many feminists still staunchly hold to it.

It is, however, a claim that has been modulated in various ways. Moira Gatens offered an early critique (reprinted in Gatens, 1996, pp.3–20), and more recently the work of philosopher Judith Butler (1990, 1993) has been hugely influential in shifting its emphasis somewhat. Her account of how gender should be seen as constructed draws heavily on her reading of Foucault and his conceptualization of discourse. Butler argues that not only is gender discursively constructed by powerfully productive discourses, but so too are bodies. That is, she pushes the argument about gender being not natural but artificial even further, and insists that we should see bodies as 'artificial' in the same way too. Bodies may seem to us to be unchangeable, inert and passive matter. But, argues Butler, that is only because discourses make us see them like that. It is discourse that creates bodies as immutable; they are produced as 'natural' precisely by the cultural. But as Pheng Cheah (1996), Vicki Kirby (1997) and Clare Colebrook (2000) all argue, Butler is pushing the argument about the natural and the cultural only so far. She is extending its brief, if you like, by arguing that more should be seen as cultural, or discursive. She is now insisting that the materiality of the body itself should be seen as constructed. But Butler is still arguing that what is significant to our understanding is what is made by the cultural.

What I am particularly interested in here is the consequences of this line of thought in terms of the kinds of knowledge it invites. For it seems to me that if it is claimed that everything is, in the end, cultural, then it is also assumed that everything is, in the end, also understandable. After all, 'culture' is about meaning, significance, knowledge. We talk it, we live it, we go to see it at the movies. It's all around us. And so it is all there as a resource for our interpretation. And interpret it we do. In the social sciences in particular, we have our own well-developed vocabulary for understanding that world. While that vocabulary might be contested, nonetheless there is a strong sense in this kind of work that if it is cultural, it can – in principle at least – be decoded. It can be understood. Its familiarity can be revealed.

Now there is nothing particularly wrong, I think, in thinking as if everything is understandable through the category of the cultural. It can have highly critical effects. What I want to do here is to spell out some of these effects. They are effects that many of us working in the social sciences take so much for granted that we do not even see them as effects. To make them a little less invisible, I want to work with a quotation from the feminist and poet Adrienne Rich. It's a short quote and one that I imagine many of you reading this chapter will be pretty comfortable with; it resembles a great deal of feminist writing both before and after Butler's interventions. She is here writing about her body:

> To write 'my body' plunges me into lived experience, particularity: I see scars, disfigurements, discolorations, damages, losses, as well as what pleases me. Bones well nourished from the placenta; the teeth of a middle-class person seen by the dentist twice a year since childhood. White skin, marked and scarred by three pregnancies, an elected sterilization, progressive arthritis, four joint operations, calcium deposits, no rapes, no abortions, long hours at a typewriter – my own, not in a typing pool, and so forth . . . (Rich, 1987, p.215)

There are several things that strike me about this. First, it's very material. Rich talks about scars, bones, teeth, skin, internal organs, posture. She pays attention to the physicality of her body in a way that sits comfortably with Butler's arguments (although Rich was inspired by a range of other feminist work, of course).

Secondly, its whole thrust is that, although the specificities of her body are very material, they are not natural. Of course, some 'scars, disfigurements, discolorations, damages, losses' may have happened naturally, that is, with no human causation, although the way in which Rich follows that list with the phrase 'as well as what pleases me' suggests that even these 'scars' and so on are assessed according to standards that are influenced by culturally constructed notions of beauty or normality. But we also learn that her bones have been well nourished, her teeth cared for. And other parts of her description can be elaborated from parts of this essay that I haven't quoted.

Thirdly, there's a sense in which all these constructions are cumulative. Each aspect of the cultural construction of her body is in her account added to the others. Thus each of them is inflected by the fact that she was born with white skin in a racist society; no doubt her bones and teeth would most likely be less well nourished if she had been born black, and perhaps her sterilization would not have been elected either. These various aspects of construction accumulate to make the point with which she begins: that her body is about specificity. For each body, born into slightly different circumstances, will be marked differently by a different set of constructions.

materiality These second and third characteristics seem to me to produce a particular understanding of the first: her **materiality**. For each element of her body is characterized and then explained to produce a full understanding of her specificity. Each part – bones, teeth, back – is given a particular history and a particular social location that together, in the way their details and intersections are known, account for her uniqueness. We could indeed cite all sorts of social histories that would enable us to understand the construction of her body in even more detail: a history of the development of the typewriter; a history of the dentistry industry in the USA; a history of gynaecology; a history of feminist campaigns about rape and abortion. We could also – and indeed Rich herself does this – think of social geographies too that would further elaborate this quote. These geographies again would be legible. They would be cartographies of categories already known: class, gender, 'race' most significantly. All these histories, geographies and categories can be deployed to produce bodily specificity because their co-ordinates are known. Their meaning is there to be had. Culture, politics and history are given explanatory priority (Cheah, 1996), hence the kinds of question and answer that this sort of understanding invites.

Let's imagine a question Rich might have asked herself as she wrote the essay from which I have quoted. It might be: *what difference does it make to my body that I am constructed as 'female'?* Her answer seems to be along the following lines. *'Female' is about gender. Gender means that I am constructed as feminine. Being 'feminine' means that my body and actions have been in large part controlled by men, my body in particular. Hence I need to talk about those aspects of my body that have been, or could have been, dominated by men. So, my pregnancies* (Rich writes a harrowing account of the highly medicalized births she and her babies underwent), *and the facts that I haven't been raped or had an abortion.* This answer is structured by what 'gender' was already known to be. This kind of answer thus makes the question a particular kind of question, in philosophical terms. *What difference does it make to my body that I am constructed as 'female'?* is a question that assumes answers are there to be had, using existing understandings, within language. It's a question that deals in *how* we can know – in epistemology (Cheah, 1996; Kerin, 1999) – and not in *what* is there to be known.

The point I'm trying to make is that, in this quote at least, the body is not a site of potentiality or excess beyond discourse or language. Instead, it speaks. It is made to speak volumes. Now, it's rather unfair to use Rich like this, since she was after all a poet, and wrote eloquently about the limits to language. However, accounts like hers have since proliferated, especially in the social sciences. They are taken for granted as ways of thinking about the body, so I want to continue my characterization for a moment longer.

In a very general sense, this kind of feminist writing about the body assumes that the body can be understood in our already existing frameworks of interpretation. It places the body firmly inside the workings of language. It uses categories and concepts that are already known. New combinations of concepts might very well produce new understandings. Indeed, certain sorts of western feminism have themselves gone through a long and slow process of having to acknowledge that 'gender' as a category should always be considered in relation to other categories such as 'race', sexuality, class and dis/ability. Nonetheless, there's a sense in which everything is brought into language, into understanding, and that there is nothing outside this linguistic framework. In this sense, there's a parallel between this kind of feminist work and the kinds of philosophy examined in Chapter 1 of this book. Both focus on ways of knowing, assuming that what can be known is framed in some way by what already is known.

I want to turn now to a different kind of feminism. Its main difference, perhaps, from that which has just been discussed is that it is much less certain that the answers to feminist questions are to be found in language. It thus asks different kinds of question, which evoke different kinds of answer. Again, although I shall explore discussions of the bodily, it is the kind of questioning this other position creates that is my main focus.

Questions and answers on the edge

The last section used a quotation from Adrienne Rich as an example of a particular way of structuring questions and answers. The assumptions underpinning that interrogative structure also produce a certain kind of writing: measured, steady, as if all can in fact be explained – given time. You might like just to return to Rich's quote to remind yourselves of its writing style, a style that's unremarkable in the social sciences even if its subject matter is not.

Now read this extract from an essay by the philosopher Luce Irigaray. She is talking about what she calls 'this *threshold* which has never been examined as such: the female sex':

> The threshold that gives access to the *mucous*. Beyond classical opposi-tions of love and hate, liquid and ice – a threshold that is always *half-open*. The threshold of the *lips*, which are strangers to dichotomy and oppositions. Gathered one against the other but without any possible suture, at least of a real kind. . . . They offer a shape of welcome but do not reduce, assimilate or swallow up. A sort of doorway to volup-tuousness? They are not useful, except as that which designates a *place*, the very place of uselessness, at least as it is habitually understood. Strictly speaking, they serve neither conception nor jouissance [Irigaray's term for sexual pleasure]. Is this the mystery of feminine identity? Of its self-contemplation, of its very strange word of silence? (Irigaray, 1993a, p.18, emphasis in original)

This piece of writing is very distinct from Rich's explanatory tone. Even if you know nothing about Irigaray's work, in this quotation you can hear hints, I think, of a very different way of thinking. First, while Rich's account is all about specificity, Irigaray's is not. She speaks of all women's bodies, and of feminine identity in general. Irigaray deals in universals in ways that often horrify feminist advocates of specificity. Secondly, the position from which Irigaray is writing is not the same as Rich's. Rich seems, if not actually to sit outside her body, at least to gaze at it with a rather contemplative or analytical stare, despite her claim to be 'plunged into lived experience' while looking. Irigaray, on the other hand, seems to be trying to write through the female body. She's offering interpretations, not only *of* female lips, but also *from* them, as if she's exploring what they can tell us. And, finally, there are those questions that Irigaray offers. She asks herself and us – her readers – questions. This makes for an element of uncertainty in her writing, in her ability to explain, that is entirely absent from Rich's account. That uncertainty is compounded by the fact that Irigaray does not answer the questions she poses. The questions are left hanging.

Irigaray's philosophical project is extraordinarily rich and I can only touch on very small elements of it here. What I am most interested in is the connection between the second and third characteristics of her writing that I've just mentioned: the connection between her use of the bodily and her unanswered questions. Broadly speaking, in her work, the body is often used as a way of pushing at the limits of understanding. Unlike the previous kind of feminist work I've just outlined, for Irigaray the body is not always explicable. It isn't always amenable, ultimately, to interpreta-tion and explanation. And this is because the body exists before and beyond its discursive construction. It isn't simply produced by discourse, as Butler claims. For Irigaray, as for other feminists like Vicki Kirby, Elizabeth Grosz and Pheng Cheah, the bodily exists actually, richly, provocatively, excessively, regardless of our particular understandings of it. It saturates our selves, including our philosophy. Their questions about the bodily are not therefore aimed at *explaining* particular bodies or particular processes of embodiment. Instead they are trying to evoke the bodily itself. And for Irigaray in particular, this entails asking questions. Questions always invite responses of some kind, and she asks questions that are open to the bodily as it exists beyond our current knowledges.

I shall begin my discussion of this kind of feminist philosophy by exploring how it thinks the body. I shall then go on to focus on the work of Luce Irigaray and her kind of questioning.

Thinking through the bodily

I am tempted to begin this section with a question of my own: why have these feminists decided to think about the body differently? There are many reasons why some feminists are beginning to think about the body as irreducible to language. First, there is the ontological claim that if the body is indeed there – if it does indeed have an existence and an integrity that are not given entirely by language or discourse – then feminists quite simply have to deal with it on its own terms. We have to think about the bodily and its natural, material specificity (Wilson, 1999). Secondly, for some of these feminists, thinking about bodies as natural immediately

sexual difference

installs **sexual difference** as inherent in and fundamental to all aspects of human (and non-human) life. Irigaray, for example, sees sexual difference as so fundamental because it is the major, naturally given difference with which human beings (and non-human beings) have to deal. She says that 'the natural is at least two: male and female' (Irigaray, 1996, p.35). Cheah and Grosz agree, saying that, 'with the exception of asexual life forms, all naturally occurring life forms are engendered from two sexes or the genetic material from two sexes' (1998, p.12). This argument subordinates all other kinds of difference to sexual difference: 'the whole of humankind is composed of women and men and of nothing else. The problem of race is, in fact, a secondary problem . . . which means we cannot see the wood for the trees, and the same goes for other cultural diversities – religious, economic and political ones' (Irigaray, 1996, p.47).

This claim has its critics, as you might imagine. Some have pointed out that human bodies cannot be so neatly divided into two, because some babies are born with genitalia that are not self-evidently male or female (see Kaplan and Rogers, 1990); others accuse her of assuming hetero-sexuality when she states that all relations are based on, and can be modelled on, relations between male and female bodies (Butler and Cornell, 1998); and still others are shocked at her marginalization of 'the problem of race' and 'other cultural diversities' (Lorraine, 1999).

Perhaps the most enduring critique of Irigaray's engagements with the bodily, though, is that they reduce feminine (and masculine) subjectivity to biology. We have already seen that making a clear distinction between natural sex and cultural gender has been vitally important to many feminisms, precisely in order to avoid this reduction. However, this distinction between sex and gender is necessary only if the body – the natural, biological body – is assumed to be passive and inert. Only if bodies are unchangeable would interpretations of sexual difference based on biology also be unchangeable. What is crucial about the arguments of Grosz, Irigaray and others, however, is that they do not see the bodily as inert. For them, a body is not just passive matter, to be worked upon by outside forces whether they are discursive or technological, linguistic or medical. Bodies are not simply the effect of discourses of gender, 'race' and class, or of socially specific practices of dentistry and gynaecology. Corporeality is not passive in this way. Instead it is active. Indeed, there's an extraordinary sense in their writing of the dynamism and potentiality of the bodily. There is nothing about the bodily – or about the biological more broadly – that is stable.

In a fascinating essay, Grosz (1999a) draws on the work of Charles Darwin to make this point. She suggests that passivity and inertia were qualities very far removed from his understanding of biology. She points out that Darwin's starting point was not stability but change: evolution, to be precise. Darwin wanted to understand how species evolved. Most of us are familiar with the most basic outline of his argument: minute and variable differences in individuals enable certain individuals to adapt better to their changing environment, and natural selection ensures that they survive while the less well-adapted do not. These advantageous differences are passed on to subsequent generations through sexual reproduction (hence the central importance of sexual difference). But the mechanisms that Darwin posited as underlying this process were all about biological transformations that were inherent and random: proliferation, multiplication, replication, differentiation, variation, mutation. Biology – life – is about change, mutability, transformation. From this, Grosz concludes that the bodily cannot be seen as determining cultural identity and practices because the body is itself mutable. It is in its nature to be so.

Grosz thus reworks what the biological, and thus the bodily, might signify in feminist arguments. Far from stasis, she insists on its dynamism. And part of its dynamism, she says, is its openness to culture. Bodies ingest culture to make themselves, and culture thus becomes corporeal. Conversely, though, Grosz suggests that the cultural needs to materialize itself corporeally. She tries to pull the natural and the cultural through each other. She does not want to reduce one to the other. She explores the corporeal as both natural and cultural, where the natural and the cultural inflect one another but do not collapse into each other. (For other, more Derridean, accounts, see Cheah, 1996 and Kirby, 1997.)

Irigaray, too, in her bodily discussions refuses to allocate the bodily to either the natural or the cultural. As Margaret Whitford (1991) points out, Irigaray uses the term 'morphology' to refer to this in-between corporeality. Her argument is a little different from Grosz's, though. Irigaray tends

bodily morphology to take **bodily morphology** somewhat more for granted than Grosz does. This is perhaps because she emphasizes sexed difference constantly, and has often written about female morphology as a means of exploring the specificity of femininity. Her use of anatomy is particular though. Like Grosz, she does not imply that anatomy, or biology, is destiny. Instead, she works with the specificity of anatomical parts to refigure them. Thus her exploration of feminine morphology chooses particular sorts of body parts that evoke certain sorts of process: in particular, relations between things that are neither separated nor fused. I shall return to this point below. For now, I want to note the way in which her bodily morphology sits on a hinge between the natural and the cultural by using a quotation from her book *I Love To You*:

> I am a sexed . . . being, hence assigned to a gender, to a generic identity, one which I am not necessarily in/through my sensible immediacy. And so to be born a girl in a male-dominated culture is not necessarily to be born with a sensibility appropriate to my gender. No doubt female physiology is present but not identity, which remains to be constructed. Of course, there is no question of it being constructed in repudiation of one's physiology. It is a matter of demanding a culture, of wanting and elaborating a spirituality, a subjectivity and an alterity appropriate to this gender: the female. It's not as Simone de Beauvoir said: one is not born, but rather becomes, a woman (through culture), but rather: I am born a woman, but I must still become this woman that I am by nature. (Irigaray, 1996, p.107)

Here Irigaray is suggesting that the sexed specificity of the body is always present as a kind of potential: 'I am a sexed being . . . female physiology is present'. However, she is also saying that the potential of that physiology must be realized: 'identity remains to be constructed' in relation to that physiology. Again, as in the work of Grosz, the body is presented as material and cultural and changeable (see also Irigaray, 2002).

In the work of Grosz and Irigaray, then, the bodily inhabits both the natural and the cultural. It hovers on the edge of understanding, only ever known through our efforts to interpret it, but nevertheless offering its own possibilities and interventions into our practices. Here we can see the relevance of the work of these feminists to this chapter's task of thinking about questions that are both intelligible and open to newness. Irigaray, for example, has said explicitly that her efforts to think through the bodily are not trying to step outside language and knowledge – as she says, 'one cannot simply leap outside that discourse'. Instead she is attempting, she says, 'to situate myself at [discourse's] borders and to move continuously from the inside to the outside' (Irigaray, 1985/1977, p.120). In other words, she places herself at the boundary of the known and the unknown, trying to allow the latter to inflect the former. In turning now to consider how Irigaray, in particular, writes through 'the body' by asking certain sorts of questions, we need to keep in mind this specific conceptualization of the bodily.

Questioning (from) the body

I have tried to show how both Irigaray and Grosz are trying to think about the natural and the cultural mediating each other. Culture is materialized in their work, and matter is enculturated. For Irigaray, this mediation is evident in her writing. Writing, for her, is not just linguistic or cultural. It is also corporeal. Her striking **writing style** needs to be approached in this context. When Irigaray writes her philosophy, her arguments are expressed as much through how she writes as through what she writes. Her writing style is fundamental to her arguments (Weed, 1994; Hass, 2000). The bodily inflects her writing. This section explores how that is the case, and what questions have got to do with it.

writing style

As we've seen, Irigaray insists on the centrality of sexed difference between bodies. So the bodily that pervades her philosophy is a specific one. She writes through the female body. This is not to say that she is claiming that her writing is determined by her particular body form. As we have also seen, she clearly states that corporeality does not shape the culture or subjectivity of an individual. Rather, she writes a morphology that is female, a writing/body both material and meaningful. This is a necessary task because, in a 'male-dominated culture', a sensibility appropriate to female bodies does not yet exist. Creating one, for Irigaray, is the feminist project (Whitford, 1994).

Irigaray's reconfiguring of the female body goes hand in hand with her critique of dominant ways of knowing as masculinist. In her earlier work, she paid most attention to the traditional canon of western philosophy as a particularly powerful 'way of knowing' that provided the foundations for many other forms of knowledge that were less explicit about their assumptions. In later work, she extended this analysis to the patterns and assumptions that underpin men's everyday speech too (Irigaray, 2000). Her analysis of this masculinism and its costs is important since it provides a context for her concern to develop a different kind of femininity. According to her analysis, the morphology of masculinity can be summed up as 'solid' (Irigaray, 1985/1977, pp.106–18). **Solid** refers to both the male anatomy and to masculine culture. Irigaray suggests that a masculine knowledge has a fear and abhorrence of anything liquid (which it designates as feminine). Instead, it desires solidity, stability and predictability. It wants certainty, not surprises. A solid discourse wants clearly defined terms, and outlaws any textual play or ambiguity. It wants to work with

solid

concepts that are clearly defined, fully knowable, with clear boundaries and no overlaps with other things. Cheah and Grosz gloss solid concepts as 'unrelated atomistic singularities' (1998, p.6). Thinking with them produces what Irigaray describes as a '1 + 1 + 1 + . . .' mode of reasoning, where each solid entity is lined up to the next in certain combination, and it is their ordering that is understood as knowledge. Irigaray also argues that this solidity structures masculine bodies. Writing of 'the value granted to the only definable form', she describes 'the one of form, of the individual, of the (male) sexual organ, of the proper name, of the proper meaning . . .' (Irigaray, 1985/1977, p.26). In making a parallel between solid thinking and 'the (male) sexual organ', Irigaray is proposing that masculine corporeality inflects philosophy. As Kirby (1997, p.75) remarks, though, we must also remember that philosophy's solidity inflects masculine morphology; as she says, the male sexual organ is only singular if we ignore its testicles. For Irigaray, then, philosophy is a masculine practice; its morphology of solids is both bodily and conceptual.

Irigaray's critique of this masculine mode of thinking has some relevance to the kinds of feminist account of the bodily explored in the previous section of this chapter. There, I suggested that there is a tendency in some feminisms to think through certainties too: to prefer to work with categories that, in their fundamentals at least, are already known. Certainly Irigaray never hesitates to make her differences from other feminists explicit (see for example her disagreement with Simone de Beauvoir, author of *The Second Sex*, which I quoted in the previous subsection). However, there is an important difference between the feminist work I described as constructionist in that previous section and what Irigaray describes as masculine modes of thinking. That difference lies in how masculine thought and feminist thought consider the relations between entities.

masculine
morphology
Irigaray's main criticism of **masculine morphology** is that when it lines up solid concepts in a conceptual chain that looks like '1 + 1 + 1 . . .', it also produces certain kinds of gap between these atomistic singularities. It makes gaps which are stable and absolute. *An Ethics of Sexual Difference* elaborates the consequences of this atomism (Irigaray, 1993a). Irigaray argues there that thinking about things in ways that produce absolute and unchanging gaps between them is symptomatic of a masculinity that fears fluidity, uncertainty and connection. For Irigaray – as for Grosz, Kirby and many others – life is, precisely, fluid, uncertain and connective. Denying this connectivity, according to Irigaray, leads only to the terrible state of the world we now live in, polluted, war-stricken and poverty-ridden, deathly (Irigaray, 1993c, pp.183–206). I would suggest that all feminisms, in contrast, think about relations between things. Feminism as a politics is based entirely on views about the relations between women and men, after all. So feminism, even when it works within the legibility of the cultural, is nevertheless always sensitive, to some degree, to relations between things. We can see this in Adrienne Rich's essay. I noted in my discussion of that

relational

feminine
morphology

permeability

piece that the categories she uses to describe and explain her self were
cumulative: each inflects the other. This is the kind of **relational** thinking
that Irigaray also advocates. Irigaray is concerned to articulate a philosophy that assumes relations between entities, not absolute gaps.

Her alternative philosophy of relations is based in large part on
feminine morphology. That is, she turns to the female body in order to
think anew. What she wants to think through is not gaps, but a kind of
relation in which entities are somewhat open to each other. Open to each
other's difference, sensitive to difference, but not overwhelmed by it. So for
example, instead of gaps she tries to think through 'a double loop in which
each can go toward the other and come back to itself' (Irigaray 1993a,
p.9). She is trying to think in terms of a connectivity between entities that
is mobile and two-way, but that also preserves the distinctiveness of
difference. Now, this might sound rather abstract. But of course Irigaray
grounds it precisely in the materiality of the body. She tries to cultivate
female morphology in ways that allow just that going towards the other
and coming back to herself. Thus she tries to write in ways that articulate
not solidity but **permeability**. She tries to figure female embodiment in
ways that are open to otherness but not fused with it. Hence one of her
most notorious essays is about lips (Irigaray, 1985/1977, pp.205–18). Lips
cannot be understood in terms of '1 + 1 + 1 . . .' because they are, as
Irigaray says, neither one nor two; moreover, they can open to other things
but they retain their integrity while they do so. She has written about the
placenta, too, as something joined and mediating, which belongs to neither
mother nor foetus but negotiates the complex hormonal, nutritional and
immunological relation between them (Irigaray, 1993b, pp.37–44).

But she does not write simply to redefine these morphologies. Rather,
the very form of her writing enacts the morphological qualities she desires.
Thus she does not simply assert a different reading of female lips, or a
different definition of their symbolic possibilities, or a different explanation
of their meaning. Instead, she tries to embody lip-ness in her text. And this
is where her questions are so important, because what they do is to carry
the permeability and openness to difference of female morphology. It is
necessary to pause here, I think, before elaborating exactly how Irigaray's
questions articulate permeability, in order to establish this point. Irigaray
obviously asks specific questions: 'a sort of doorway to voluptuousness?',
we've heard her say, for example, 'is this the mystery of feminine identity?'
And equally obviously, the terms of those questions – 'doorway', 'voluptuousness', 'mystery', 'feminine', 'identity' – have (some sort of) substantive meaning in the context of her work. But what I am trying to
emphasize here is that the *form* of Irigaray's questions is just as central to
her project as their content. That is, the structure of her questions is also
crucial to their production and effect. Of particular importance, I think, is
the fact that she so rarely answers the questions that she poses. This refusal
to answer gives her questions a certain open-endedness. They are open to
responses because they are indeed questions. But those responses have to

come from elsewhere, since Irigaray herself does not provide them. Answers to her questions have to come from something or somewhere else.

Readers of Irigaray's texts have to look for answers to her questions in three other places in particular, I think. They have to look at the concepts she works with in her overall arguments; they have to divine her own position; and they have to think about their own responses to her work. And when you make these connections as you respond to Irigaray's questions, 'permeable' effects are generated.

First, the concepts Irigaray employs have a certain openness or undecidability in relation to other concepts; secondly, her own position is uncertain in its relation to her writing; and thirdly, as a reader of Irigaray's text, I am rendered open to her arguments.

Concepts are never defined once and for all in Irigaray's work. You cannot grasp what they mean by looking for definitions of them. You can define them only by default, as it were; since she never stops to clarify her own terms, you have to deduce their significance from clues, hints, suggestions, implications. Many of these clues are offered in the form of questions she doesn't answer. Her questions exemplify a style of writing which, as Irigaray (1985/1977, p.79) says, 'tends to put the torch to fetish words, proper terms, well-constructed forms [and] resists and explodes every firmly established form, figure, idea or concept'. Read the quotation from her that opened this section of this chapter again, where Irigaray is talking about female lips. We can understand better now why she wants to describe them as 'strangers to dichotomy and oppositions', why she is interested in thresholds, mucous, half-openness. These are all morphologies of permeability, neither solid nor solid's opposite, fluid, but in-between, open to both. And her questions are half-open too. Are lips a doorway to voluptuousness? Are they the mystery of feminine identity? Irigaray is giving us certain clues here, since she's phrasing the questions in particular ways. She's not suggesting that lips are a doorway to an engulfing chasm, for example, as some of her masculine philosophers imply. But precisely what she *is* suggesting isn't certain either. I can't answer yes or no definitively to her questions. They feel to me more like suggestions that Irigaray is giving me, resources, potential ways of thinking about the relation between meaning and matter.

If Irigaray's questions make her concepts permeable, they also make her own position uncertain. And this uncertainty is amplified by another permeable relation between things: in this case, the relation between her and the text she is commenting on. She sees herself as a writer open to the texts she interrogates, and this openness she has described in terms of asking those texts a question:

> The only response one can make to the question of the meaning of the text is: read, perceive, experience. . . . *Who are you?* is probably the most relevant question to ask of a text, as long as one isn't requesting a kind of identity card or an autobiographical anecdote. The answer would be:

how about you? Can we find common ground? talk? love? create something together? What is there around us and between us that allows this? (Irigaray, 1993c, p.178)

Who are you? she asks of texts, and she assumes a response, a form of communication between her reading and the text's writing: *how about you?* Irigaray is suggesting here that this kind of questioning engagement with the other – in this case, with what is read – produces a mediation between the two, something created together. Her request not to receive an 'identity card or an autobiographical anecdote' refers to her critique of solid concepts, since both ID cards and (some kinds of) autobiography describe people using clear and unambiguous categories. In contrast, her own integrity, her own self, is modulated through her encounter with something different from herself. Her writing does not, then, mirror herself; instead it articulates her engagement with other work. It reminds me of her figuration of the placenta: the placenta, too, is something that mediates between two other things. So 'Irigaray herself' is not solid in her questioning encounters with other writers. She shift-shapes in response to them. She's not solid.

Finally, as Elizabeth Weed (1994) points out, the permeability of Irigaray's concepts extends to the relation between her texts and her readers. As a reader, I'm never quite sure that I've understood her properly. And of course it's precisely that sense of 'proper' that Irigaray dislikes so much: remember her association of 'the proper name, of the proper meaning' with 'the (male) sexual organ'. So I follow her allusions and ironies and references and arguments as best I can and then she asks me a question. She asks a question and I have to respond from where I am, in relation to her. I don't know if I'm 'right' or not, if I'm being 'proper' or not. But of course that doesn't matter. What does matter to Irigaray's project – and it matters both in the sense of being significant and being material – is that her writing and I are doing something together at the edge of what is presently understood. It's no wonder, then, that reading her is difficult and even disconcerting. It's meant to be.

Irigaray's questions thus evoke permeability. They are open to newness because their terms are always in relation to something else, and that relation affects each term. Thus her concepts shift according to the context in which they are evoked. Her own position is open to the texts with which she engages. And her reader's position is rendered porous in the way she always invites your participation. She doesn't let you read unscathed. This porosity to otherness is written through the female body. Lips and the placenta, among other parts, corporealize this mode of relationality. They are used as both a source and a figure for a particular kind of questioning. On the edge of understanding, their morphology allows a questioning that also rests on the pivot between what is known and what is new.

Conclusion

Like the others in Part I, this chapter has been about questioning. Here, however, I have explored the relation between philosophy and research questions by focusing on the work of one philosopher for whom questioning is a fundamental part of her work: Luce Irigaray. As I have tried to show, the form of Irigaray's questions is integral to her wider arguments about the production of knowledge. She argues that much of our existing knowledge, language and understanding is structured in masculine ways, and that philosophy in particular is shaped by masculinity quite profoundly. Her analysis of this masculinity suggests that it is deeply dysfunctional for humane living in a world full of differences. But she also suggests that there are some existing resources to rethink relations between differences. In seeking ways to re-imagine more open, receptive and per-meable relations between things, one resource Irigaray draws on extensively is the bodily. She evokes a bodilyness that is open to difference and otherness. This is an openness that does not lose its own integrity in the other – it is not swallowed into it – but neither is it an openness that itself swallows and engulfs. Irigaray insists that we can learn this kind of relationality, that we can train ourselves into it, because it is there potentially already in our bodies. A placenta, or lips (for example, and here lips need not only be female), can be re-formulated, re-materialized. And articulating this particular kind of relationality is the point of Irigaray's questioning. Her questions are most often unanswered. And that openness makes all the components of her text – author, writing, reader – open to each other. Her concepts aren't solid; she is somewhat elusive; she makes her reader think with her. In this way, her body of questions articulates her philosophy.

Irigaray's work, then, is a very clear demonstration of the conse-quences of a particular philosophical position for the kinds of question a research project might ask. Irigaray's ontological assumptions about what exists, and her epistemological claims about how we do know it and how we might know it, drive her particular form of questioning. This has been the case with all the philosophers discussed in this part. Rorty, Foucault, Deleuze and Derrida each make quite fundamental claims about the form of our knowledges and, should you adopt any one of them, from their claims follow certain consequences for the asking of research questions.

Further reading

If you want to start reading Irigaray herself, I suggest her book *I Love To You* (Routledge, 1996). It contains a range of different aspects of her work: parts of it echo her 'difficult', questioning style, on which this chapter concentrates (although in rather diluted form); parts of it refer to her linguistic research; parts of it are practical, politicized suggestions for change; and parts of it are just wonderful pleas for a new way of living. The best secondary account of Irigaray's work, I think, remains Margaret Whitford's *Luce Irigaray: Philosophy in the Feminine* (Routledge, 1991), although it does concentrate mostly on Irigaray's relation to psychoanalysis. For more wide-ranging discussions of her work, see the collection of essays edited by Carolyn Burke, Naomi Schor and Margaret Whitford called *Engaging with Irigaray* (Columbia University Press, 1994), and the book by Tina Chanter, *The Ethics of Eros* (Routledge, 1995).

CONCLUSION TO PART I

Part I has explored what for many is often regarded as a straightforward process: the development of a research question. Rather than take you through the pragmatics of refining a research question in the way that so many textbooks on research methods tend to do, however, we have chosen to approach the asking of questions from a different angle: one that explores the difference that philosophy makes to how we go about generating research questions.

At a basic level, all that we have tried to do is raise awareness of the different possible ways of asking questions. In doing so, we have asked you to pause and reflect upon your own manner of questioning. When you settle upon a question or a form of words that feels comfortable, what assumptions have you made about their relationship to the world that you are in? Is it all about achieving a better 'fit' with the world? Is the quest one of exercising our imaginations to come up with a form of words that breaks with past associations – a kind of gestalt-switch – that shifts the focus of our attention on to something entirely new and novel? If so, what weight or importance have we attached to this experimental use of language in the research process? Does the assumption that language is the only tool at our disposal restrict our research possibilities?

If the answer to that question is yes, then a different set of assumptions come into play, where the world is less something of our own construction and more something that draws us out of ourselves, not only to surprise, but also to answer back. On this view, the world intervenes in our knowledge; it exceeds our descriptions of it by confronting us with the sheer messy, slippy, surprising business of living in it. Whatever easy assumptions we may have made about being able to 'know' the world are now themselves open to question. Chapter 2 raises this possibility and in doing so invites you to consider research questions as less than the words which compose them and more about the question mark at the end – as a provocation for someone who is caught up in the vicissitudes of the world.

What assumptions you make about your place in the world, whether you are inextricably caught up in it or inevitably independent of it with language as your only means of access, will thus have consequences for how you go about the process of research. The kinds of question that we might ask – even down to whether an interrogative statement style of probing is appropriate – stem from the assumptions that we make about what exists and how we claim to know what we know.

This is most apparent in Chapter 3 where issues of ontology and epistemology open up for examination the very form in which questions are asked. Asking questions which presuppose an answer is itself an assumption that we make all too readily, as indeed is the assumption that there is only one way to pose a research question. In thinking about the embodiment of our questioning, different assumptions come into play that presuppose an openness not always present in those who stop at the boundary lines drawn by language. Put another way, if you believe as a researcher that you cannot get in between language and the world to come up with a better question, then what is openness for some is for you likely to be treated with scepticism. But that is precisely why philosophy has consequences for how we go about the business of research.

Whatever the assumptions in play, however, a research project is not something that lasts for ever. Whether short or long term, there comes a moment early on in the project when it is necessary to fix a question or indeed a cluster of key words, simply because it is necessary for you to move on in your research. Perhaps somewhat surprisingly this has more to do with taking responsibility for your endeavours than anything to do with the production of the 'right' question or key words. While you will invariably find yourself revising, refining and revisiting whatever question or questions you decide to run with, the responsibility that you have at this stage of the research process is one of taking a decision – to make a cut, so to speak – and to live with it until you or the world, or both (depending upon the philosophical assumptions that you hold, of course) change your mind. Asking questions is an iterative process; it would be surprising should you remain with your first efforts. It would be equally surprising and perhaps more difficult, however, should you fail to exercise your judgement to arrive at a research question, no matter how provisional, before you move on – or rather move out – into the 'field'.

PART II
Investigating the field

INTRODUCTION
Sarah Whatmore

The business of 'investigating' stands as the kernel of what research is often thought to be about, the part sandwiched between the desk-bound tasks of 'formulation' and 'writing up'; the one where you get your hands dirty. The aim of this second part is to blur this apparently simple sequence of stages in the research process while preserving the importance of the moment in which you have to engage with and, by the same token, intervene in the world of your research. The chapters employ the ideas of Latour (in Chapters 4 and 5), Stengers (in Chapter 5), and Rabinow and Spinoza (in Chapter 6) to set up a series of questions and guides that not only ask you to interrogate the accepted sequential nature of research, but remind you of the consequences of adopting philosophical lines of inquiry to how you approach work 'in the field'.

Significantly, the chapters offer ways of re-positioning the researcher in relation to the empirical work about to be undertaken. They encourage us, for example, to think of fieldwork as 'engagement'; they open us to the idea that such an activity involves a variety of encounters (as Chapter 4 suggests with the help of Latour). Such a view moves us towards a position where researching is far more than discovering a passive world – a position, you perhaps recall, that would follow should you be persuaded by the ideas of Rorty or Foucault, discussed in Chapter 1. To take Rorty, say, into the field would mean that work would focus on the word rather than extend, as it were, into the world, and thus be limited to the sifting through existing language; there would be no risk that the world might bite back – because of its perceived passivity. In contrast, through an engagement with the work of Stengers, Chapter 5 demonstrates what might be gained if we re-think this stage of the research process so as to allow non-human and material worlds into the research process from the outset. The process then becomes more about the co-fabrication or joint generation of research materials.

As this suggests, the Latourian/Stengerian line of inquiry calls for reflection on the human *and* material worlds *active* in empirical work. Furthermore, in her critique of the humanistic legacy that has long informed many qualitative research methods (a flavour of which has just been given), Stengers' approach helps us to ask questions about how we might better appreciate the role of a *variety of entities* (that is, not simply the human researcher) in the conduct and outcome of research (as you will see in Chapter 5). The prompt to think about a range of entities adds to initial fieldwork-type questions (such as 'How much data do I need?') the issue of *what counts as data*. This type of thinking reverberates through to the nature of the research question made at the outset – 'what does my question allow me to do here, "in the field"?', 'what does it close down or open up when it comes to empirical work?', and so on. In this way we see how research is very much an iterative process: it's about shaping and reshaping, moving on and returning, thinking of the consequences that accompany philosophical choices.

By questioning the accepted spatial divisions – work 'in the field', the library before that, and then 'the study' – that inform the familiar sequence and the linear progression through them, you'll see how the chapters' engagement with ideas produces a number of related philosophical issues and associated crafts to help to rework this moment in the research process. For instance, if we accept the Stengerian line of argument demonstrated in Chapter 5, then it is not tenable to view fieldwork as being about the discovery of pre-existing evidence. Rather, viewing research as producing what she terms a 'knowledge event' means that we understand this encounter between the *uncertainties* of human and material worlds in more generous terms. After all, preoccupied as we are with our 'own' research project, it's all too easy to imagine ourselves exclusively at the centre of things. Part of the skill we thus learn along this route is to work a degree of humility into this important part of research, a lesson that might be foregone if this moment were to be informed by other assumptions about the world.

And, as the chapters note, if we accept that human and material worlds actively combine in doing research, then quite complex ethical issues are sure to be involved. Moreover, if we are persuaded by the philosophical discussion in Chapter 4, and recognize the *range of encounters* made through our engagement in fieldwork, then our co-constitution of research materials, and the power relations this necessarily involves, produce a *variety of ethical issues*. How we address these requires us to exercise judgement (as Chapter 4 again reminds us) and serves as another illustration of how philosophically informed *crafts* – the craft may be to judge the *appropriateness* of a research method – are exercised as we 'map materials into knowledge' (to employ the words of Chapter 5).

From an initial discussion of the ethical dilemmas recounted by the anthropologist Paul Rabinow as he reflects on his own fieldwork,

Chapter 6 takes us further into a discussion of ethics and research. As the conversation develops, we learn something of the easily passed-over craft of reading philosophical texts, something you will also come across in Chapter 4. There, you will see that only part of Latour's work is interrogated: the skill is not just to know which part to question but what specific question to have in mind when doing so. Such a craft is refined further in Chapter 6, where it is exercised in relation to the writings of the philosopher Spinoza. The chapter considers how Spinoza's wide-ranging ideas might inform a present-day approach to ethical responsibilities in the research process – and how, it should be added, we might accomplish such a task without the fear of drowning in abstract ideas. From the complicated thought of Spinoza the chapter shapes a philosophical stance that may help us to think ethics actively through the research process. It is a stance, moreover, that invites us to *re-imagine* the space of the encounter and thereby to 'cultivate good judgement' in the process of doing research, rather than to adopt an 'off-the-shelf' formula provided by one of a growing number of ethics committees.

In this chapter, as with the others in this part, the role of the imagination in an engagement with philosophical ideas is shown to be crucial to re-invigorating this moment in a research project.

4

Imagining the field

Doreen Massey

Introduction

In most research projects there comes a moment when you must leave your own room, your literature review, your formulation – which will still be provisional – of the question, and 'go out to encounter directly' your 'object of study'. Whether this latter is a sector of an economy, an archive, a social process or, indeed, a region, the activity frequently goes by the name of 'doing your fieldwork'. The aim of this chapter is to coax you into reflecting upon your 'field', and your relationship to it, from a philosophical perspective and thereby to enrich this moment in the overall craft of doing research.

How do you imagine (implicitly, in your mind's eye) your field? What **fieldwork** kind of engagement with your subject matter is involved in **fieldwork**, and is it any different from any other? What, precisely, are you up to when you 'go out into the field'?

All the scare quotes around words and phrases in the preceding paragraphs are there to indicate that much of our habitual terminology of fieldwork deserves further investigation. Indeed, precisely, they raise philosophical issues.

The field vs the cabinet

The whole activity of doing research is frequently imagined in terms of 'exploration' and 'discovery'. The language recalls an earlier age, of voyages and expeditions, and much of the imaginary of that period still frames our implicit conceptualizations of the process of investigation. The notion of 'fieldwork', and the complex of heterogeneous understandings of that term, are central to this. The mention of 'fieldwork' still evokes the idea of 'going out there' to address directly, 'in the real world', your chosen object of study. It is a distinct moment in the overall process of doing research. But even in those early days the relationship between work 'in the field' and the production of knowledge was the subject of fierce debate.

Debate

Alexander von Humboldt (1769–1859) was one of the most significant and thoughtful, as well as passionate, of 'explorers'. His aim, in his extensive travels in Latin America, was both 'exploration' in a classic sense, and a wonder at the landscapes in which he found himself, and also precise scientific recording and measurement. Felix Driver writes of 'Humboldt's vision of scientific exploration as a sublime venture and his emphasis on geographical analysis as a means of scientific reasoning' (Driver, 2000, p.35). He was also a man equally at home in his study, pursuing further his 'scientific reasoning' and philosophical enquiry. He had a 'commitment to a synthesis between scientific observation and scholarly learning' (2000, p.53) which, although exceptional, was influential. In particular, he influenced Charles Darwin, whose *On the Origin of Species* appeared in the year of Humboldt's death.

Yet half a century before that book was published, an attack was launched on this approach to 'doing science'. It came from Georges Cuvier (1769–1832), also a naturalist but one whose mission was to create a new science of 'comparative anatomy'. Cuvier's methods involved detailed anatomical investigation of the internal physiological structures of flora and fauna as specimens, and also of fossils. His workplace was the dissection rooms in the Museum of Natural History in Paris. In 1807 Cuvier vented his anger against the scientific claims of explorers in the field in a highly critical review of a report of Humboldt's field research (Outram, 1996). It was a key moment in a debate which was to last for decades (and, I would argue, in some senses still goes on) and it wound issues of epistemology, and more generally the nature of science and what could be classified as science, together with spatiality, or the various geographies through which the scientific endeavour comes to be constructed.

At the very heart of this debate was a relation to 'the field' and 'fieldwork'. As Dorinda Outram writes: 'The concept of the field is a complex one, . . . the idea of "the field" is pivotal in its union of spatial metaphor and epistemological assumptions' (1996, p.259). The challenge thrown down by Cuvier to men such as Humboldt raised crucial questions which still reverberate: 'Where was their science located? Indoors or out? Were the systems of explanation created by the work of indoor anatomists superior to the intimate knowledge of living creatures in their habitats which was traditional field natural history?' (Outram, 1996, pp.251–2).

Here is Cuvier's opinion:

> Usually, there is as much difference between the style and ideas of the field naturalist ('*naturaliste-voyageur*'), and those of the sedentary naturalist, as there is between their talents and qualities. The field naturalist passes through, at greater or lesser speed, a great number of different areas, and is struck, one after the other, by a great number of interesting objects and living things. He observes them in their natural

surroundings, in relationship to their environment, and in the full vigour of life and activity. But he can only give a few instants of time to each of them, time which he often cannot prolong as long as he would like. He is thus deprived of the possibility of comparing each being with those like it, of rigorously describing its characteristics, and is often deprived even of books which would tell him who had seen the same thing before him. Thus his observations are broken and fleeting, even if he possesses not only the courage and energy which are necessary for this kind of life, but also the most reliable memory, as well as the high intelligence necessary rapidly to grasp the relationships between apparently distant things. The sedentary naturalist, it is true, only knows living beings from distant countries through reported information subject to greater or lesser degrees of error, and through samples which have suffered greater or lesser degrees of damage. The great scenery of nature cannot be experienced by him with the same vivid intensity as it can by those who witness it at first hand. A thousand little things escape him about the habits and customs of living things which would have struck him if he had been on the spot. Yet these drawbacks have also their corresponding compensations. If the sedentary naturalist does not see nature in action, he can yet survey all her products spread before him. He can compare them with each other as often as is necessary to reach reliable conclusions. He chooses and defines his own problems; he can examine them at his leisure. He can bring together the relevant facts from anywhere he needs to. The traveller can only travel one road; it is only really in one's study (*cabinet*) that one can roam freely throughout the universe, and for that a different sort of courage is needed, courage which comes from unlimited devotion to the truth, courage which does not allow its possessor to leave a subject until, by observation, by a wide range of knowledge, and connected thought, he has illuminated it with every ray of light possible in a given state of knowledge. (cited in Outram, 1996, pp.259–61)

Geographical exploration and discovery were central in the development of empiricist methods of modern science and, as Livingstone (1990) argues, they continue to be an important background imagination shaping the practice of research in geography and other disciplines. In this view, we go out into the field to 'discover' things. Cuvier's response was that real scientific discovery can only take place away from the field, in the study. Why? There are three reasons given in that quotation which it is important to pull out here:

Study		Field
the possibility of comparison	vs	the specificity of the field
nature as specimens	vs	nature in action
distance from the fullness of the field	vs	embeddedness within the field

There are other (related) oppositions, implicit or explicit, within that passage by Cuvier which you might at this point just note: between mind and body (an important issue which will be examined by Sarah Whatmore in the next chapter); and between specified genders (an issue which we shall return to in this chapter).

What is going on in this passage? There were clearly all sorts of oppositions in play: between theoretical speculation and confronting the empirical world; between a kind of isolated systematic logical clarity and an inevitable openness to the 'thousand little things' of the real world out there. The struggle here was over power and legitimacy between different kinds of scientist and different kinds of scientific practice. It is a debate, I think, which continues to reverberate; in some sciences in precisely this form ('you can't be a proper anthropologist/geographer/. . . if you haven't been out in the field'), and also in other guises (see below).

But studying this debate from the vantage point of doing research today we might also read it differently. Much of our research will involve *both* the field *and* the cabinet (and, after all, Humboldt insisted on both and Cuvier had to have his 'samples' collected somewhere). So I would suggest that what we might understand as also going on here is a differentiation between two distinct 'moments' in the overall process of doing research; and one question consequently raised is how we think about the relation between these moments – crudely put, between going out and obtaining your 'material'/'data' and what you do with it when you get back. Each 'moment' involves a distinct manner, or mode, of addressing our object of study. 'Fieldwork' is one such moment, and the focus of this chapter is, in part, on the nature of its relation to other steps in the research process.

Spatialities of knowledge

These are not only 'moments', a temporal differentiation; what was also crucial to the distinctions being contested was the spaces/places of the production of knowledge. The 'geographies of knowledge', in the most general sense of those words, have often been argued to be integral to the kind of knowledge which is produced, and to its subsequent status and reception. In this debate about fieldwork, indeed, there is a whole range of spatialities (some explicit, some implicit). What is more, they structure both the epistemological presuppositions and the practice of research. They are real **spatialities of knowledge-production.**

spatialities of knowledge-production

First, and most importantly, there is a key contrast in spatialities between the modes of investigation in play in Cuvier's argument. At its starkest, it is a contrast between immersing oneself in the field and distancing oneself in the study or laboratory. Thus Outram argues that Cuvier is:

> . . . saying that the knowledge of the order of nature comes not from the
> whole-body experience of crossing the terrain, but from the very fact of

the observer's *distance* from the actuality of nature. True observation of
nature depends on not being there, on being anywhere which is an
elsewhere. At bottom, Cuvier is fighting an epistemological battle.
(Outram, 1996, p.262)

This establishing of *distance* is crucial. This was the period of the
emerging hegemony of that geography of knowledge which insisted on a
gap between observer and observed, between knower and known; and saw
the production of the idea of objectivity. What this may develop into is the
establishment of a gap in kind between known and knower: writes Cuvier,
'it is only really in one's study (*cabinet*) that one can roam freely throughout the universe'. This is not just an 'elsewhere'; it is a kind of nowhere. A
gap which (it is supposed) lends placelessness, a lack of locatedness,
objectivity. But, the reply might come, from those committed to 'being
there', by doing one's thinking and one's science in the field itself, it
is possible to capture the complexity and the ongoing movement of the
world one is studying. Each position makes a different kind of claim to
knowledge: the objectivity (supposedly) lent by distance; the verisimilitude
(supposedly) lent by immersion. (And considering these different kinds of
claim to knowledge may raise again the question of your question – in the
continual back-and-forth between designing your fieldwork and refining
your question you need also to consider the kinds of claim your research
may propose to make.)

Traces of that opposition between objectivity/distance and immersion
are still in play today. A questioning of the possibility of positionless
objectivity (the so-called 'God trick') has led some to argue against
distancing *tout court*. This kind of argument is implicit in some feminist
approaches, which express a distrust of 'the view from above', or urge us
to concentrate on 'local' investigations. It is mirrored in the opposition
between structure and street – as in Michel de Certeau's (1984) exhor-
tation that we abandon the view from the skyscraper to plunge into the
real complexity of the lived life below. Sometimes, to the knowledge-
claims being made by this argument is added the claim that such a position
in and among (from the situation of) the 'objects' of one's research is also
to be preferred on ethical or political grounds.

But as Meaghan Morris (1992) points out, this is a false opposition.
On the one hand, distance, or height, or standing on top of skyscrapers,
cannot lend 'objectivity'; it is still a view from somewhere. However high
you climb, however much distance you put between yourself and your
object of study, you will still be located somewhere. You cannot pull off
the God trick. Objectivity in that sense is not possible. On the other hand,
there is no such thing as total immersion; there will always, still, be a
perspective, some things will be missed. You will still be producing a
particular knowledge. So maybe that opposition of extremes (between total
removal and total immersion) is itself unhelpful. Moreover, abandoning
that opposition opens up other, perhaps more productive, questions. If

some 'distance' is inevitable between knower and known, how do we conceptualize it and how is it to be negotiated? And if 'total immersion' is impossible, how do we negotiate our engagement? These questions will run through the later sections of this chapter. But, before that, there are other spatialities of knowledge-production to consider.

material geographies

The second spatiality concerns the symbolic significance of the **material geographies** of knowledge. In many cases, the material spaces/places of the production of knowledge are both constructed and conceptualized as reflecting the nature of the knowledge-production with which they are associated. Cuvier's museum was conceived as a heavenly place of order 'outside' the real world. Over the ages in the western world there has been a tradition of certain forms of knowledge being produced in places 'set apart' from the world – in monasteries, on science parks, in ivory towers. And it can be argued that such locations both reflect the epistemological relation of distancing and use this isolationist spatiality as an adjunct to the legitimation of this form of knowledge and as a reinforcement of the status of its producers. (Chapter 9 will consider in more detail this issue of legitimation and status.) The very place of research can be one of the sources of its authority. Being aware of the locations of your research, and of their social meaning, can itself induce reflection on the nature of the process in which you are involved. Indeed, one of the points you might pull out of this chapter, and use to reflect upon your own research process, is this relation between particular activities of research, and types of knowledge, and their geographical location.

Finally, our imaginaries of 'fieldwork' itself are often very strongly spatialized. (The notion of the field as being 'out there' is essential to the construction of Cuvier's argument.) And each of these spatial imaginaries will encapsulate a relationship, maybe only implicit, of inquiry and of power. Johannes Fabian (1983) has analysed what might be called this 'epistemological positioning' of the field within anthropology. He argues that for anthropologists the field is not only (classically) geographically distant, it is also usually imagined as temporally distant too; that anthropologists imagine the societies they are studying as 'further back' in historical time than the scientist themselves. This manoeuvre of the imagination has significant effects, most obviously in that it increases the supposed distance between observer and observed (and thus, on the model above, increases objectivity). This, as Fabian (1983) notes, is only anthropology's way of doing what all other sciences do. (It is, of course, also internally contradictory, for the anthropologist's actual practice '*in* the field' is to engage with, talk to, these people whom he or she has imaginatively placed in another time.) The imagination of the field is thus a significant element in the articulation of the relationship between the anthropologist and the peoples being studied. It substantially affects, recursively, the nature of the encounter. It is for this reason that addressing the spatio-temporal imaginary within which 'the field' is placed is an important part of doing research.

For this to be true, it is not necessary that your fieldwork takes place in some distant part of the planet; it may rather involve studying other texts, or archives, or your own home neighbourhood. Strongly accented spatialities may nonetheless be in play. The East End of London, and many other working-class areas, have frequently been figured as the Heart of Darkness, for example, into which ventures the intrepid researcher. Or again, perhaps more likely these days, one's field may be imagined as 'exotic' or as 'peripheral' or, even worse, as titillating or eye-catching. All these ways-of-imagining are mechanisms of distancing researcher from researched, and thereby – even if inadvertently – of establishing a particular relation of power.

Discovery/Construction/Transformation

The constraints of discourse

Those debates which began in the latter half of the eighteenth century continue today and have significant influence upon the way in which western scientific practice is structured. But, as is common in fierce debates, the early protagonists, as well as disagreeing strongly on major questions, also shared some significant assumptions. For them the aim of science was to find out about the world. The vocabulary of discovery was strong. Cuvier writes of 'truth' and of 'reliable conclusions'. The assumption is that the aim and the possibility of research are to produce an accurate representation of 'the world out there'. At this point in your research this becomes a critical assumption to confront. After all, the whole burden of connotation with which the very term 'fieldwork' has come down to us through the centuries is that this is the moment of going out into that world to investigate it.

And yet, in Chapter 1 you have encountered philosophers who in various ways would challenge this view that our language is, or can demonstrably be, 'a mirror of nature'. The argument of Richard Rorty is that we cannot connect with a world of experience outside language; that what we have available to us, as researchers, is language 'all the way down'. On this view, then, we cannot plunge into the truth of the real (the background imaginary which so much of the history of fieldwork has bequeathed to us); there will always be a gap which we cannot cross. Rather, our task as researchers is to produce the new through the process of inventive rearticulation of language. Here is a strong challenge: 'the field' is not out there waiting to be discovered; rather, it is already linguistically constructed and the researcher's aim must be imaginatively to reformulate this construction in such a way that new avenues can be opened up, new ideas and practices can flow. Discovery: construction. Indeed, we have already begun to recognize the power of 'construction' in the last section, though without commenting upon it in this form. Fabian's argument about anthropology, for instance, is precisely concerned with how we do not just 'encounter' the field but construct it, imaginatively, linguistically. Rorty is arguing for re-imagination in productive ways.

Now, it's all very well to agree with Rorty as one reads him (he does, appropriately, given his philosophical position, have immense powers of rhetorical persuasion) or to argue his case in a seminar. But what does this position mean for the craft of research? Most tellingly of all, what does it mean when you come to the moment of 'fieldwork'?

For me, there are a number of things that Rorty argues that can have an important impact upon both how we conceptualize and how we practise that element of research which we call fieldwork. First of all, it emphasizes the need to be aware of prior linguistic construction. This is significant, whether or not we agree that there is an unbridgeable gap between language and something else 'beyond'. But if you are a strict Rortyian your engagement in fieldwork cannot lead to claims of discovery, or about how things really are. Rather, you will seek to persuade your audience to understand differently, to articulate the linguistic constructions in such a way that they make a different kind of sense. This will mean, perhaps even more strongly than is usually the case in research, that you are self-consciously engaging a debate, an already constituted under-standing (academic or popular or political). There is an emphasis (though again this need not by any means be confined to Rortyians) on conceptual experimentation. This does not, even in Rorty's insistence on linguistic construction, mean that anything goes. There must still be rigour, con-sistency and relation to purpose. And, finally, that sense of purpose is also very important in a Rortyian approach: you want to redescribe *in order* to disrupt the hegemonic imagination, open up new ways of thinking, remove blockages to potential new forms of practice.

Those who do not accept Rorty's philosophical position may respond that they agree with, and value, many of these things (the significance of reconceptualization, the importance of a sense of purpose), but query, at this moment of fieldwork, the role of 'the world out there' in all this. Does it not have the capacity to surprise us? To force our reconceptualizations? In Rorty's pragmatist universe it is the researcher who seems responsible for all the surprises, who is the only active agent in this process. What about all the arguments in Chapter 2 about the need to go outside ourselves, to break out of the prison house of language, to stop seeing ourselves as the centre of everything? The notion of an ambulant science, maybe even the notion of surprise, implies the possibility of an unknown into which we may venture. But if our encounter is language all the way down, even the unknown (if there can strictly be said to be such a thing) will come to us immediately framed by the concepts we already have available to us.

That latter point is, of course, even more strongly made by Foucault (see Chapter 1), particularly in his earlier work. While Rorty is pretty ebullient about our freedom to redescribe, Foucault points to the power in and the powers behind dominant discursive practices. In Chapter 1 the concern was with how the questions we ask are constrained by the discursive rules and conventions already available to us. In fieldwork, this same argument points to the limits upon our freedom to re-imagine, to reconceptualize.

This is especially to be recognized to the extent that fieldwork is thought of, as it so often is, as a voyage 'into the unknown' (Driver, 2000, p.268). And once again the terminology of discovery can provide food for thought. Much has been written about how the Europeans who first landed upon the shores of what was to become the Americas came to terms with what they found. They were indeed faced with what was, to them, the unknown. On the one hand, all they had at their disposal, linguistically and conceptually, was what they had brought from Europe. So, both in order to make some sense of what they found, and in order to be able to communicate it back home to an expectant European public, as well as demanding European paymasters, they had to struggle to arrange this new reality into the terms which they already knew. The discursive constraints were very real. Wayne Franklin (1979, 2001) has analysed this struggle as it faced Hernán Cortés. He writes of how this rebellious Spanish conquistador had to communicate back to Charles V in 'canons of allowable speech [which] shaped the manner in which he perceived and acted in the world of Mexico' (Franklin, 2001, p.120). In other words, the discursive regime, outside which he could not think, moulded the reality he confronted. But also, for himself, he had to struggle to make sense. Franklin writes of Cortés undergoing 'a formidable cognitive test' (2001, p.120) and argues that 'we can . . . see his literary efforts as an . . . attempt to fill the almost aggressive silence of the West with words, to convert "noise" into meaningful sound' (2001, p.120). Yet that last sentence gives a clue also to an opposing process: that, in Franklin's interpretation, Cortés was not the only agent in action. There were tensions between word and thing: 'the voyager found himself so far beyond the bounds of his known world that knowledge and words alike were threatened with a severe breakdown' (2001, p.125).

It is in this context that we can appreciate why, as pointed out in the last section, such voyages were so significant in the establishment of the importance of empirical enquiry – and why in its day this was a liberatory, even revolutionary, move. For the philosopher Francis Bacon (1561–1626 – in other words, two centuries before Cuvier), the voyager, by the very fact of discovering new things not immediately capturable within the old, set ways of European thinking, was a brilliant exemplar of the possibility of breaking free from the ancient established authority of book-bound scholasticism. For him, 'the library as a symbolic enclosure of authority stood opposite to that "road" which he urged his readers to pursue. By breaking through the enclosures of traditional space, the American traveller also was breaking the bonds of received language' (Franklin, 2001, p.125).

I wanted to come back, full circle, to Bacon here, and to the dawn of the age of empiricism and of 'the field out there', for one particular reason. It indicates how philosophical shifts are themselves historically embedded. And this in turn is a caution to us: both not too scornfully to deride 'past' positions nor to be too confident of the 'truth' of the newest arrival.

Of course, in your own fieldwork there may be rather less of this journeying into the pure unknown. But you may well be attracted precisely by an element of the not (yet?) understood. Sometimes the aim of research may be to disrupt the reassurance of the apparently familiar (where, you suspect, the very familiarity can be obscuring) precisely by *rendering* it strange. You may have posed a question, as discussed in the last chapter, which precisely tries to remain open to the unfamiliar, even to 'hover on the edge between the known and unknown'. Indeed, it can be argued that much of the writing of Alexander von Humboldt, which embraced the minute documentation of 'scientific data' alongside the expression of a sensuous exhilaration in the landscape, was his way, precisely, of maintaining this position. More simply, you may just wish to insist upon an element, at least, of 'finding out' (note your position here in relation to those who insist upon the prison-house of language). If so, all the foregoing arguments would urge upon you an acute sensitivity to the fact that your field, and much that you find therein, will come to you already organized into a frame of reference. One can never be totally questioning (partly because it is likely to become circular, and partly because you do need to finish your research at some time) but do question, be aware, as much as you can. (It is also the case, of course, that one often cannot be aware of all the constraints and confinements.) On the other hand, the tale of Cortés may enable you to open up a space of engagement, where you may become aware that maybe you are forcing well-worn categories, or categories and concepts to which you are committed, upon recalcitrant material, where the world speaks back. And once again, pondering all this will give you another opportunity to refine your question further.

Bringing the world back in

Let us pause for a moment and consider again an issue which was raised in the previous section: the need to be explicit, and reflective and critical, about the spatiality of knowledge within which one is working. At this point I am thinking particularly about the imaginary spatialities through which we express epistemological positions. Thus Outram argued that in Cuvier's day the ideal positioning for the achievement of objectivity was in a 'heavenly' location removed from the particularities of the world one was studying, a location which was intended precisely to obviate the 'problem' of locatedness. There was a gap in kind between the scientist and the field. Rorty also imagines a gap, and again it is a gap in kind, but this time it is between reality and representation, between 'the world out there' and language. (In developing this line of thought in second-stage pragmatism, Rorty was part of a wider movement called the 'linguistic turn'.)

This is a very general epistemological position, in that it concerns the whole of our relationship, as linguistically able (indeed often linguistically defined) human beings, to the world beyond us. What we are exploring in this chapter, however, is 'fieldwork' and 'the field'. Two points immediately arise. First, the term 'fieldwork' has greatly extended in its meaning from those days when Humboldt set out for Latin America. Today it is often used in a more general way, to indicate original empirical work. Your field may be an economic sector, a set of people, a group of social processes, or an archive or other texts. Nonetheless, fieldwork is still a specific activity within the wider research process. And that indicates the second point: are not discourses and texts, books and tables and diagrams just as much of 'the real world', and are not other stages of your research (your literature search perhaps) also engagements with that world?

One approach which takes this position is perhaps best exemplified in the work of Bruno Latour. Latour is a philosopher and social scientist and his writing, and his intellectual contribution, span a huge range. By asking awkward questions, and by maintaining a steady focus on practices, he has attempted to overturn a number of ways of thinking which have often been taken for granted. He has stressed both the **multiplicities** involved in all practices and processes (often using terms like 'collectives') and the **effectivity** (the 'actant' status) of things other than human beings. He has become particularly known for his contributions in the spheres of actant network theory (ANT) and science studies. The wider philosophy of Latour will be explored in later chapters. Here, however, I want to take advantage of the fact that on occasions Latour has addressed specifically the question of fieldwork and its relation to (its setting within) a wider practice of research. Indeed, I want to focus on one chapter of his book, *Pandora's Hope* (Latour, 1999) – Chapter 2, 'Circulating reference' – in order to interrogate Latour in a particularly focused way, and in relation to just a part of his work. Doing it this way, however, allows some important issues to emerge concerning fieldwork. Later you can put them in the context of his wider work.

margin notes: **multiplicities**, **effectivity**

In this chapter, Latour does a very Latourian thing: he pays 'close attention to the details of scientific practice' (1999, p.24). He does his own field research on a group of scientists doing *their* field research, which concerns the shift of the border between forest and savannah at Boa Vista in Amazonia. For Latour, it is 'a chance to study empirically the epistemological question of scientific reference' (1999, p.26). It is a detailed study, documented in detail.

And what emerge are a picture and a proposal. Latour jumps into that supposed gap between the field and the written-up research to investigate the practices which he argues it in fact entails. He points out the numerous distinct operations which it involves (we might think of operations such as: deciding how to sample, collating information under different headings in your filing system, fixing on the key questions for an interview or series of interviews). Latour argues that each of these distinct stages in the research process involves a *transformation*. You turn the object before you into something different. You make it *mean* something which will feed into the next stage of research, for which it will in turn become an object, to be worked on further. At each stage of research, in other words, what you have before you (whether it be, for example, an interviewee or a set of interview notes) has characteristics both of being a 'thing' and of being a 'sign' (1999, p.60). At each stage you take the thing created at the previous stage (say, your interview notes) and work on them to produce a new sign – maybe a redistribution of the transcript under a sequence of headings. At each stage, says Latour, something is lost (locality, particularity, materiality, multiplicity, continuity) and others things are gained (compatibility, standardization, text, calculation, circulation, relative universality). In his terms, there is both 'reduction' and 'amplification'. At each stage there is an engagement, a transformation, a process of creation. One should never speak of 'data' as something given, argues Latour, but of 'achievements'.

Now, for Latour the implication of the elaboration of all these steps in the research process (this chain of transformations) is that we must challenge that spatiality of knowledge which envisages an uncrossable gap between two polar extremes, of 'real world' on the one hand and 'representation' on the other. Thus, he argues:

> The philosophy of language makes it seem as if there exist two disjointed spheres separated by a unique and radical gap that must be reduced through the search for correspondence, for reference, between words and the world. . . . While following the expedition to Boa Vista, I arrived at a quite different solution . . .
>   . . . Phenomena . . . are not found at the *meeting point* between things and the forms of the human mind; phenomena are what *circulates* all along the . . . chain of transformations. (Latour, 1999, pp.69, 71; emphasis in original)

Not only is every object both 'thing' and 'sign', depending on its positioning within the process of research but, insists Latour, 'There is nothing privileged about the passage to words' (1999, p.64). This, then, is a radically different spatiality of knowledge from Rorty's: 'at every stage, each element belongs to matter by its origin and to form by its determination; it is abstracted from a too-concrete domain before it becomes, at the next stage, too concrete again. *We never detect the rupture between things and signs*' (1999, p.56, emphasis added).

This view also alters the way in which 'the field' itself is spatialized. Latour is very clear that there is a difference, for his scientists, between the field and the room in the university to which the information will be taken. Indeed, in his characterization of reduction and amplification he makes some of the same distinctions that Cuvier makes. He writes also of the room in terms of the advantages of comfort, in terms of being the place where all the 'achievements' (recordings, interviews, documents, for instance) can be brought together for the unifying gaze, and where they can be shuffled around while the researcher thinks (1999, pp.36–8). Elsewhere again he writes of 'disciplining' the field. What Latour adds, though, is an emphasis on each stage as a distinct kind of engagement, where a different mixture of things, signs and activities is enrolled, and also an emphasis on each stage as being open, both through its position in a chain of trans-formations and because each operation (through its artefacts and categories) is produced through and therefore connects out to a wider world of research and scientific production. 'The field', then, begins to seem less like a space which one goes to and subsequently leaves. Rather it is a much more complex structure which one transforms; it is still present, in transformed form, in your written report (1999, pp.70–1), and the processes of transforming it are present, too, in every operation 'within' the field. The field and the cabinet, then, are distinct certainly, but also are utterly linked through a chain of your own production.

There is much here that can enrich the way we go about fieldwork. It encourages an awareness of each operation. It points to the need to consider what each operation is really doing. (As you collate notes from interviews, or records of observations, for instance, you are transforming them into a particular distillation: creating something, engaging with the object to produce a new sign.) You need therefore to be aware of both what you are gaining and what you are losing and aware, too, of the collectivity and materiality of each operation. It is in the next chapter that these stages (what is sometimes lumped together under the term 'data collection') will be considered. Here, what is important is to note that in this view there is no huge uncrossable gap between you at your desk reading 'the literature' and a field 'out there'.

An adherent of the linguistic turn might want to respond to this onslaught, and it is important that we give them some right of reply. First of all, one could argue that what has happened here is that a big gap has been reduced to a lot of little ones (within each transformation). Even if we recognize the constitution of phenomena as inevitably hybrids of thing and sign, there remains the question of where the 'sign' aspect derives from. This study of Amazonian fieldwork is very much an empirical inquiry. Latour gives full recognition to the necessary dependence on concepts and categories inherited by the researchers from the earlier studies and from a range of fields. But here those categories (elements of wider discursive frameworks) are taken as given (as indeed in practice they often *are* taken). But what about a piece of research that aimed at reconceptualization? What of re-signing, of 'redescribing lots and lots'? The lack of attention here is ironic given Latour's own conceptually innovative record. Indeed, on the first page of this chapter he tells us that he is going off with this bunch of scientists because 'I want to show that there is neither corre-spondence, nor gaps, nor even two distinct ontological domains, but an entirely different phenomenon' (1999, p.24). In other words, he goes off with a real purpose: to redescribe.

Yet, and to circle round again, in his *own* field research *into* field research Latour is disarmingly unreflective. By simply describing, by 'paying close attention to', by examining in detail (1999, p.24), he will give us a more realistic picture. What of the concepts and categories, the discursive regimes, which he brings to this close paying of attention? Later, he acknowledges that he is posing as 'a simple spectator' (1999, p.72). Nevertheless it is important to recognize that the injunction just to look at what researchers do is also, itself, an epistemological position.

Relating to the field

'The field' itself is a spatial concept with material, practical, effects. Whatever imaginary you operate within (and it would be difficult to manage without one), it will have implications. It will have effects on your relationship to the field, on the nature of your own identity as a researcher, and on the range of practices and behaviours which are thereby enabled. It will also raise questions of power and responsibility. We have already touched upon this, particularly in the discussion of spatial imaginaries of fieldwork: anthropologists displacing their field to the past; the imagining of the field as 'exotic', and so forth. Those imaginations stand at one extreme, perhaps. In them, the field is at some distance; it is a bounded space separated from the academy where other stages of research are performed; you the researcher are not implicated in it; you just go there and, even more significantly, you leave. Such an imagination is likely to induce, or to reflect, an assumption of power on the part of the researcher. This may not be at all deliberate, but imagining the field as 'exotic', for instance, raises all kinds of questions, about objectification, about the assumption of a right to investigate, about the centrality of the imagination of the researcher, for instance. At the other extreme, Katz (1994), writing of ethnography and of the difficulty of drawing boundaries 'between "the research" and everyday life; . . . between "the field" and not; between "the scholar" and subject' (1994, p.67), argues that she is 'always, everywhere, in "the field"' (1994, p.72) and she explores the issues of relationships and of power which necessarily have to be faced.

The work of Bruno Latour, stressing the myriad of small but crucial transformations which connect field and study, so that the moment of study is in the field and the Amazon forest and savannah were brought back (transformed) to his study, has already begun to raise questions about that 'here–there cartography' of doing fieldwork. What his work clearly does is to challenge that **territorial cartography** where the field is a bounded space. Here it is open and porous, and connected by a chain of practices (and also by the complex networks, human and non-human, within which those practices are set) to the rest of the research process.

territorial
cartography

Here spaces are constructed through relations. And once the question of 'relations' is on the agenda, then not so far behind should come questions concerning the nature of power within those relations. How, then, can we relate the disruption of the settled territorial cartography to questions of power? Of particular importance here have been some strands of feminist philosophy.

It is often indeed argued that field*work* is classically characterized as a masculine activity, while the *field* itself is positioned as feminine. There are all kinds of source for this, including the frequent historical associations between going into the field and military endeavour, on the one hand (see, for instance, Driver, 2000), and the counterposed connoting of the field itself as passive and available for entry on the other (see, for instance, Clifford, 1990). Matters are, however, also more complicated than this, and go deeper philosophically.

Thus Georges Cuvier was clearly all too aware of the prevailing heroic, manly image of the fieldworker and feels he is obliged to struggle, to assert, in competition, the 'courage' required of intellectual labour, and the different kind of manliness that characterizes sedentary scientific production. Whatever these scientists are doing, it has to be understood as masculine. And indeed the distancing, universalizing, procedures of the cabinet have subsequently been taken to task for their 'masculine' structurings. One might reflect that what is at issue is representational power rather than any essential masculinity or femininity. One of the things most evident, here, about 'masculinity' is its mutability. Similarly, within the discipline of geography, while there is an extraordinarily strong tradition of characterizing fieldwork as a manly rite of passage, more recently other geographers, including many feminists, have used 'fieldwork' precisely to challenge some of the existing orthodoxies (see Hyndman, 1995; Sparke, 1996). (Shades here of Francis Bacon.) So the means and mechanisms of gendering are by no means simple.

Nevertheless there is a consistency, although of a different kind. In the opening paragraphs of this section, a distinction was made between the field conceptualized as a separate and enclosed entity and the field as more clearly constructed in relation to the researcher and to other stages in research. The first conceptualization is characteristic of a way of thinking which was introduced in Chapter 3, where the world is imagined as consisting of 'atomistic singularities' (Cheah and Grosz, 1998, p.6). Things are what they are, and only then may they come into contact, interact. It is a way of thinking which has been much challenged by feminism. Moreover, in this particular matter of field and fieldwork, as has also been pointed out by feminists, not only is the field a separate place, already given, but the relation between field and fieldworker has often been viewed in dualistic terms. The field is everything that the fieldworker is not, and vice versa. The fieldworker is active, thinking, part of culture. The field is passive; it is the real world; it is nature. Field and fieldworker, in other words, are counterpositionally characterized through some of the classic dualisms of western thought: dualisms that counterpose mind and body, culture and nature (and, indeed, possibly, the real and representation). As the last chapter pointed out, to this way of thinking what is not natural is understood as cultural; and nature is passive while culture is active. The imagination of the field outlined at the beginning of this section depends upon such dualisms.

One of the reasons why it is important to be aware of the form of this classic imagination is that it has significant implications for the distribution and nature of power between fieldworker and field. The fieldworker is the only active agent. The field itself actively contributes nothing; it only offers up. Neither field nor fieldworker are (imagined to be) changed by the encounter.

Moreover, the complex concatenation of dualisms structuring much of western philosophy has positioned 'the feminine' as the passive pole, along with body and nature, as against the active masculinity associated with culture and mind. For a whole variety of reasons, therefore, feminist philosophers have been at the forefront of challenging these presuppositions (see, for example, Lloyd, 1984, and the collection edited by Nicholson, 1990). As the last chapter pointed out, just about all strands of feminist philosophy 'think about relations between things'. Indeed, one of the most significant lines of argument is that we should think about things as constituted *through* relations.

If these challenges are applied to our imagination of field and fieldwork, then all kinds of further questions arise, questions which pertain to the formation of the identities of each term and questions about power and responsible behaviour. Indeed, further questioning can problematize (or enrich) the situation even more. For there is another characteristic of what we might call the 'classic' imagination of the field which deserves attention and which relates back to our earlier discussion about discovery/construction/transformation. If you take a position that the world out there, or more specifically your object of study, can speak back, that it too is an active agent in this process of research, then what is at issue is a real *two-way* engagement. Many imaginations of the field have pictured it as static, as synchronic. A revision of that imaginary would make the field itself dynamic; and it would make field*work* into a relation between two active agents. It would recognize it as a two-way *encounter*.

Now the question of 'the ethics of the encounter' has been the subject of much philosophical attention which will be addressed directly in Chapter 6. But some initial points arise already from the discussion in this chapter.

Thus, as a first point, this encounter, in the actual practice of doing fieldwork, may take a huge variety of forms. In this chapter, the issue has **fieldwork as an** emerged out of a very general discussion about the nature of **fieldwork as** **engagement** **an engagement**. We have also seen, however, that there are debates even about the initiating terms of that engagement (whether one can have direct access to something called the real world, and so forth). Moreover, the nature of the fieldwork varies dramatically between disciplines and between individual research projects. Much will depend on the nature of your research question. The encounter may be focused through interviews with other human beings (but then the latter may be among the most powerless people on the planet or they may be the power-brokers of major corporations or international institutions). Or the encounter may be through already constituted statistical sources, or through an archive. Or, and this is important to stress, the encounter may not be with human beings or their representatives/representations at all: there is also an ethics to the encounter between human and non-human. The immediate point is that what constitutes an encounter will vary, and thus very different ethical questions will be raised.

Secondly, although I have stressed in this chapter the significance of the implicit, but powerful, spatialities of our imaginations of this practice of fieldwork, I personally am wary of attempts to address the problem through a spatial response alone. For instance, a common response across the social sciences to, say, the gap between field and academy is to claim that one stands in-between. 'Between-ness' and a whole set of associated tropes has become very popular. In my own opinion, such metaphorical 're-spatialization' alone will solve nothing. It leaves unaddressed the issue of the character of the social relations constituting that space. 'Between what?', one might ask (between two separate and still not mutually implicated atomistic entities?). And what role is this 'between-ness' enabling? (It could be mediator, translator or powerful orchestrator.) In other words, the 'political' questions concerning ethics and relative power remain

power relations unspecified. All spaces are constituted in and through **power relations** and it is this co-constitution which must be addressed (imagining spaces as relational poses the question of the nature of the relations): it is this which so much of feminist philosophy has been trying to stress.

Thirdly, the ethical issues of the encounter are not easily resolved. This is true in two senses. One is in a rather practical way: it is often, though not always, going to be the case that it is the researcher who has the initiating power to define a field in the first place. The aim is not to 'remove' power from the situation (which is impossible given its constitutive nature in social relations; and power is enabling as well as constraining) but to work on its nature and distribution and to recognize the inequalities which will almost inevitably remain. But, in another sense, these questions are not simply resolvable precisely because they occur in practical, particularized situations. On the one hand, there may be an ideal, an absolute imperative, against which you would like to behave; on the other hand, there are the real constraints and particularities of this specific situation. Jacques Derrida has written of this kind of structure and argued that what it involves is a necessarily double or contradictory imperative (see, for instance, Derrida, 2001/1997). There is no 'resolution' to this situation in the sense of being able to have recourse to a foundational rule or an eternal truth. Rather, the truly ethical or political element consists precisely in being forced to negotiate between these imperatives. Your 'resolution' of this negotiation is unlikely to be amenable to assessment as 'correct' or 'incorrect'. Rather, on Derrida's argument, what will be at issue will be appropriateness to the particular situation.

judgement

And this raises a final point, which will be taken up more fully in Chapter 6. What is involved here is **judgement** and the sense of responsibility of you, the researcher. The lack of single, correct answers does not mean you have to plunge into an endless vortex of self-doubt. (The same point was made in a previous section about reflexivity.) There will, moreover, be others to talk to, other work to read and consider, and established sets of guiding conventions (we might imagine these last as temporally congealed forms of society's thinking-so-far on the question). In the end, however, this is one of many occasions on which considered, informed judgement is a crucial element in the craft of being a researcher.

Further reading

In *Geography Militant: Cultures of Exploration and Empire* (Blackwell, 2001) Felix Driver explores in great detail the history of fieldwork within geography. Johannes Fabian's *Time and the Other: How Anthropology Makes its Object* (Columbia University Press, 1983) provides a particular example of how anthropology imagines the field and positions us in power relations to it. In *Pandora's Hope: Essays on the Reality of Science Studies* (Harvard University Press, 1999) Bruno Latour follows the practices of scientists 'in the field', 'back in the study' and the journey between them, as a basis for wider arguments about the nature of the research process. In relation to this chapter you might like to focus on Chapter 2, 'Circulating reference' (pp.24–79).

5
Generating materials
Sarah Whatmore

> How to succeed in 'working together' . . . where phenomena continue . . .
> to speak in many voices; where they refuse to be reinvented as univocal
> witnesses. (Stengers, 1997, p.90)

Something solid to go on

What 'data' do I need, how much is enough and how should I go about
obtaining it? These are the sorts of question that vie for your attention
along with the pressing demands of refining a topic and formulating an
approach to it as your research gathers pace. In the early career of a
research project or thesis it is not uncommon to experience a kind of
vertigo as theoretical ambitions heighten with the momentum of your
reading, while their relation to the 'real world' seems to become increasingly remote. This is the moment in which the idea of data as something
solid to go on is at its most seductive. Standard accounts of the research
process suggest that all you have to do now is go out and 'collect' some of
it. Indeed, for some types of research, such as statistical analyses of disease
patterns or medical service use, the identification of a viable 'data set' is
often treated as a prerequisite for defining a topic and the kinds of question
you can ask. Taken at face value, the business of data 'collection' that
abounds in introductory texts on research methods bears an uncanny
resemblance to the activity of squirrels in the autumn, gathering up acorns
and hoarding them as treasured stores of winter food. Whether interviewing actors *in situ*, manipulating the digital population of census
returns, or trawling documentary archives for traces of past lives, data
collection mimics this squirrel–acorn relationship as you scurry about after
nuggets of 'evidence' just waiting to be picked up, brought home and
feasted on at a later date. This rodent model of data collection has already
been challenged by Doreen Massey's interrogation of the space–times
of 'fieldwork' in the previous chapter. Moreover, in practice, I'm not sure
that many social scientists would recognize this as a description of their
own experiences of doing research. But its hold on our sense of what we
should be doing is perpetuated to the extent that these experiences are

written out of, or as deviations from, this model in research accounts and methods manuals.

This chapter adopts the notion of 'generating materials' to further unsettle this stance towards the activity of doing research and its implicit distribution of energies, in which the researcher does all the acting while the researched are merely acted upon. This alternative formulation suggests that data, like questions, are produced, not found, and that the activity of producing them is not all vested in the researcher. I trace some of the consequences of this reformulation for 'doing' research. For a start, it trips up the apparently straightforward notion of research as an *investigation of the world* which positions the researcher at one remove from the world and renders 'it' a passive object of study. But the purpose of the chapter is not just to unsettle and trip up conventional ways of thinking about how research is, and should be, conducted. It also sets out to provide some way-markers and tactics for those of you who may want to pursue the **generating** consequences of these arguments as you set about **generating materials** for **materials** yourselves. In thinking through this process I draw on the writing of the contemporary philosopher Isabelle Stengers, which I will introduce in a little more detail in the section 'Stengers at work'. In particular, I work through some of the implications of her account of research as a process of knowledge production that is always, and unavoidably, an *intervention in the world* in which all those (humans and non-humans) enjoined in it can, and do, affect each other. This suggests a mode of conduct that, as she puts it in the quotation with which this chapter opens, demands a more rigor-**co-fabrication** ous sense of, and commitment to, research as a **co-fabrication** or 'working together' with those whom we are researching.

Towards a more-than-human social science

Some aspects of this line of argument may seem familiar in so far as they resonate with the well-established concerns of humanistic critiques of scientific methods and their empirical emphasis on the 'objective' measurement of observable phenomena and their interrelations. Such methods – so these critiques go – are inappropriate to social research, because people, unlike any other object of study, are purposeful agents whose own understandings of their actions in the world must be incorporated into, and even allowed to challenge, research accounts of them. Humanistic critiques have spawned a rich variety of social science research practices called qualitative research methods, from focus groups to discourse analysis, in which the spoken and written word constitute the primary form of 'data' (see Seale, 1998; Limb and Dwyer, 2001). These arguments have been well rehearsed in relation to one of the most widely used methods of generating data in the social science repertoire – the interview. For example, Holstein and Gubrium mobilize them against what they call the 'vessel-of-answers' approach to interviewing found in many research methods manuals, particularly its emphasis on 'neutrality' as the ideal mode of conduct to prevent the interviewer from 'contaminating' what the interviewee has to say:

> In the vessel-of-answers approach, the image of the subject is epistemologically passive, not engaged in the production of knowledge. If the interviewing process goes 'by the book' and is non-directional and unbiased, respondents will validly give out what subjects are presumed to merely retain within them – the unadulterated facts and details of experience. Contamination emanates from the interview setting, its participants and their interaction, not the subject, who, under ideal conditions, serves up authentic reports when beckoned to do so. (Holstein and Gubrium, 1997, p.117)

But Stengers' philosophy of science is of a different order. Her imperative of 'working together' in the knowledge production process is not derived from any appeal to the uniquely human qualities of the research subjects with whom social scientists have predominantly concerned themselves. Rather, it amplifies the ways in which all manner of entities, non-human as well as human, assembled in the event of research affect its conduct, exceed their mobilization as compliant data and complicate taken-for-granted distinctions between social subjects and material objects reproduced through scientific divisions of labour. Thus, thinking through research in the company of Stengers challenges some of the methodological assumptions associated with the humanistic legacy of qualitative research practices in the social sciences, as well as those of the scientific methods that they critique. Such disputes have been staged for the most part in *epistemological* terms, that is in terms of the kinds of 'how can we know?' question that we saw in play in Chapter 1. This staging restricts the terms of any answer to the relationship between language, as the currency of human thinking and knowing, and matter, as the stuff of the world out there. Questions about 'how can we know the world?' hereby become reformulated as questions about 'how do we represent (or, in Rortyian terms, redescribe) it?' By contrast, Stengers picks up the argument in Chapter 2 that our disposition towards the world we study is better conceived as one of craft than discovery. If we are immersed in the world through bodily exchanges of various kinds, rather than at a distance from 'it' mediated only by language, the philosophical question is recast in *ontological* terms – 'how does the world make itself known?'

The philosophers and social theorists interrogated in Part I will have given you a sense of some of the many and varied ways in which this interval between word and world has been traversed. Gillian Rose's discussion in Chapter 3 of the discursively 'constructed' bodies that populate certain variants of feminist theory provides a useful example. To greater (e.g. Rorty) or lesser (e.g. Foucault) extents and with important exceptions (e.g. Deleuze), many of those whose ideas you have encountered thus far in this book focus questions about the uncertainties of human knowing as if these uncertainties were confined to the properties of human cognition and language. Meanwhile, the stuff of the world remains 'out there', untroubled and untroubling, waiting impassively for us to make up our minds and making no difference to the knowledge production process. It is a stance captured in Rorty's claim that 'it is language all the way down' (discussed by John Allen in Chapter 1). By contrast, Stengers redirects attention to the uncertainties generated by the complexities and energies of the material world, including those of human embodiment. In this, Stengers' project is at

word–world odds with the terms of dispute set in train by the **word–world settlement**
settlement and stylized as a choice between two positions – 'constructionism' (what we know is an artefact of human thought) versus 'realism' (what we know is an artefact of the real world). Rather, her philosophical imperative of 'working together' challenges the intellectual entrenchment of this settlement and its hold on the terms of exchange between social scientists and natural scientists in the late twentieth century, illustrated with such venom in the so-called 'science wars' (Gross and Levitt, 1994).

'Working together' in practice

Given their philosophical divergence, it is perhaps unsurprising that, with one important exception, Stengers' work has made relatively little impression on the English-speaking social sciences. For the most part, her philosophical project has not yet been 'domesticated', in the sense of having been made useful to social theory and research agendas. The exception is the research community and literature of science and technology studies that have flourished over the last two decades or so, particularly that in Europe. Her influence is most in evidence in that gathering of energies which gelled momentarily into actant network theory (ANT), associated with the work of such notable (if increasingly reluctant) intermediaries as Michel Callon, Bruno Latour, John Law and Annemarie Mol (see Law and Hassard, 1999). Here, Stengers' project finds resonance in substantive research concerns with the practices and artefacts of scientific knowledge production, and in theoretical commitments to rethinking the very idea of society as an exclusively human domain distinct from that of a material world of things. Science studies have long since over-spilled their early confines as an interdisciplinary niche through lively conversations with sociologists, geographers, anthropologists, historians, literary theorists and others (not to mention scientists). Stengers' philosophical influence has travelled through such conversations, most forcefully in the work of Latour. The interweaving of their projects is apparent from Latour's frequent references to her work, a compliment that is returned in her writing, and from his foreword to the English translation of her book *Power and Invention* (1997), a book which Stengers dedicates to him (and Felix Guattari). In light of this, I shall revisit Latour's essay, 'Circulating reference' (1999), discussed in the last chapter, as a way of making connections between what is at stake in the approach you adopt to 'data' and the issues raised about constituting the 'field'.

Without being directly derivative of them, ANT can be seen as giving methodological expression to Stengerian principles through its trademark adaptation of *ethnographic* research methods to the study of scientific conduct. Originating in anthropology, and now well established through-

ethnography out the social sciences, **ethnography** is distinctive in its approach to what constitutes 'data', paying as close attention to social practices (what people do) as to social discourses (what people say). It also attaches particular weight to 'doing fieldwork', requiring the researcher to spend significant periods of time working with those whom they are studying, engaging in their everyday routines and exchanges – a process formalized as 'participant observation' (Cook and Crang, 1995). In this sense, ethnography can be argued to come closest to the notion of 'generating materials', as opposed to 'collecting data', of any method in the social sciences. ANT amplifies two currents in this body of research practices. The first concerns the spaces of fieldwork or the question of 'where' to engage in generating materials discussed in Chapter 4. Here, emphasis is shifted from working in single locales, such as a laboratory, to 'multi-sited' fieldwork that traces networks of association connecting several (Marcus, 1995). The second concerns the objects of study or 'what' to count as relevant material. Here, a 'symmetrical' approach is adopted that redistributes attention from exclusively human actors, what scientists say and do, to the host of non-human devices, codes, bodies and instruments that are active parties in 'doing' or practising science (Callon, 1986).

In this chapter, I want to outline some key elements of Stengers' philosophy of science and illustrate their implications for generating materials should you want to follow them through. In particular, I will elaborate three related elements in Stengers' philosophical vocabulary, which, as you will expect of philosophers by now, is uniquely her own.

mapping into The first is the idea of '**mapping into knowledge**', an approach to **knowledge** knowledge production that by-passes the word–world settlement, and the constructionist/realist choices it sets in train, by positing research as an event co-fabricated between researcher and researched. The second element is her criteria for what constitutes good research, which centre on researchers placing themselves 'at risk' in terms of entertaining, and even inviting, the non-compliance of those whom they are studying. The third element is her commitment to what she calls 'cosmopolitics', a politics of knowledge in which the admission of non-humans into the company of what counts invites new alignments of scientific and political practices and more democratic distributions of expertise. In the closing section of the chapter, I will return to the still pressing anxieties of 'what data do I need, how much is enough and how should I go about obtaining it?' with which I began, to outline the lessons and pitfalls of reworking these anxieties through Stengers.

Stengers at work

As a philosopher of science based at the Free University of Brussels, Stengers has worked closely with scientists, including an early and influential collaboration with the Nobel prize-winning chemist Ilya Prigogine in a book published in English under the title *Order Out of Chaos* (Prigogine and Stengers, 1984). Her subsequent work, which is only now being translated, exposes more directly her philosophical allegiances. The first of these is *Power and Invention* (1997), a collection of essays, most of which appeared in French during the 1980s, and the most recent is *The Invention of Modern Science* (2000). Here, she refers directly to the philosophers whose thinking has most inspired her own. These include historical figures such as Lucretius, Leibniz and Whitehead, about whose work she has written (see Prigogine and Stengers, 1982; Stengers, 1994), and older contemporaries such as Michel Serres and Gilles Deleuze, with whom she has engaged. The common thread she identifies in their work is: '. . . the attempt to speak of the world without passing through the Kantian tribunal [see below], without putting the human subject defined by his or her intellectual categories at the centre of their system' (Stengers, 1997, p.55).

However, Stengers is anything but an 'ivory tower' philosopher and her writing is alive with a political militancy and scientific passion that make her a public figure in her native Belgium. These interconnections are most apparent in her untranslated work, notably the series of essays published under the umbrella title *Cosmopolitiques* (1996).

The movement of Stengerian energies through the social sciences that I sketched in the previous section maps my own journeys into her work too. ANT furnished a provisional opening that was intensified for me by a research collaboration with Belgian colleagues on food scares (Stassart and Whatmore, 2003). I find her writing daunting and compelling in equal measure. There is something relentless in the rigour of her thinking, combined with a style that obstinately refuses to be read lightly such that, if you persist (and it can be tempting not to), you find yourself forced to follow arguments past the comfort zone of your own habits of thought. Her main philosophical protagonists are not post-structuralists but less fashionable philosophers of science, such as Kuhn and Popper, and the science establishment that clings to the authority of the Scientific method. In this sense, she is not a philosopher who is readily made to serve the purposes and problems that social science readers bring with them to her texts. Stengers is also difficult to read for other reasons, in part because something of the tenor and wit of her writing is lost in translation and in part because she anticipates a familiarity in her readers with the intricacies of scientific, philosophical and science studies literatures that is quite formidable. Nevertheless, if you stick with it, I think her work can be instructive for connecting enduring debates in the philosophy of science to the growing theoretical and methodological emphasis in social research on knowledge *practices* as the currency of 'non-representational' approaches to the study of social life (Thrift, 2002).

'Mapping into knowledge'

For Stengers, knowledge production is not about translating between the pre-constituted and self-evident constituencies of word and world, mind and matter, subjects and objects, in which the act of knowing is always an act of mastery. Rather than taking these divisions as given, she sees them as particular outcomes of philosophical interventions by eighteenth-century thinkers such as Kant and the ways in which these were harnessed in the methods of inquiry institutionalized by professional science as it emerged in the nineteenth century. Stengers describes this Scientific method (with a capital 'S') as a stance towards knowledge that 'unilaterally' makes it possible 'to subject anything and anyone at all to quantitative measure-ments' (2000, p.23). Such measurement procedures presuppose and reinforce what kinds of knowledge count, what kinds are forbidden and what is authorized to be mutilated 'in the name of science', like the 'innumerable animals [that] have been vivisected, decerebrated [brain removal] and tortured in order to produce "objective data"' (2000, p.22). Thus Stengers' objection to the 'Kantian tribunal', a term which she invests with Stalinesque overtones, is not just a philosophical nicety but a concern with the abusive consequences of the word–world settlement. Her alterna-tive to a knowledge production process engaged in filtering the indifferent stuff of the world through human ideas, theories and categories is one not of mastery but of *modification*, in which all these components are mutually reconfigured.

Stengers' approach can be located in the very different philosophical traditions identified above. In particular, she adopts a Deleuzean term to describe the way in which all the parties assembled in the research process, researcher and researched, bodies and texts, instruments and fields, condition each other and collectively constitute the knowledge 'event'. On this account, 'evidence' does not pre-exist scientific inquiry (Stengers, 1997, pp.85–6), both the scientist and his/her object of study are (re)con-stituted through the activity of research. Thus, the philosophical choice posed by Stengers is, as Latour puts it, between those philosophies that hold the real and the constructed to be opposites, like fact and fiction, and those that hold them to be synonymous aspects of fabrication (Latour, 1997, p.xiv). In this vein, the business of 'generating materials' becomes one of how to 'map phenomena into knowledge' (Stengers, 1977, p.117). Here she contrasts the mappings of science-in-practice, the routines and crafts of scientific work which she characterizes as 'labyrinthine', with those reproduced in (and as) *the* Scientific method, which she characterizes as 'triumphant'. Both are in the business of making connections but, where Science is looking for 'interconnections . . . between [already] separated populations of phenomena', science-in-practice is more concerned with configurations that 'string together at once all the phenomena and those who study them without distributing *a priori* . . . what is significant and interesting, and what . . . can be ignored' (1997, p.117).

Latour's essay 'Circulating reference' (1999) provides a vivid illustration of what Stengers means by 'mapping into knowledge', emphasizing, among other things, the complex space–times of the **research event** discussed in Chapter 4. In it, he gives an account of a scientific expedition to the edge of the Amazon rainforest. Describing his own part in the expedition as that of a 'participant-observer', he reminds us of the debt that his methodological approach to studying this expedition owes to ethnography. He details in words and images (black-and-white photographs) the many small but consequential displacements through which the soils that the scientists are studying are transformed into samples, charts, numerical and textual records of observations. Each displacement involves a mobilization of the world, like the maps and aerial photographs from which a field-site is discerned; the grid squares and markers that organize the collection of 'samples'; and the specimen boxes and classificatory schemas that carry these field-materials away. On this account, the exchanges set in motion in the research event never seem to separate out into words (signs) and things as neatly or thoroughly as they are supposed to, or to begin or end in 'the field', but rather constitute what Latour calls a 'circulating reference'. As he suggests,

> . . . we never detect the rupture between things and signs, and we never face the imposition of arbitrary and discrete signs on shapeless and continuous matter. We see only an unbroken series of well-nested elements, each of which plays the role of sign for the previous one and of thing for the succeeding one. (Latour, 1999, p.56)

Latour's essay makes the consequences of Stengers' notion of 'mapping into knowledge' for the treatment of research 'data' more tangible. Data emerge here not as nuggets of the 'real world', or as so many 'discursive constructs', but rather as intermediaries or 'third parties' between researchers and researched that are as material as they are meaningful. What difference might this stance towards 'data' make to, say, the practicalities of interviewing? Among other things, it could enable you to be explicit about the displacements involved in your own mobilizations of the talk generated by interviewing as 'data'. Consider, for example, the displacements between the interview encounter rich with bodily habits and cues; the tape-recording that transports its sounds alone; the transcription process that distils these sounds into words on a page; and the quotations from the transcript that make an interviewee 'present' in your research account. In place of 'raw data' that, so to speak, takes the words out of an informant's mouth, the interview/tape/transcript/quotation emerge as intermediaries constituted *between* the researcher and researched; talk

research event

and text; devices and codes that take on a life of their own as they travel through the knowledge production process.

But it is also worth taking a little time to think about what work the photographs do in Latour's account of 'fieldwork' (see also Mike Crang's discussion of photographs in Chapter 7). Among other things, they provide snapshots of science-in-practice that show various members of the scientific team and a variety of devices (like the soil-corer) and documents (like maps) working together in the making of measurements. The photographs have the effect of making the 'doing' of research present in the text, emissaries of the energetic exchanges between bodies and instruments, soils and plants that are set in motion in the research event. In other words, they extend the register of what it means to 'generate materials' from one in which only human talk counts, to one in which bodies, technologies and codes all come into play. In direct contrast to Rorty's insistence that 'the world does not speak, only we speak' (see Chapter 1), Stengers and Latour are adamant that 'good' research practice is

> . . . actually a matter of constituting phenomena as actors in the discussion, that is, not only of letting them speak, but of letting them speak in a way that other scientists recognise as reliable. . . . The real issue is . . . the invention and production of . . . reliable witnesses. (Stengers, 1997, p.85, emphasis in original)

I now want to look more closely at how Stengers conducts this shift from 'data' as passive evidence in the hands of the researcher to active witnesses in the collective research event.

'Being at risk'

being at risk Stengers' principle of '**being at risk**' provides a litmus test for distinguishing between well and badly constructed propositions, a term she derives from Whitehead (1978), as opposed to true and false theories. If you recall from the first section, theories premised on the word–world settlement bridge the interval in representational terms. By contrast, propositions admit many different kinds of element into the company of the research event (gestures, devices, bodies, sites, etc., and words too) and seek to establish practical relations between them in terms of the articulations afforded by their different properties in combination. To pass Stengers' 'test', a scientist/researcher must demonstrate that 'the questions raised by [their] experiment/research are at risk of being redefined by the phenomena mobilized by the laboratory or theory' (Latour, 1997, p.xvi). In other words, the production of questions discussed in Part I is recursively linked to the business of generating materials. This Stengerian principle applies equally to natural and social sciences, human and non-human objects of study, marking out 'bad' scientific practice as that which does not give the researched a chance to answer back. This might be giving people being asked by sociologists to complete a questionnaire an opportunity to redefine the terms of what it is that is being interrogated, or the bacterium under the microbiologist's microscope the opportunity to demonstrate other capabilities than the one under scrutiny. In either case, the crucial criterion is that the researched are permitted, by the way the research is conducted, to resist being aligned to only one scientific 'truth', as if this exhausted their potential as either agents or evidence. This is what Stengers means by 'univocal' witnesses (1997, p.87).

One of the examples that Stengers gives is that of the work of the Nobel-prize-winning biologist Barbara McClintock, who was engaged in the 1950s' revolution in microbiology, working on the singularity of the genetic material of corn. She uses this example to address the question posed in a short essay entitled 'Is there a women's science?' McClintock's working practice was not to commence her research as a means to make the world fit her models, but rather to search for ways of permitting the world to contradict the theories that biologists brought to bear on it. Stengers describes the delight recorded in McClintock's laboratory journal, and detailed in Evelyn Fox-Keller's biography of her (1983), 'when she knew that the corn had, if I can put it this way, "intervened" between her and her ideas' (Stengers, 1997, p.111). For Stengers this joy or passion (she uses the French term *jouissance*) of the scientific craft occurs when the materials the scientist is working with force an unexpected possibility into the exchange. It is a joy less of knowing than of *not* knowing that she argues is a defining feature of scientific knowledge practices, but one that invariably gets written out of scientific literature and education. This happens, Stengers suggests, by the unexpected being retrospectively accounted for as the consequence of an ultimately rational method or correct theory (1997, p.88). The joy of *not* knowing is disciplined out of Science by training and, more specifically,

> . . . learning never to say I but we, never to present research methods as the expression of choices but the expression of unanimous and impersonal consensus; never to admit that an article's object is contingent not . . . the result of what was being aimed at from the beginning. (Stengers, 1997, p.113)

The question for Stengers becomes one of how to hold on after the event to those moments in which researchers find themselves lost for words in the face of some unexpected possibility that bodies forth in the knowledge production process. Her answer lies in shifting the onus of what it means to 'know', such that 'to understand means to create a language that opens up the possibility of "encountering" different sensible forms, of reproducing them, without for all that subjugating them to a general law that would give them "reasons" and allow them to be manipulated' (Stengers, 2000, p.157).

At this point the idea of data as 'third parties' in the relationship between researcher and researched discussed above becomes critical to acknowledging that, as intermediaries, they are only ever partial and incomplete mobilizations of the phenomena enjoined as the 'object' of research. Rather than a mute world being rendered compliant evidence of theory 'x' or 'y', Stengers insists on the capacity of worldly phenomena to exceed their alignment in the knowledge production process. It is in this sense that 'good' science should allow 'phenomena [to] continue to speak in many voices; [to] refuse to be reinvented as . . . objects in the Kantian sense' (1997, p.90). Here, Stengers' criteria for discerning 'good' research propositions from 'bad' ones come very close to the characteristics of the 'ambulant science' advocated by Deleuze and Guattari in *A Thousand Plateaus* (1987/1980), as discussed by Nigel Clark in Chapter 2. There are also interesting parallels, though not ones that Stengers herself makes, with Irigaray's use of the term *jouissance* and her celebration of an 'openness to the new' discussed in Chapter 3.

While she makes her argument in relation to, and through, natural science examples, unlearning the conventions of 'writing out' the unexpected from research accounts is no less significant a challenge for social scientists. What difference might the principle of 'being at risk' make to how you conduct and use research interviews? One of the implications of Stengers' argument, to which she repeatedly returns, is writing research differently, developing a style that better holds on to the open-endedness of what is said and done in the research event and the multiplicity of sometimes incommensurable 'truths' that it admits. But this is getting ahead of ourselves and trespasses into the domain of Part III. In terms of interviewing itself, it might encourage you to experiment with practices like cumulative interviews with the same person or collective encounters like focus groups, which amplify the frictions, discrepancies and silences in the talk generated between researcher and researched. Such variations on the standard one-off individual interview also permit more opportunities for research subjects to engage with, and object to, transcripts of the talk generated from previous encounters and your analysis of them, thereby making these intermediaries more 'reliable' in Stengerian terms.

If Rorty's argument that it is 'language all the way down' removes any substantive basis for lending more or less credence to scientific as against other kinds of knowledge-claim and leads him to resort to irony, Stengers' philosophy invokes substantiation as an evaluative criterion but appeals to humour as a bulwark against any scientific claim to a monopoly of the 'truth'. By humour she means,

> . . . learning to laugh at reductionist strategies which in impressing research institutes and sponsors turn the judgements they permit themselves into brutal facts; learning to recount histories in which there are no defeated, to cherish truths that become entangled without denying each other. (Stengers, 1997, p.90)

The important point here is that the imperative and exercise of such 'humorous' tactics is not restricted in Stengers' account to practitioners of science alone. It is not a matter of self-regulation within the research community. Rather, as Latour notes (1997, p.xvii), she looks everywhere for the conditions where the power of scientific knowledge-claims is counterbalanced by the intervention of those whom scientists speak for and about – the 'lay public', in whose name science is conducted, and the objects of scientific study (including people) themselves. This takes us to the third element in Stengers' philosophical vocabulary that I want to outline here.

'Cosmopolitics'

Stengers' philosophy of science is bound up with a politics of knowledge that spills beyond the communities of science and through the wider fabric of civil society and governance. It is for this strange mix of science, philosophy and politics that she contrived the 'beautiful name' – *'cosmopolitics'* (Latour, 1997, p.xi). As the literary theorist William Paulson notes of her project:

> . . . it is not enough to decide to include nonhumans in collectives or to acknowledge that societies live in a physical and biological world as useful as these steps may be. The crucial point is to learn how new types of encounter (and conviviality) with nonhumans, which emerge in the practice of the sciences over the course of their history, can give rise to new modes of relation with humans, i.e. to new political practices. (Paulson, 2001, p.112)

cosmopolitics   As a 'learning process', Stengers' **cosmopolitics** are thoroughly collaborative. On the one hand, they have been elaborated through ongoing conversations with science and technology studies, and with Latour in particular, as is evident in the extensive cross-referencing to each other's work. Both share a concern with developing a politics of knowledge that is not restricted to an exclusively human constituency but rather involves 'the management, diplomacy, combination, and negotiation of human and nonhuman agencies' (Latour, 1999, p.290). On the other hand, the political in Stengers' cosmo*political* project is also manifestly informed by her involvement in activist campaigns, for example, on the politics of drug (ab)use and the treatment of AIDS, an activism that marks her out from Latour.

Thus, if Stengers' philosophy of science is at odds with the Rortyian inference that scientific knowledge-claims are no more or less intrinsically compelling than any other, she is no less critical of the stratagems of scientists who would bolster their authority by exempting their knowledge-claims from political dispute. As she puts it: 'Because we now know the connivance of . . . scientists with all forms of power capable of extending the scope of their judgements, . . . new constraints have to condition the legitimacy of inventions in "the name of science"' (Stengers, 2000, p.158).

Cosmopolitics, then, is precisely a project about recasting the intellectual and social terms of engagement between science and politics. The shift it seeks to make is from a problematic that presumes a gulf between science and politics even as it sets about bridging it, to one that takes their entanglement as given and redirects attention to the democratization of expertise (Stengers, 2000, p.160). Here,

> . . . it is a question of inventing apparatuses such that the citizens of whom scientific experts speak can be effectively present, in order to pose questions to which their interest makes them sensible, to demand explanations, to posit conditions, to suggest modalities, in short, to participate in the invention. (Stengers, 2000, p.160)

An example of cosmopolitics in action can, I suggest, be found in the work of the economic sociologist Michel Callon (1998), whose substantive research interests lie in the organization of markets.

Callon has been closely associated with ANT (as well as being a colleague of Latour's), but has turned its distinctive methodological energies to the study of economic knowledges and processes. In his recent work he develops the notion of 'hybrid forums' to describe the proliferation of public spaces in which scientific expertise, and the commercial and regulatory practices that it underpins, are becoming the subject of intense dispute. These forums are 'hybrid' both because the questions raised mix economic, political, ethical, legal and technological concerns in new and complex ways and because of the variety and heterogeneity of social interests engaged in them (lay persons and experts; parents and consumers; pressure groups and civil servants). Take the case of the vigorous public resistance to genetically modified (GM) foods in Europe in the late 1990s. Callon (1998) suggests that amidst the many counter-currents in play, it was less the health and environmental 'risks' of this technology *per se* that fuelled public dispute, than their association with monopolistic corporate markets and the impoverishment of producer practices and consumer choices that they entailed. Such forums exposed both the contested nature of the science informing the assessment of the risks and benefits of GM, and the relevance of other kinds of knowledge to the terms of dispute. In so doing, they forced a redistribution of competencies and rights in the politics of knowledge-making, expressed not least through the explosion of new market practices like organic, animal welfare and other certificated 'quality' food networks that variously proscribed GM (Callon et al., 2002, p.195).

But Stengers' cosmopolitics do not just place scientific knowledge practices on trial while those of other members of the polity are left untouched, but rather require that concerned citizens also put at risk their own opinions and convictions (Stengers, 2000, p.160). What difference might this stance towards the politics of knowledge production make to the conduct of social science research? One such difference concerns the distribution of powers and affects *between* researcher and researched in the research event. By way of illustration, you might work through the consequences of reframing the question raised earlier about the methodological importance of the photographs in Latour's essay, 'Circulating reference' (1999), in cosmopolitical terms. In making the 'doing' of research present in the text, such a framing should encourage you to interrogate more closely whose eye is behind the camera lens, whether the picture-taker is singular or plural and to what extent, if at all, they figure in the images of the research account.

In the case of Latour's essay, we learn on the first page that the camera is 'his' and it is his eye behind the lens in all twenty-odd black-and-white photographs (1999, p.24). While he is at pains to position himself within the research event by constant reference to the collective 'we', it is nonetheless the case that he never appears in front of the lens. Thus, for example, he notes that as he 'snaps the picture' of the scientific team, the pedologist René is enlisting him as an 'alignment pole' to take a topographic bearing with an instrument that can be seen pointing directly at the camera in the photograph (1999, p.41). By the same token, none of the photographs in the essay is witness to any of the other scientists in the party assuming the role of photographer. Stengers' cosmopolitics should encourage you to work more reflexively with such visual methods (Pink, 2000). This might include harnessing the skills associated with the social usage of camcorders and disposable cameras by inviting research subjects to position themselves behind the lens, and by subjecting yourself to their picturing of the research event. In this, her emphasis on inventing apparatuses to democratize participation in the production of knowledge finds resonance in Nigel Thrift's discussion of the ethics of Spinoza in the next chapter, with its emphasis on the affective relationships between manifold beings. For both of them, ethics (and politics) are better understood as relational activities and practical accomplishments, rather than as individual stances or universal rubrics.

Conclusion

The urgencies and dilemmas of questions about the kinds and quantities of research material you need and how best to generate them, do not disappear with the wave of a philosophical wand. But neither is it possible to abstain from situating the activities of data generation in philosophical terms – there is no 'philosophy-free' option even in this seemingly most practical aspect of research conduct. Different philosophical resources are consequential for 'doing research' and for the ways in which you formulate and address these questions. Working these consequences through the particularities of Isabelle Stengers' philosophy of science holds both lessons and pitfalls for social scientists, not least because her own scientific reference points are characteristically those of thermodynamics or psychiatry rather than society. In other words, her's is not a ready-to-wear philosophy that fits the questions that social researchers are predisposed to bring to it. Rather, her work might best be approached as a rigorous attempt to articulate some principles for 'good' research conduct in terms of the generation and treatment of 'evidence' in any field of inquiry. These principles, notably those of 'working together' and 'being at risk', have now been transposed to numerous social research contexts, including literary studies (Paulson, 2001), economic sociology (Callon, 1998) and political science (Barry, 2002), as well as science studies, and provide useful intermediaries for engaging with her work. Revisiting the questions about 'generating data' posed at the start of this chapter in turn, where might Stengers take us?

The first question – 'What data do I need?' – is clearly one that is directly linked back to Part I of this book and the 'kinds of question' you want to ask. What Stengers offers here is a way of keeping these questions open through the research process by allying them to an insistence on the produced-ness of 'data' and the creative and sometimes contrary possibilities generated in and by exchanges between researcher and researched. Her work has been taken up in the social sciences to emphasize the importance of non-human witnesses in the research event and to inform methodologies that extend the register of what counts beyond both the human and the said. While it is not antithetical to taking language and cognition seriously as human competences that afford a vital site or mode of engagement with the world (see Paulson, 2001, p.118), neither does it privilege them over the bodily repertoire of senses and practices that make us human. For this reason, many social scientists will always find this a philosophical pill that is hard to take.

The second question – 'How much is enough?' – is in no small measure a logistical question of how much time you have to spend on generating materials and 'being in the field', given the time and resource constraints of your research. These, too, are very much part of practising science, even if they figure nowhere in the rarefied conventions of the Scientific method or the 'big questions' of the philosophy of science. These constraints might be the schedule and/or budget for the production of a research report commissioned by government; the institutional regulations on the maximum allowable period of registration as a student before a thesis has to be submitted; or the duration of a research grant to support your activities. But however long or short the time you have to spend on such activities, you will not be alone if you find yourself feeling overwhelmed by the sheer volume of materials generated or its recalcitrance in the face of your efforts to fashion it into some kind of order. But, in Stengers' terms, this is not an entirely unhealthy state of affairs, in the sense that the research objects mobilized in your research should be troublesome intermediaries in the research process. As Nick Bingham elaborates in Chapter 8, it is just such intermediaries that prompt you in new and unexpected directions and keep your analysis 'at risk' as you engage in what commonly passes for 'writing up' your research.

And, finally, the third question – 'How should I go about obtaining data?' – has shifted through this encounter with Stengers from a rodent activity of 'collecting' bits of the world and bringing them home, to one of generating materials in and through the research event. This has been a recurrent theme through the whole of Part II. This process of what Stengers calls 'mapping into knowledge' involves, as we have seen through Latour's example of 'circulating reference', precarious displacements between matter and meaning, things and signs generated by and through relations between researcher and researched. It is a process that entails rethinking the space–times of research in important ways, not least those of 'the field' interrogated in Chapter 4. But it is also a process that you might want to think about more reflexively than is evident in Stengers' (or Latour's) own writing about this process, in terms of how you situate yourself in the research interventions you describe and the ethical implications and possibilities of so doing. It is these ethical considerations that are brought into focus in the next chapter.

Further reading

For those interested in a taste of Stengers' philosophical writing, her essay, 'Is there a women's science?', in *Power and Invention: Situating Science* (Minnesota University Press, 1997, pp.123-32) is a useful starting point. Latour's essay, 'Circulating reference', in *Pandora's Hope: Essays on the Reality of Science Studies* (Harvard University Press, 1999, pp.24–79) provides a highly readable exposition of the notion of research as a process of 'working together' through an ethnography of a scientific expedition. For an economic illustration of the politics of knowledge associated with Stengers' approach it is worth looking at the article by Callon et al., 'The economy of qualities' (2002).

6
Practising ethics

Nigel Thrift

Introduction

One of the questions that bears down on you quite quickly as your thesis or other piece of research develops, is your relationship with those you will encounter in the field. 'The field' can, of course, include a wide range of actors with whom you may have a relationship – not all of whom by any means will necessarily be human (although until quite recently it was widely assumed that they were the only actors who could have an active say) – and a whole series of different methods of inquiry which demand different kinds of stances to human actors and other others. Similarly, the field can include numerous, very different kinds of situation in which these relationships need to be negotiated in very different ways. But one thing stays constant: that is the need to produce encounters from which some measure of enlightenment is possible for you, but which is not at the expense of those others whom you count as respondents (and which may even be to their advantage). In other words, we need to think about the *ethics* of encounters – the effort to formulate right and wrong modes of behaviour – remembering that responsibility does not end with leaving the field but lasts beyond (and sometimes well beyond) the end of the thesis or other piece of research you may be conducting. This chapter is intended to show up some of the ethical dilemmas that can arise in the field and how to think them through *and* think through them. Note the use of the word 'dilemmas': you should not expect there to be any easy answers. Generally speaking, there will be no one right answer and what may often be quite agonizing situations will not be resolved but rather will rumble on uneasily and ambiguously through the rest of your life: did I do the right thing? You will never have the satisfaction of knowing that you did the right thing because no easy definition of 'right' exists.

Because of these dilemmas, much fieldwork can actually be quite painful. There is not only that sense of dislocation of values which you take for granted – which comes and goes – but also the difficulty of negotiating with people when you don't know all the small and unspoken ethical ground 'rules' that make up everyday life, rules which you have arduously to construct.

Though fieldwork is often portrayed as a classical colonial encounter in which the fieldworker lords it over her/his respondents, the fact of the matter is that it doesn't usually feel much like that at all. More often it is a curious mixture of humiliations and intimidations mixed with moments of insight and even enjoyment as you begin to imagine the world you have chosen to try to inhabit. Note the use of the word 'feel': fieldwork is often a profoundly emotional business, a constant stew of emotions, ranging from doubt and acute homesickness to laughter and a kind of comradeship, which are a fundamental part of how you think the situations you are in. Note also the use of the word 'imagine': fieldwork is also about the act of imagination, about thinking the powers and limits of the bodies around you.

But fieldwork comes loaded up with its own mythology. In the early 1980s, when I was a part of a field-oriented School in Australia which focused on one of the key anthropological heartlands, Papua New Guinea and the Pacific Islands, fieldwork was a veritable rite of passage which required the fieldworker to undergo the validation of great hardship in order to bring back authentic knowledge: I well remember the chillingly routine discussions about which awful disease (invariably hepatitis) the fieldworker had barely survived. Encounters with 'natives' were a part of this codifying regime, but those encounters were rarely written about for themselves: 'natives' were informants who told the fieldworker about local practices and 'cosmologies' and then, generally speaking, kept out of the way as the western shaman worked out what was really going on. Of course this is, to some extent, a caricature – but not as much of a caricature as you might think.

But things were already changing. A series of books were appearing which were attempting to recast fieldwork as a much less certain (and much less macho) exercise. There was good reason for this. In particular, fieldwork had, almost simultaneously, moved out of the classical field territories like Papua New Guinea and the Pacific Islands and into the cities and back into the West, and had also, in an age of widespread decolonization, become much more conscious of its colonial origins. The result was that the field could no longer be equated with the past, the classical distancing move that Doreen Massey notes in her chapter. It is no surprise that in this context Paul Rabinow's *Reflections on Fieldwork in Morocco* (1977), a now classic autobiographical account of a period of doctoral fieldwork, had become a key work. It was located in the Maghreb in a barely post-colonial Morocco among people who were a cosmopolitan mix of native Moroccans and French ex-colonials and it was a work that concentrated on encounter and the dilemmas that encounter threw up.

I am going to start this chapter by considering Rabinow's account of encountering the 'field' in a little more detail because Rabinow was so acutely conscious of the dilemmas of encounter that are faced there. His book is often considered to have started off the great inward turn that preoccupied many anthropologists in the 1980s, much of which consisted of concerns about whether it was possible to have encounters with others which were not inevitably, in some sense, colonial in form and content and had some genuine ethical weight.

But then, in the second part of the chapter, I want to move on to consider how we might use philosophy to begin to think through some of the dilemmas of encounter. Of course, a lot of philosophy revolves around precisely these dilemmas, so we hardly have to start from a blank slate. In fact, so much philosophy is concerned with these issues that it is possible to get involved with them to a degree that many might see as a fault: whole theses on the dilemmas of the field have been written which are, in effect, long philosophical disquisitions. Indeed, for a time in the 1980s, it often seemed as though a subject like anthropology, which prides itself on being field-minded, had turned itself over to debates about little else.

I will therefore be approaching the subject of the field through the work of a philosopher who may, at first sight, seem rather an odd choice, namely Benedictus de Spinoza (1632–77). Spinoza held a series of views which are, to put it but mildly, out of tune with our times. He was wedded to a strict notion of reason, based on logical inference. He believed that the ordering of the universe was causally logical and deterministic. He held up as a model of good philosophy the kind of work carried out by Euclid, in which the world was able to be reduced to a series of simple mathematical axioms by considering 'human actions and appetites just as if it were a question of lines, planes and bodies' (*Ethics*, Spinoza, 1996/1677, Part III, Pref.). He therefore believed that 'humankind's blessedness lay solely in the applied conclusions of mathematical deduction in every possible arena of perception, including that sphere of mental activity we call the moral . . .'

ethics　(Gullan-Whur, 1998, p.189). As a result, his view of **ethics** – the effort to formulate principles of right and wrong behaviour – seems very strange to us now. Like a number of contemporaries, he wanted to render ethics scientific, by basing it on an entirely naturalistic and deterministic understanding of human passions and behaviour. But he went farther in aiming to marry ethics to science in one further respect as well, in that:

> He sought to construe natural scientific understanding itself (also describable for him as 'knowledge of God') as the highest virtue. . . . His ethical vision is one in which scientific understanding allows us to participate in a peaceful and co-operative moral community with other co-inquirers, sharing and taking joy in one another's achievements without being disturbed by one another's weaknesses. (Garrett, 1996, p.307)

So why has a seventeenth-century philosopher like Spinoza enjoyed such a remarkable intellectual comeback in recent years, a comeback sufficient to be able to paint him as a very modern philosopher indeed? Not least, I think, because he provides a way in to problems of *ethics* which short-circuits so many of the problems that we routinely come up against in trying to sort out what can be counted as right and wrong in any situation. And he did this by imagining a new space in which these problems take place, which transforms their content and allows us to think about them in new ways. A brief account of Spinoza' s work will therefore take up the second part of this chapter. In it, I want to show, in particular, how Spinoza, by re-imagining spaces of encounter, has provided a resource for re-thinking how we are ethically and thus what a 'good' encounter might consist of: I will illustrate this by briefly coming back to an episode from Rabinow's fieldwork in Morocco.

But, in the third part of the chapter, I want to move on from Spinoza's work to consider how ethical dilemmas are often conceived now. Back in the 1960s, when Rabinow was doing his fieldwork, ethical judgement was usually still construed as a matter of individual choice, but that is no longer the case. Since that time a new kind of 'audit culture' has grown up, based around the production of 'correct' templates for prac-tising encounter, in the shape of the rise of the dictates of the ethics committee (and the considerable resistance to some aspects of this new institution put up precisely by anthropologists like Paul Rabinow). I want to ask whether this new kind of culture of ethical judgement, which you are very likely to come up against, really promotes good encounters or whether it actually, in its desperation to avoid mistakes, closes down some of the main means by which we learn about others and other cultures, and therefore violates the Spinozan principles I will set out in the second part of the chapter.

Doing fieldwork

Paul Rabinow's book, *Reflections on Fieldwork in Morocco* (1977), described a series of situations which are common to fieldwork – not least the pretty obvious fact that people around you don't want to notice you as you believe that you should be noticed. That sense of disenfranchisement from a culture sits rather oddly with the other obvious fact that you have to negotiate a relationship with that culture which will allow you to obtain the material that will allow you to do your research.

Most particularly, Rabinow, in a long anthropological tradition of recounting his encounters with just a few individuals (Metcalf, 2002),
co-produced   stressed that fieldwork knowledge was **co-produced** from a process of interaction in which both the fieldworker and the informant participated, a process of interaction which might well change both participants' thinking by building fragile and temporary *commonplaces* predicated on building temporary ethical understandings. However, equally, Rabinow was not starry-eyed about these encounters. He did not believe in the kind of reversal of roles that was typical of anthropologists who had become worried that just about every breath they took expressed colonial values, so that the informant was always right. He was willing to assert his own

ethical stance in certain circumstances. For example, on one occasion Rabinow was returning from a wedding early in the morning with one of his key informants, the acerbic and direct Ali, and another acquaintance Soussi. Rabinow was feeling ill and more than a little exasperated at Ali's lack of thought for his situation, and the persona of an all-accepting anthropologist was in these circumstances starting to break down. Rabinow began, however passively, to respond and 'push back', resulting in Ali insisting on getting out of the car and walking the rest of the way home. This spat could well have threatened some of the fieldwork, but not only Ali's, but also Rabinow's, ethical codes were being violated:

> At the wedding, Ali was beginning to test me, much in the way that Moroccans test each other to ascertain strengths and weaknesses. He was pushing and probing. I tried to avoid responding in the counter-assertive style of another Moroccan, vainly offering instead the persona of anthropologist, all-accepting. He continued to interpret my behavior in his own terms: he saw me as weak, giving in to each of his testing thrusts. So the cycle continued: he would probe me more deeply, show his dominance and exhibit my submission and lack of character. Even on the way back to Sefrou he was testing me, and in what was a backhanded compliment, trying to humiliate me. But Ali was uneasy with his victories, and shifted to defining the situation in terms of a guest–host relationship. My silence in the car clearly signalled the limits of my submission. His response was a strong one: Was I happy? Was he a good host?
>
> The role of the host combines two of the most important of Moroccan values. As throughout the Arabic world, the host is judged by his generosity. The truly good host is one whose bounty, the largesse he shows his guests, is truly never-ending. One of the highest compliments one can pay to a man is to say that he is *karim*, generous. The epitome of the host is the man who can entertain many people and distribute his bounty generously. This links him ultimately to Allah, who is the source of bounty.
>
> If the generosity is accepted by the guest, then a very clear relationship of domination is established. The guest, while being fed and taken care of, is by that very token acknowledging the power of the host. Merely entering into such a position represents an acceptance of submission. In this fiercely egalitarian society, the necessity of exchange or reciprocity so as to restore the balance is keenly felt. Moroccans will go to great lengths, and endure rather severe personal privation, to reciprocate hospitality. By so doing, they re-establish their claim to independence.
>
> Later in the day, I went down to Soussi's store in search of Ali to try and make amends. At first he refused even to shake hands, and was suitably haughty. But with the aid of Soussi's mediation and innumerable and profuse apologies on my part, he began to come round. By the time I left them later that afternoon it was clear that we had re-established our relationship. Actually, it had been broadened by the confrontation. I had in fact acknowledged him. I had, in his own terms, pulled the rug out from under him – first by cutting off communication and then by

challenging his gambit in the car. There was a fortuitous convergence between my breaking point and Moroccan cultural style. Perhaps in another situation my behavior might have proved irreparable. Brinkmanship, however, is a fact of everyday life in Morocco. And finesse in its use is a necessity. By finally standing up to Ali I had communicated to him. (Rabinow, 1977, pp.47–9)

Subsequently, Rabinow's work has been criticized by a number of writers precisely for this ethical assertiveness, most notably by feminist writers who have argued that, as a man, Rabinow occupied a privileged subject-position which allowed him to produce a discourse about the construction of ethical commonplaces that had never been open to them. Certainly, Rabinow's gender and standing as a North American anthropologist had an important influence on his ability to interact relatively forcefully in Moroccan society and assert his own ethical standpoint, since each of these characteristics come with particular power relations engrained in them. Moreover, considerable work by writers like Carol Gilligan (1990) has claimed that western men and women approach the question of practical ethics quite differently: whereas men tend to be oriented to an ethic based on an autonomous sense of self and an associated morality of justice, women tend to be oriented to a connected sense of self and an associated morality of caring. (However, Gilligan's work is not itself immune to criticism; not only has it been accused, like Irigaray's work in Chapter 3, of a certain essentialism, but it has also been criticized precisely for its insensitivity to cultural difference (see, for example, Killen and Hart, 1995).)

So how does the work of a philosopher such as Spinoza chime with forays into the field like Rabinow's? I want to argue that not only does Spinoza give us some very useful resources to think a little more complicatedly about the practice of fieldwork, but that through his emphasis on the construction of common advantages of good encountering through the exercise of feeling and imagination, he provides an ethical stance that is much more in tune with what the experience of fieldwork is (or at least should be) like.

Doing Spinoza

Benedictus de Spinoza has been claimed as a notorious atheist – and as a 'God-intoxicated man'. He has been adopted by Marxists as a precursor of historical materialism and by Hegelians as a precursor of absolute idealism. He is often considered to have been one of the great figures of continental European rationalism (along with Descartes and Leibniz) and yet he has also been judged to be a thoroughgoing irrationalist. Some have argued that he is the founder of modern ecophilosophy (Naess, 1975, 1977), and others that he is some kind of political revolutionary. In the light of these and many other widely differing interpretations (Moreau, 1996), it doesn't seem an awful sin to say that Spinoza was also a kind of geographer. For his thought consists of a series of propositions that seem inexorably bound up in spatial figures which are more than incidental in that they are used to transform how we should think about thought and consciousness. In particular, for Spinoza, the world is in constant movement, involved in a constant process of self-construction. It is always *becoming* because matter is internally disposed to create its own motion. So Spinoza believed that every corporeal thing was nothing other than a proportion of motion and rest, so that everything is always to a greater or lesser degree active.

In his posthumously published *Ethics*, Spinoza set out to challenge the model put forward by Descartes of the body as animated by the will of an immaterial mind or soul, a position which reflected Descartes' allegiance to the idea that the world consisted of two different substances: extension (the physical field of objects positioned in a geometric space which has become familiar to us as a Cartesian space) and thought (the property which distinguishes conscious beings as 'thinking things' from objects). In contrast, Spinoza was a monist, that is he believed there was only one substance in the universe, 'God or Nature' (he actually used this phrase) in all its forms. Human beings and all other objects could only be modes of this one unfolding substance; they could not be split off from it as something else. Each mode was spatially extended in its own way and thought in its own way and unfolded in a determinate manner. In Spinoza's way of thinking, '*every* mode of extension is identical with a corresponding mode of thought, so that everything is thinking as well as extended' (Garrett, 1996, p.4). So, in a sense, in Spinoza's world everything is part of a thinking and a doing simultaneously: they are aspects of the same thing expressed in two registers. Individual human minds and bodies, for example, ultimately derive from a fundamental unity of composition. In a famous passage from the *Ethics*, Spinoza puts this proposition baldly:

> The mind and body is one and the same thing, which is conceived now under the attribute of thought, now under the attribute of extension. Whence it comes about that the order of the concatenation of things is one, or, nature is conceived now under this, now under that attribute, and consequently that the order of actions and passions of our body is simultaneous in nature with the order of actions and passions of our mind. (Spinoza, 1996/1677, Part III, Proposition 2, note)

In turn, this must mean that knowing proceeds in parallel with the body's physical encounters. Spinoza is no irrationalist, however. What he is attempting here is to understand thoughtfulness in a new way, extending its sphere of activity into nature. Human activity is no longer, as he put it, a kingdom within a kingdom. Rather, it is one part of a much greater dominion. Spinoza's metaphysics was accompanied by an original notion of what we might nowadays call human psychology.

Straightaway, we have to note that Spinoza does not work from a model of the human individual and then simply power that model up. Rather, human psychology is manifold, a complex body which is an alliance of many simple bodies and which therefore exhibits what nowadays would be called **emergence** – the capacity to demonstrate powers at higher levels of organization which do not exist at others. This manifold psychology is continually being modified by the myriad encounters taking place between individual bodies and other finite things. The exact nature of the kinds of modification that take place will depend upon the relations that are possible between individuals who are also simultaneously elements of complex bodies. Importantly, Spinoza describes the outcome of these encounters by using the term 'emotion' or '**affect**' (affectus) which is both body and thought: 'By EMOTION (affectus) I understand the modifications of the body by which the power of action of the body is increased or diminished, aided or restrained, and at the same time the idea of these modifications' (Spinoza, 1996/1677, Part III, definition 3).

So affect, as a property of the encounter, takes the form of an increase or decrease in the ability of the body and mind alike to act, which can be positive and increase that ability (and thus 'joyful') or negative and diminish that ability (and thus 'sorrowful'). In this way, Spinoza detaches 'the emotions' from the realm of responses and situations and indexes them instead to action and encounters. They therefore become firmly a part of nature, of the same order as storms or floods: 'as properties which belong to [nature of mind] in the same way as heat, cold, storm, thunder and the like belong to the nature of the atmosphere' (Spinoza, 1996/1677, Pref. C492). But affect will present differently to body and mind in each encounter. In the attribute of body, affect structures encounters so that bodies are disposed for action in a particular way. In the attribute of mind, affect structures encounters as a series of modifications arising from the relations between ideas which may be more or less adequate and more or less empowering (see Brown and Stenner, 2001).

This emphasis on relations is important. Though Spinoza makes repeated references to 'individuals', it is clear from his conception of bodies and minds and affects as manifolds that for him the prior category is what he calls the 'alliance' or 'relationship'. So affects, for example, occur in an encounter between **manifold beings**, and the outcome of each encounter depends upon what forms of composition these beings are able to enter into. Therefore, as Brown and Stenner put it:

> The method begins from a point that exceeds individualism . . ., concerning itself instead with the 'necessary connections' by which relations are constituted. Spinoza challenges us to begin not by recourse to biology or culture, or indeed any of the great dualist formations, but with the particularity proper to an encounter . . . (Brown and Stenner, 2001, p.97)

emergence

affect

manifold beings

This way of proceeding from relations and encounters has many echoes in contemporary social science. It shows up in work which is concerned to find common complexes of relation, such as that informed by contemporary philosophers like Gilles Deleuze (who was a Spinozan through and through, see Deleuze, 1988a/1970, 2001/1981). It shows up in work that is challenging the nature–culture divide as found, for example, in the writings of Bruno Latour which, just like Spinoza, questions a discrete human substance. It shows up in work which is challenging what counts as thinking, both in arguments that the characteristic of 'thinking' should be extended to many more objects and in the emphasis on affect as a part of thinking. It shows up in the much greater emphasis being given to expression, as found in work on, for example, performance and performativity. And it shows up more generally in the way in which social science is now saturated by metaphors of movement. In other words, at this time it is possible to say that Spinoza has become a common philosophical ancestor for many different social science projects which are attempting to produce architectures which deal in constant reorganization, redistribution and revaluation and in which space and time are no longer fixed categories of intelligibility.

But what, you might well be asking at this point, has all this got to do with ethics? I think it is fair to say that Spinoza's thought gives us some tools to think about what makes for right action in the face of ethical dilemmas, tools which are at a tangent from those that are usually to hand but which, when brought together, supply us with what Gatens and Lloyd (1999) so nicely call a 'vulnerable optimism', which can offer a freedom to construct and explore common ground. And I want to end this account by pointing to just one more element of Spinoza's thought that up until now I imagination   have kept in reserve, and that is his notion of **imagination** as a positive mental capacity.

For Spinoza, imagination is essential to the flourishing of human beings. Indeed, it is a touchstone of leading a responsible life. Imagination may be considered as a set of constitutive 'fictions' which are, on the one hand, an individual way of knowing arising out of different bodies and their idiosyncratic associational paths and, on the other, the 'imagery which becomes lodged in social practices and institutional structures in ways which make it an anonymous feature of mental life' (Gatens and Lloyd, 1999, p.39). Imagination is, then, a continual reworking of the materials of common perception which 'reflects both the powers of the body, over which the mind has no causal influence, and the powers of the mind to understand it and gain freedom through that understanding' (1999, p.36). And the exercise of the imagination can, of course, have real consequences: though they are subject to the same material necessities, the lives of those who use their imagination well are very different from those who do not. In turn, Spinoza takes an important part of the exercise of the imagination to be working on the circulation and concatenation of affects – understanding and transforming them through 'fictions' and by this exercise allowing affects themselves to communicate, as well as ideas. The stress on the importance of the imagination also makes it easier to see that Spinoza's notion of ethical *responsibility* shifts away from simple declarations of praise or blame (which rely on notions of individual sites of freedom with independent causal force). In its place, we are encouraged to understand and work with processes of the formation of individuality (so-called 'trans-individual' understanding), in which we take on the responsibility to become something different by expanding our and others' subjectivity.

How might Spinoza's *Ethics* help us here in thinking through field-work dilemmas? Most particularly, by pointing to the importance of the *imagination* in producing good encounters. As you will remember, Spinoza sets great store by the goal of improving the intellect by improving the imagination. In fieldwork, it often happens that the best exchanges come from encounters in which the participants have to exercise their imagination, thereby producing something hybrid that very likely did not exist before; new hybrid 'interface cultures' can blossom, however briefly, bringing insight to *both* parties.

Or at least that is the goal. In reality, what this can mean is a fairly brutal calculation by the parties to a fieldwork encounter of what they can get from it (including the possibility that the researcher is deluding themselves in believing that those being researched have any interest whatsoever in the research or believe that it is anything other than a mild nuisance which they feel it would be polite to humour). But this is too cynical and I want to return to Paul Rabinow's *Reflections on Fieldwork in Morocco* to show that this does not have to be the case. For, in his period of fieldwork, a genuine friendship grew up with one of the villagers, Driss ben Mohammed, who continually refused to work as an informant. But Rabinow and he were able to find a space of respect:

> Casually, without plan or schedule, just walking around the fields, ripe with grain or muddy from the irrigation water in the truck gardens, we had a meandering series of conversations. Ben Mohammed's initial refusal of informant status set up the possibility of another type of communication. But clearly our communication would not have been possible without the more regularized and disciplined relationships I had with others. Partly in reaction to the professional situation, we had slipped into a more unguarded and relaxed course over the months. (Rabinow, 1977, p.143)

space of thoughtfulness

In other words, over a period of time Ben Mohammed and Rabinow were able to perform a **space of thoughtfulness** and imagination, however temporary and fleeting, different from that of either of their two cultures.

This is exactly what is now being tried across the social sciences and humanities – in compressed form and often involving more actors – through the use of various performative techniques. What is being looked for is not a new theory, or a new social epistemology, or a new rhetoric, but rather a theory/method of practical-critical activity which, by its very nature, is shared (e.g. Deleuze, 1988a/1970; Guattari, 1995; Newman and Holzman, 1997). The emphasis is put on *expression* because it is assumed that the process of sharing requires the construction of new things: there is no world of already defined things there for the mirroring, but rather the energy of the forces of bodies – bodies as understood in the Spinozan sense – heading off for unknown and risky destinations. As Massumi puts it, when describing the writings of Deleuze and Guattari, two of the chief modern philosophical inheritors of this Spinozan approach:

> They insist on the term 'ethics', as opposed to morality, because the problem in their eyes is not in any primary fashion that of personal responsibility. It is a basically pragmatic question of how one *performatively* contributes to the stretch of expression in the world – or conversely prolongs its capture. This is fundamentally a *creative* problem. (Massumi, 2002, p.xxii, emphasis in original)

The kinds of method that can stretch expression contain something old (sheer good writing would be one) and something new. Much of the new is only just being born but it includes methods drawn from performance and from various kinds of three-way psychotherapy (in which the researcher and the researched are moderated by a third party who both acts as a witness and an adjudicator). But it is not being born in the most propitious of circumstances for, at the same time (and perhaps not co-incidentally), research methods like fieldwork are being made subject to a new tapestry of ethical regulation which, if strictly adhered to, would close down many jointly expressive possibilities because it assumes that there is only one way of proceeding.

Manufacturing ethics

audit culture   Across academia new forms of **audit culture** are growing up (Power, 1998; Strathern, 2000). These forms of culture are means of systematizing the academic labour process so that it is measurable and predictable, and therefore open to greater control. This goal is achieved through an attendant army of new kinds of audit professional, a number of whom are 'dealers in virtue' who are there to audit academic ethics. Once these cultures take hold, they tend to grow as the new cadres of activist audit professionals spread out in search of further fields in which to apply their skills of scrutiny. Not least among the elements of the academic labour process that is open to this professionalization of scrutiny is ethics. For, increasingly, virtue is being audited. Some writers would go farther. They argue that there is now a global market in ethics, of which developments in academia are but a small offshoot, produced by growing competition to accumulate symbolic capital. So Dezalay and Garth (1996, 1998), for example, speak of a new global project of 'elitist democracy' which intends to produce a 'market in humanitarianism' by stressing correct ethical stances, which an elite of professionals will then enforce. In other words, ethics has become a highly articulated trans-national form. Dezalay and Garth take the example of international commercial arbitration as the prototype of a global system of private justice which allows ethics entrepreneurs to flourish, under the guise of a lofty disinterestedness. This is a new circuit of accumulation of ethical capital which will instigate an era of 'philanthropic hegemony'. Human flourishing becomes big business.

Whether things are really quite as bleak as Dezalay and Garth – and other writers like Hardt and Negri (2001) – argue when they write of an enforced humanitarian universalism circulating in a newly global civil society – and the 'surplus of normativity' that accompanies it – there seems little doubt about the manifestation that they would choose to concentrate **Research Ethics** on as the best example of this tendency in academia, that is the **Research** **Committee** **Ethics Committee**. The ethical judgements of such committees have their roots in the so-called Nuremburg code on ethical research on human beings that was drawn up at the Nuremburg trials following the Second World War as a counter to the numerous atrocities committed by Nazi doctors in the name of science. But their main impetus sprang from various scandals in US biomedical research in the 1960s and 1970s. It did not take a battery of professionals to identify that unethical practices were rife in this paternalistic culture (such as the discovery in 1972 that doctors in Tuskegee, Alabama, had withheld treatment for syphilis from roughly 400 black men since the 1930s in order to document their symptoms) and, as a result, after a National Commission on Medical Ethics was established by the US Congress in 1973, a whole new area of bio-ethics appeared (Rothman, 1991). Ethical linkages were made easily in a rights-based culture that had already been sensitized to these kinds of issues by the civil rights movement. They were fuelled by massive increases in the national bill for healthcare arising out of the increasing application of high technology (Rothman, 1997) and they were topped off by the interest of lawyers in extending litigation to new and profitable areas. As a result, practices of biomedical research that had formerly been tacit became subject to analysis, scrutiny and regulation. A whole new industry of bio-ethics was born, at whose centre was the increasingly ubiquitous ethics committee (or as it is usually known now in the USA, the Institutional Review Board or IRB) which was meant to screen all medical research for its ethical consequences for 'human subjects'. This new ethical/audit knowledge is enshrined in the *Protecting Human Subjects* handbook (Office for Human Research Protection, 1993), a regularly updated secular bible which is meant to be used to screen all biomedical research for possible risk, evidence of consent, efficacy of selection of subjects and privacy and confidentiality. In turn, the handbook also sets out how to set up an Institutional Review Board which not only acts as a gatekeeper but also monitors and observes in its own right (see also Amdur and Bankert, 2002).

Similar events have happened in many other countries around the world, though often at a somewhat slower pace. In the United Kingdom, for example, most biomedical, scientific and social scientific learned societies have had codes of ethics for a good number of years, covering issues such as informed consent, deception, privacy and respect for local cultural values. But it is only now that some British universities are setting up ethics committees, in part at the prompting of the Wellcome Trust, the chief biomedical funding body which is insisting on the presence and enforcement of a code of ethics as a condition of funding.

I do not want to argue that ethics committees are *de facto* a bad thing in the biomedical sciences. Given the proven past levels of sometimes quite appalling patient abuse, that would indeed be a difficult case to make. But the problems begin when this bio-ethical apparatus is transferred wholesale into the realm of the social sciences (and so on to activities such as ethnography and other qualitative methodologies which the social sciences are increasingly prone to use) and the humanities, as has increasingly occurred in the USA and now looks set fair to do in Europe. For, in these spheres of knowledge, what counts as ethical practice may sometimes be very different. There have, indeed, been impassioned debates in the USA on precisely this issue. The growing bureaucracy of some 4,000 ethics committees operating in US universities, hospitals and private research facilities has imposed a rule-based biomedical approach generally based on the *Protecting Human Subjects* handbook. The concern is that this actually violates certain ethical precepts that only become clear when doing social science research.

As might be expected, there is a range of positions in the debate. To begin with, there are, of course, certain situations where most social scientists would have little difficulty in condemning a research practice: for example, in anthropology a controversy erupted not long ago concerning an anthropologist who, in studying indigenous populations in Central America, was alleged to have staged violent feuds. In another case an economist introduced money into a currency-less society just to see how people would react (Kancelbaum, 2002). But while situations such as these are clear-cut, there are plenty of others that are not.

One position is to argue that there is no real problem: 'Louise Lamphere, the president of the American Anthropological Association . . ., says that it is second nature – and should be – for graduate students in her department to submit research protocols to the campus IRB each time they start a project' (Shea, 2000, p.30). But others would argue that this is too simple a stance and that there are many ethical instances which are much more blurred than this. For example, what does informed consent mean if you are researching crowds of protesters? Asking a crowd of protesters for their informed consent is not exactly a practicable option! Another example, researching contraceptive methods, highlights cultural and gender differences in what constitutes ethical ground and further complicates what counts as risk (see Kancelbaum, 2002).

A further position would be to argue that ethics committees' rules and regulations, originally designed to be applied in closed situations such as hospitals and laboratories, are very often simply not practicable in the field. Would many of the classic ethnographic works of twentieth-century social science ever have made it to the printers if they had been subject to eagle-eyed IRB regimes? What seems certain, at the very least, is that research protocols need to be adjusted if certain kinds of urban ethnographic work are ever to be carried out again. And there is a real possibility that, as one Berkeley academic put it, bodies like the IRB will 'turn everyone into low-level cheaters' (Shea, 2000, pp.31–2).

But it is important to note that some social scientists do try very hard to interact with those whom they are researching in ways that show that informed consent can be an ethical position and not just a matter of ticking the boxes and getting the signatures. Mitchell Duneier's prize-winning book *Sidewalk* (1999), a study of working-class reading habits in Greenwich Village, New York, is a case in point:

> [Duneier] dutifully got IRB permission. . . . But when his project broadened to include panhandlers and homeless book vendors, [he] improvised. The booksellers knew he was a scholar, but he did not carry a backpack full of consent forms. Still, he took steps to protect them. In his notebooks and diaries, Duneier concealed the identities of his subjects. He stored tapes of conversations in an out-of-state location, where they were beyond reach of the police. After he had written a draft of his manuscript, he rented a hotel room in New York and read long passages of the book to everyone he planned to mention – sometimes for eight or nine hours at a sitting. 'I did get informed consent – in my case it was really informed', he says. 'I showed them the manuscript. I said 'Here's what I am doing with the words and photographs'. He then asked his subjects if they would be willing to sign forms that explained IRB rules and outlined the risks and benefits of appearing in the book . . .
>
> Duneier emphasizes his concern with research ethics. 'I think the procedures I adopted are reasonable and fulfil the spirit of informed consent in a more meaningful way than the routine signing of advance consent forms,' he says. . . . But he still wonders whether he could ever have gotten IRB approval in advance for a study of this kind. (Shea, 2000, p.31)

The example of *Sidewalk* shows not only the considerable ethical sensitivity of Duneier's encounters with others (and, very importantly, disadvantaged and relatively powerless others), but also something else – the creative quality of invention which Spinoza so wanted to promote. But the example also shows just how very difficult it is and will be to slide this quality past the apparatus of ethics committees. For, above all, such committees attempt to render the ethical outcomes of research encounters predictable. At least on certain dimensions, what comes out of an encounter must be known in advance. And the apparatus is therefore likely to smother what is often so valuable about these encounters: the sense of being there and interacting as something more than just researcher and researched in ways which must be relatively unpredictable in order to have any value. Take the case of an activity like ethnography. Part of the value of the exercise comes from the risky relationship with 'data' that Sarah Whatmore outlines in her chapter, with not knowing what exactly will turn up and therefore not knowing exactly what ethical stance to take. Indeed, in certain cases that value may lie – precisely as Paul Rabinow found in the Maghreb – in having one's own ethical certainties shaken up.

So what can be done? One task is to work on the rules of research ethics committees so that they become more amenable to social science research. The need for informed consent is usually interpreted by ethics committees as requiring a form signed by the subject (rather like a patient undergoing an operation), even though the ethical guidelines of a number of social science organizations offer alternatives and even though most social scientists would agree that it is the quality rather than the format of consent that is at issue (Coomber, 2002). Another task is to find creative ways of getting around some of these guidelines. But it is much easier for senior scholars, like Paul Rabinow, to do this than for graduate students (Shea, 2000, p.32). A third is to turn to the rapidly growing body of work, arising out of or inspired by **performance**, which tries to make more out of research encounters and thereby co-construct knowledge by asking questions that might never have been thought of by either party (Thrift, 2000, 2003; see also Chapter 9). What this work attempts is to provide ways of coming together which can form new ethical spaces, a theme taken up in Chapter 9. This is not some grandiose reformulation of the whole basis of western moral thinking. Rather, it is an attempt, often for a very short span of time, to produce a different sense of how things might be, using the resources to hand. In western thinking, for people to achieve ethical solicitude, they have to have a coherent – for which read bounded – culture resting on cartographic parameters of considerable antiquity within which encounters can be resolved (Campbell and Shapiro, 1999). But it is possible to think very differently – as I have tried to show in the case of Spinoza – and to allow various aspects of difference to remain dynamic rather than become definitively coded. The numerous aspects and sensory registers of performance can allow us to 'embrace contingency and enigma, assuming that problems are historically contingent, that subjectivities are unstable and never wholly coherent, and that spaces need to be continually negotiated rather than physically or symbolically secured' (Campbell and Shapiro, 1999, p.xviii).

Whether they do, of course, is up to *us*, for thinking alone, as Spinoza realized, is an impossible act.

performance

Conclusion

The problem I tried to outline in the previous section of this chapter is the double ethical compromise that developments like ethics committees promote: on one side, they produce a normative regime that takes responsibility away from the researcher and, on the other side, they promote an arrogation of responsibility. The researcher only has to think through the multiple dilemmas that continually infest his/her practices – and which can become a source of a mutual enlightenment – in a partial and restricted way. No wonder that these committees produce a certain unease; there is no easy answer but we live in a world in which the formulae provided by audit all too often make the answer seem as if it is just that.

In this chapter, I have tried to think about ethics by heading in another Spinozan direction. What this means, above all, is cultivating the faculty of

good judgement **good judgement** in the course of encounters. But can good judgement be cultivated? I think it can – and not only because this is what the processes of social ordering do all the time. Indeed, it is precisely what some contemporary work is trying hard to do, using a variety of affective techniques. In particular, this work attempts to set up good encounters by training bodies and minds to react in open and constructive ways, taking a stance of what has already been termed a vulnerable optimism towards the world (see, for example, Varela, 1999; Irigaray, 2002). Notice straightaway the Spinozan emphasis on bodies as well as minds. Contemporary work aims to engrain in the body's non-conscious being resources for good encountering (through the use of body techniques learnt from sources as diverse as yoga and dance) in order to extend the range of thoughtfulness beyond cognition and into intuition. But it also works to train conscious thought as well, through the usual academic technologies certainly, but also through other technologies drawn from performance, such as acting out encounters in various ways which are meant to both embarrass and enlighten (Atkinson and Claxton, 2000). Taken together, these trainings can begin to develop both spaces and dispositions in the field (such as knowing when to wait for a response, knowing when and when not to foreclose a situation, knowing when to be playful and when to be serious, and so on) in ways that can open out the ethical possibilities of an encounter and allow both the researcher and the researched to trust their judgement and so be carried along by it. Subjectivity expands when we take on such responsibility. To come back again to Spinoza's geometrical imagination, we must write of restless bodies endlessly making new modes of thoughtfulness.

Further reading

If you wish to explore more of Spinoza's thinking, then a short and helpful guide is provided by Genevieve Lloyd in her *Routledge Philosophy Guide to Spinoza and the 'Ethics'* (Routledge, 1996). In the first chapter of *Reflections on Fieldwork in Morocco* (The University of California Press, 1977) Paul Rabinow reflects on how and why he came to do fieldwork and how his own sense of ethical behaviour was subsequently moulded. In 'A geography of unknown lands' (2003) Nigel Thrift provides an account of an ethical project which, in part at least, relies on a Spinozan approach. His dissatisfactions with moral and political certainty led him towards a new kind of ethical performance which can remake the world but not in its own image. This paper can be found in Duncan and Johnson (eds) *Companion to Cultural Geography* (Blackwell, forthcoming 2003).

CONCLUSION TO PART II

The focus of Part II has been the encounter in the field and how, with the help of philosophical influences, we may be able to re-imagine the production of knowledge made through field*work*: the nature of the encounter between researcher and the objects of research, and the ethical issues that arise through such encounters. In Chapter 4, for example, 'fieldwork' was identified as a potent space in the practice and imagination of scientific knowledge production conventionally associated with the idea of *discovery*. Moreover, by working with the idea of fieldwork as engagement, the space of the 'field' is seen not to pre-exist the research process but actively to be constituted in and through such activity. If nothing else, the blurring of the all too easily imagined line dividing field and cabinet has been one productive outcome of an engagement with philosophical materials.

One of the main ways in which the line was re-imagined was through a dialogue with the work of Latour, whose approach to the ideas and materials generated though the research process helped us to appreciate them as transformed into what he terms circulating references, which connect the sites of study, field and computer in complex ways. This theme was taken further in the following chapter, where the research process was seen to be less an investigation of the world, which philosophically positions the researcher at one remove from the world, than an *intervention* in the world, in which all those enjoined in it can and do affect each other.

The introduction of such ideas into a reflection on the work that goes on 'in the field' was shown to have further implications. Thus, for example, what thinking alongside philosophical influences helped to provoke was a re-appreciation of what is quite often referred to as 'data collection' as instead a process of 'generating materials'. In Chapter 5 this alternative take on this stage in the research process was informed by the work of Isabelle Stengers. Her work reminded us of the importance of ontological approaches to framing the relationship between researcher and researched. This was achieved by working with her principles of 'working together' and 'being at risk'.

We went on to see how such ideas and what they mean – the *consequences* that accompany them – cannot be confined neatly to this stage of the research. This sort of thinking, its openness to iteration, upsets a linear view of the process of research. The implications of these philosophical arguments for the politics of knowledge production and the distribution of expertise are quite real. This view was reinforced in the discussion of how different *ethical stances* inform different research practices (the subject of Chapter 6). One of the voices engaged was that of Spinoza. Through a discussion of his approach to ethical thinking and the implications of his notion of 'co-existence', we were able to reflect on some of the ethical dilemmas that may arise in the conduct of research and begin to *re-imagine* them in productive ways. This was achieved notably by working with the fieldwork accounts of the anthropologist Paul Rabinow. While such discussion may have at times seemed quite abstract, it was shown how these issues have very real implications – consequences – for the formal conduct of research (an issue raised in part through Rabinow's work), particularly given the marked move towards the formalization of concerns with ethics, witnessed by the rise of research ethics committees in the USA.

The chapters in Part II have offered a number of ways to recognize further how ideas developed through an engagement with philosophical materials, can help us to gain a fuller appreciation of just what it is we do and what's at stake when we engage in research, here at the moment commonly referred to as empirical or field*work*. In doing so, Part II has demonstrated some of the skills and crafts, learnt through working alongside thinkers such as Latour, Stengers and Spinoza, that should help you to cultivate and to exercise better *judgement* in the conduct of your research as a whole.

PART III
Writing practices

INTRODUCTION
Michael Pryke

Perhaps you will not be surprised to hear that research has to be brought to a completion; there has to be an end point; it cannot go on forever. Although it's a process that has its own anxieties, there has to be closure of some kind. You have to write up your research. You've worked away at a research question, slogged your way through secondary materials, perhaps interviewed numerous people, then listened to the tapes for hours on end, transcribed them, made notes on notes . . . and now, finally, you get the chance to practise making sense of it all and to write your 'findings' into the world.

Too often, however, a number of arguably unhelpful assumptions are made about the whole process of concluding research, particularly what is expected from analysis and writing – unhelpful because of what the assumptions smooth over. How often, for example, do you hear 'Just do it!' barked when the question of writing-up is raised? The root of the impatience is perhaps not that difficult to trace. It lies in the viewpoint that fairly clear-cut rules can be followed, that the task is about plain speaking, the easy delivery of the facts assembled during the empirical work. In fact, one gets the distinct impression from those who are persuaded by this view, that if writing research is to be done properly, executed effectively, then all traces of the messiness of the research done to date, all of the mediations followed and explored, should be left outside writing, at the door of the study, as it were. Much the same points could be made about the way in which a researcher is often encouraged to view analysis and the potential audiences for whom the research is written.

The chapters in Part III wish to tell a different story. They want to suggest that there are other ways to think about – and to continue to think through – the situated activities of analysing and writing. Just as a wide range of questions was seen to be in circulation, so there is a variety of ways in which to reflect on the last stages of research. Chapter 7, for example, demonstrates what might be gained if analysis acknowledges the very stuff of research – all the notes, the transcripts, and so on, all jumbled and untidy – and suggests that much might be lost if such products of research are too rapidly and thoroughly cleaned. Chapter 8 shows that far from being unproblematic, writing – writing up – is an active method of inquiry, just as much as was engaging in empirical work. Chapter 9, meanwhile, dwells on the influences that run through the contexts of writing, and the relationships and responsibilities that are made in the act of preparing research for reception.

What are the consequences of the philosophical influences discussed in the chapters to follow? Well, what we hope you will gain is a range of ways to re-address the mode of thinking that would have us believe that analysing, writing, the contexts of writing up and the responsibilities a researcher has to his or her audience are philosophically unblemished, workaday matters. As you will see in Chapter 7, we are encouraged, through Benjamin and de Certeau, to think of analysing as an active, involved, material process, not one that positions the researcher above and distant from the messiness of analysis. With their help we are free to fancy such thoughts as 'Do we really need to be in *total* control of the materials we are analysing?' If we listen to their ideas we see scope to work into this stage of the research process such notions as recombination, recontextualization, translation and transformation of materials – the vocabulary Benjamin and de Certeau came up with as they ran through their minds what analysis involves for them. Such a set of ideas in turn gives support (and authority) to those who wish to re-examine just what it is that makes for 'good analysis' and why conventional approaches might need to be attended to. From Derrida and Latour in Chapter 8 we learn through their different styles to think reflexively about writing otherwise. From them (and others) we at least become aware of the philosophical underpinnings that make writing seem so matter of fact. We gain the ability to work at alternatives, should we so wish. Similarly, in Chapter 9 Bourdieu, Fish, Said and Spivak allow us to gain an appreciation of a range of ways to re-appreciate the contexts of writing and to entertain other approaches to the question of researcher and audiences. And while this point marks the completion of one stage of research, if you are wishing to disseminate your work, then this is also the beginning of that work and another set of responsibilities, as well as an extension of those already begun. Overall, in unmasking what is disguised as a transparent process, Part III demonstrates how philosophies can help us productively to analyse, write and respond in other ways, otherwise.

7

Telling materials

Mike Crang

Introduction

In Part II of this book you have been concerned with field*work* but now
you are ready to move on and address what to do with material you have
created out in the field. The way this chapter will approach this is by
thinking about the actions involved in analysis: the stage when you make
sense out of the material you have so painstakingly gathered. However, I
am not going to present a discussion of the criteria of a 'good' or 'valid'
analysis, since there are many types of epistemological theory that underlie
different sorts of analysis. That is, there are theories about how we know
what we can claim to know, about how we judge truth claims and assess
the reliability or validity of our work. The sorts of claim you can then
make and the type of analysis needed are thus going to vary according to
your approach, your questions and hence the data, and the sorts of answer,
you need. So rather than work through a list of philosophies and their
assumptions about validity, this chapter will focus on the actual activity of
analysis, as a material process, an idea we will come back to shortly in the
next section. When we write research proposals and timetables we often
pencil some period for 'analysis of data'. This chapter is going to unpack
this process, first by suggesting that analysis is a messier business than
this suggests and, secondly, by highlighting the tangible processes of
interpretation.

There is a certain moment of pleasure that often occurs in projects
when we complete fieldwork and with satisfaction look at the mass of
accumulated materials – be they questionnaires or field notes, tape or
transcripts, copied documents, pictures or whatever – and think of what
we have achieved. This is the lull before the storm, the moment before a
rising anxiety starts tapping on our shoulders (well, it does mine anyway)
and asks what are we now to do with all this stuff. How are we to turn this
mass of material into some cogent, hopefully illuminating, maybe even
impressive, 'findings'? And, of course, we realize the one thing they are not
is findings – findings, like questions, require work. It is better to think that
through analysis we make interpretations, not find answers.

The process I am going to discuss is one of producing order out of our
materials, of making sense. And this making sense is a creative process.

Now this is not to say that our materials are in total chaos beforehand, as often quite the contrary is true; our materials are structured by our questions, our methods, by our respondents, by external forces, say in official documents, and so on. Yet, to make them work for us, we have to reconfigure them, perhaps decontextualize then recontextualize different parts to make them say new things.

This chapter is structured around some of the key tensions in this process of disciplining our material, of creating order from our work and sustaining that order. The next section offers a way into these tensions by considering what counts as analysis. Then we shall look at the way most accounts see order emerging from data and suggest that some sort of 'natural order' does not automatically flow from the materials you have gathered. We move on to consider the disciplining of materials, by looking at pre-existing order and disorder in our material using an example of archival work. In the following section we offer an alternative vision from Walter Benjamin, who in many ways sought to present disorder as a finding, or to reveal the fragmentary nature of order. We then present a critical look at how fragments are made into smoother wholes through the work of Michel de Certeau. The aim is to think about the implications of how we shape our material. This is not, then, about assessing the limits or applicability here of different analytical techniques, but rather the generic processes of analysis. The chapter is going to suggest that this is a creative process of producing meaning, and one where we need to be clear about what is involved in producing order. One outcome of this analysis of 'analysis' is to suggest that thinking and analysis are not abstract processes or theoretical models or rules that occur purely in our heads, but involve the manipulation and orchestration of a range of materials that occur in specific places. It suggests that we need to start with the actual stuff of our interpretations, in terms of how we get to grips with (literally and figuratively) all the material we so diligently made in the field.

What counts as analysis?

If for a moment you do not believe that the issues of how you store, write down and recompose material have an impact, then just imagine doing all your interpretation in your head, as though you were forbidden any notes. Imagine trying to communicate your ideas without writing or drawing at all. So if we acknowledge that the techniques of writing, storing and moving information play a role in 'processing' our material, it seems beholden upon us to understand what role they play. Now with statistics there are well-worn rules, but my aim here is to think how we get to the stage of statistics or of a final report. Just cast your eye over an imaginary desk: scattered about are index cards – perhaps with just a title of a work, perhaps quotes – elsewhere are long-hand notes from a library book on file paper, perhaps photocopies marked up with coloured pens, the odd post-it note sticking from a book to mark a key passage, all burying a well-worn and intermittently legible field diary. Let me dramatize it further, let us suppose we are part of a team. Then we have notes to other members, notes from other members and photocopies with their red biro, overlain by our fluorescent highlighter. What the stuff on our desk and our fellow team-members seem to be asking is: 'What counts as "**analysis**"?'

analysis

We might begin our answer by suggesting that these material objects are the means through which ideas are bandied about – between team members most obviously but even just sustaining our 'internal' dialogue. In fact if we look at how 'information' has been defined, we can see that it is linked to a range of specific material practices (Nunberg, 1997). Thus for example, when we ask each other whether we have got sufficient data, or in a research proposal we talk of information, what we are actually referring to are specific forms of acceptable or even permissible data. Thus conversations, our memory of the weather, often our emotions, or even gossip we hear, tend not to be counted as information or data. However, by following certain rules of analysis, say, by putting those observations in a field diary (bound between covers or maybe just floating on bits of paper) or when interviews become tapes, which in turn become transcripts, they become sanctified as information: they become data. To this way of thinking about analysis, then, what counts is clear-cut. Yet, this approach tends not to recognize the range of materials from which ideas may emerge. Some pieces of paper are indeed clearly formal records or 'calculations', but others might be, say, a scribbled note in a margin 'compare this idea with X', some bits of paper might be laser-printed, and some even with formal headings and citations, but others may be much more informal, or a formal record might be annotated. There is, then, a need to think about the variations and types of material used in paper work and what each signifies – the informality of a post-it note, the finality of a signed thesis for submission (Pellegram, 1998). Typically, then, if we are to follow this approach further, analysis tends to be a progression from 'data' through informal notes to more and more formal outputs, the shape of which will be taken up in the next chapter. Yet, what gets dignified with being 'data' is itself an issue worth reflecting on for, as we have seen, the work of the field itself transforms material into 'useful' (to us) information. So our material has already begun to be shaped prior to analysis. Our analysis then goes on by phases, becoming more and more formal outputs. If we recognize this prior stage, then we should question accounts that divide research into discrete 'theory', 'empirical' and 'analytical' sections – as though we might say 'and now the analysis bit'. Instead, we might think of the analytical approaches as activities, as the practice of weaving the material into a text.

What this implies is a set of fuzzy rather than clear-cut boundaries around our 'analysis' as a stage in the research project. So let's keep thinking of our papers, notebooks with more or less fastidious field notes and jottings, possibly some newspaper cuttings, maybe our notes on some archival sources. All these we might call data (though we might indeed want to tidy them up before suggesting they were really ready to stand up to scrutiny as data). Moreover, such tidied notes may well already contain our reflections, either explicitly or implicitly, for instance in our decisions on what is worth including or discarding, and quite probably then our thinking through of the questions we are posing. Our notes thus bear traces of our starting to recompose them. We may well then have notes specifically thinking through material, specifically notes on reflections. Now, this suggests a different approach to analysis, one that has been called **grounded theory** 'grounded theory' (Strauss, 1987). This approach encourages us to keep writing these so-called theoretical memos as we transcribe and work to code and mark up materials. They are designed as an aide to our evolving thought; so we do not forget ideas that seemed important and we can develop them systematically.

Let's move this on a stage and suppose these notes and materials begin to be put together into drafts, by taking, say, lots of informant quotes on a topic, some bits of literature, all the time trying to develop an argument. If you are like me, then, you will have one go, look at it with disgust and move it all around. If you are part of a team, like me, other people will make suggestions and more or less helpful comments. What we are doing is reworking, re-working (and re-re-working) drafts. Analysis is not simply an issue of developing an idea and writing it up. Rather, it is thinking by writing that tends to reveal the flaws, the contradictions in our ideas, forcing us to look, to analyse in different ways and rethink. The question that quickly emerges is how on earth are we meant to separate 'analysis' from 'writing' – a question I often pose to students who say they plan to finish their analysis before they 'write up'. And this blurring of clearly marked sections in the interpretative process has grown greater with the advent of word-processors. As Jacques Derrida notes, this has enabled a new rhythm to working through materials:

> With the computer, everything is so quick and easy, one is led to believe that revision could go on indefinitely. An interminable revision, an infinite analysis is already signalled, held in reserve as it were. . . . Before crossings out and superimposed corrections left something like a scar on the paper or a visible image in the memory. There was a resistance of time, a thickness in the duration of the crossing out. (Derrida, 1999, p.8)

There is now an immediacy, a de-distancing, that brings the objective text closer to us yet at the same time makes it somehow 'weightless'. It seems we can play with meanings almost endlessly, composing and recomposing our material. With echoes of Chapter 2, this seems a state of boundless play, in one sense exhilarating, yet also scaring and debilitating in equal measure, since after a while it can be quite difficult to recall whether something occurred to you, when it occurred and how the idea developed and, amid all these proliferating versions and permutations, we must eventually send one final (at least for now) interpretation out into the world. In fact one of the temptations of analysis is just that: to keep playing around, to keep seeing if something else better might be done, if more might not be included, if only there was a little more time. But whether it be writing a chapter for a book, or a dissertation, eventually time pressures tend to push to a closure, however provisional, however many holes we think may still be lurking in our interpretation.

Analysis as building theory

As the previous section suggests, analysis depends on a variety of things and, as the stress on re-reworking drafts emphasizes, a natural order does not just leap out of the material. This section is going to develop our discussion of analysis by looking at thinking through some qualitative materials. And to ensure that I do not make this into just a token or a foil for some later 'cleverer' approaches, I am going to use research I have actually done to exemplify this. What I am going to try to illustrate is the effort and dynamics it takes to produce – what I at least like to think was – a coherent account from materials. The issues I will be flagging are not to do with either the mechanics or straight epistemology but with a range of choices a researcher faces about how they shape the material. In later sections I will suggest some alternative strategies to the ones I used on this occasion.

So let us envisage a researcher sitting at a desk. This person has been doing fieldwork. He/she has, in fact, been told that this stage is complete and it is time to move on to 'analysis'. He/she might be quite relieved that someone else is telling him/her to do this. For this part of his/her research, he/she is staring at something like 400 pages of transcript, two field notebooks, some notes from newspapers and observation records (oh, and an archive of some 5,000 photographs, but that topic is for the next section). The pile on the desk has a comforting solidity, neatly (and laboriously) transcribed and numbered by line, labelled by source. Yet it also has to be made into something that will justify the project to both academics *and* the respondents. And, as will be discussed in Chapter 9, the analysis can be driven by, in this case, two divergent audiences and in fact two products will come from this analysis – an academic piece and a piece to return to informants. More immediately, let us suppose we have been reading something on grounded theory as a style of analysis (for example, Strauss, 1987, or for my own summary of the approach adopted, see Crang, 1997, 2001).

We thus set out to read our materials intensely, working through them line by line, writing notes to ourselves in margins, on cards and so on, as we develop a set of categories about what was said, categories that form the building-blocks of an interpretation. Here I want to focus upon a couple of issues in the background of this process. First, one of 'where do the categories come from?' and secondly, 'what we do with them?' The first is something of a vexed issue, with Strauss pushing a process of constant comparison, where we develop categories to describe parts of our materials and then test them to see if they hold water. Thus we look at the data, develop an idea and see if it holds true – hence the idea of 'grounded theory'. This is somewhere between deduction – testing a previously formed question – and 'abduction'. The latter is the term used by the philosopher C.S. Peirce, for developing knowledge where we are not trying to falsify hypotheses, but to develop plausible explanations through the data, to examine which ones are worth following up – what in Chapter 1 we saw discussed as the way in which we pose questions that anticipate answers. Well here, too, we are posing questions of our data that may lead us down different paths. This runs counter to what others claim should be nearer induction, where we let our categories form through the data and we do not impose our ideas upon it. This is a vexed issue. Indeed, the first book defining 'grounded theory' was written by Anselm Strauss and Barney Glaser (1967) who later parted company over which way to lean, with Glaser rejecting 'forcing' our concepts on to the data. The issue here is very much whether, or how far, the analytic framework we develop should come from our agenda or emerge from our materials. For our researcher this issue is compounded by the fact that respondents really wanted to see just what they said, never mind some university-type's ideas; while for the academy a different set of rules and audience expectations tend to dominate. So the ethical issues raised by Nigel Thrift in Chapter 6 are not confined to the field and they are present in our analysis as we think about our responsibilities in relation to people with whom we worked – to ask what information different people want, and possibly whether some information may harm the interests of some people.

So far we have really been discussing the basic blocks of analysis, and we now have to think how they are put together. So the next step is to think through the relationships between these blocks. One obvious pattern is categories and subcategories, and then sets of continuums and oppositions – so some categories grade across from one to another, others indicate opposite sentiments, say. So we think, we work, we sift the ideas as we move large number of bits of paper or text around. If we are using software to do this on screen then the limits to categorizing and recategorizing are fewer, which is both liberating and tormenting. In the end, however, something must be produced. So our researcher begins to put related categories together and try to string an argument across them. One approach is to build directly out of the categories we have used to manage our data. This results in collating relevant material into a series of subheadings based on our categories that form the thematic parts of our analysis. Our researcher puts all this together and produces a document of some 80,000 words. It quickly becomes apparent that there is a need both to select among the material and also to transform the categories into a linear argument. Sometimes it is easy, for example when one group of material leads into another, but inevitably we end up selecting which bits follow which and which bits are important.

So, as in Chapter 1, which spoke of Rorty and pragmatism, analysis is not just holding up a mirror to give a 'true picture', but a practical action of describing and relating things to answer specific needs and questions. And so the crux of analysis becomes transforming these chunks and bits of material – some empirical, some theoretical – into a plausible and persuasive whole. Having broken down our field data into topic-based 'chunks' or fragments, they get recontextualized and rebuilt into an interpretation. In other words, this process of analysis works by taking an existing pattern of material and breaking it down, and then recomposing a new one. I want to look at this recontextualizing in a little more detail, drawing upon work in archives.

Analysis as disciplining material

The sense of contexts and relationships between bits of information can be examined a little more clearly if we use literature that thinks about archives – both as an empirical source and as a scholarly practice. You will recall that confronting the researcher are not only piles of notes but some 5,000 pictures, all archived, and many now collected and published. The question of analysis does not just mean looking to see what is in the pictures, but rather to ask questions of *why* pictures are included or excluded from the archive, *why* that one is chosen to be put next to another, *why* one is published, in what forum, and so forth. Historical researchers have thus argued that studying collections means we end up studying how they label and organize the world. Allan Sekula has pointed out that this tends to mean creating relationships of equivalence by reducing knowledge to bits of commensurable information or, as Pinney put it, the catalogue is a 'linguistic grid enmeshing otherwise volatile images' (cited in Rose, 2000, p.559). As Gillian Rose has argued, we need to think rather carefully about how cataloguing and archiving work is used to frame and discipline material, with the result that each document is classified under a specific scheme, is made uniform and thus into a coherent collection. Documents and materials, which outside the archive had one set of meanings, are invested with new ones and are now transformed within

archive   it. Rose (2000) argues that we need to see the **archive** as very much one of the areas where knowledge is shaped, but that the 'disciplining' of knowledge through the collection's categories does not always succeed since, for instance, the presence of the researcher with his/her own questions, background and knowledge may disrupt the neat categories. She suggests that analysis thus combines three sets of orders: that of the archive itself; the visual and spatial resources of its contents (the actual pictures held in it); and the desires and imperatives of the researcher. Put together, this suggests that the meaning we gain from material in an archive exceeds its classifications (Rose, 2000, p.567).

Let us take the account of Alice Kaplan (1990) working in Parisian archives to illustrate the way in which the division of data and ideas can be over-stated, with archives being all too glibly labelled as 'data' over and against a cerebral, **'speculative theory'** (1990, p.104), and how ideas, circumstance and theory come together. She notes that the tendency is to write up what you found, what you concluded, and not the processes in between – of finding and thinking. The result tends to be a suppression of the actual practices of thinking, which again leaves data and conclusions seemingly sharply divided. This tends to take out what Chapter 1 used Rorty to describe – the fragility and contingency of our ideas. Hence, we tend to edit out how our ideas evolved in non-linear fashions, since to proceed in this way would 'not only gum up the narrative, it would threaten its credibility, by showing on what thin strands of coincidence, accident, or on what unfair forms of friendship, ownership, [and] geographical proximity, the discoveries were made' (Kaplan, 1990, p.104). So archives are not just about disciplining and stratifying meanings, they are places where connections – between ideas, different kinds of facts and emotions – are made. In some sense the archives are anti-disciplinary places where tracking down materials leads to surprising connections, new sources in obscure locations, even for Kaplan. Midnight walks retracing the steps of a writer on Montmartre, which gave her new insights on her subject's outlook, led Kaplan into a maze of frustrations and sudden elations as her ideas developed. Kaplan concludes that the 'archive is constituted by these errors, these pieces out of place, which are then reintegrated into a story of some kind . . . [these incidents] are fragile but necessary contingent ingredients to archival work' (1990, p.115). She suggests that developing ideas is not separate from the archive, nor is it entirely a disciplined process, but one that starts connecting diverging elements. The issue for us here is to see that in all our work, however contemporary, in our offices, files and studies, we to tend to be producing archives, albeit less systematically and more chaotically than official ones. We, too, are collating documents, taking and transforming them, reordering them in our new classification schemes, taking 'ownership' of them and making them speak to each other in new relationships.

Analysis as assemblage, ideas as montage

So how might we see this leading to different ways of working, different ways of making sense of the world? Well one approach is to think about us writing through materials – both theoretical and empirical. Let us think how, through the course of a research project, you have developed sets of notes – maybe filed on a computer, maybe on A4 sheets, maybe on cards, annotating books and papers you have read. From these you are going to

(margin note:) speculative theory

try to stitch together an argument and an account about the topic you have studied. Let's look at an example of this sort of process.

The theorist Walter Benjamin worked in Paris in the 1920s and 1930s and is often associated with the Marxist Frankfurt School of critical theory, though he was never formally a member of it. Benjamin was a voracious reader of theory, journalism and historical documents – indeed almost anything became 'data' for his project on reconceptualizing urbanism. Benjamin offers us an example of interpretation pursued almost entirely through notions of conjunction and recontextualization, arguing that it was by taking what seemed common and unexceptional and putting it in a new context – alongside other unremarkable events and information – that you could reveal previously hidden dynamics. He spent considerable amounts of time working through the relationships between finding and making order, as well as the techniques of representing his ideas. His working method was to file items from a vast variety of sources in different registers (called *Konvolut*). Each responded not to a 'source type' but rather to a theme of analysis. He likened his work to that of a collector because for him the key element of his work was not finding new material (though he researched archives tirelessly) but its transformation back in the 'cabinet': 'The true method of making things present is to represent them in our space (not represent ourselves in their space)' (Benjamin, 1999, p.206, H2, 3). That is, he argues, we reconfigure things, materials from their original contexts and recontextualize them in new relationships and thereby produce insights. This transformation is not 'distancing' data from the field but creating it afresh. He describes, perhaps with too much relish, the 'dark pleasures of discovery' (Benjamin, 1979, p.314), working in the archives, suggesting that these delights are not derived from specific pieces of information, but are very much created through the process of finding the archival materials which become invested with meaning and gain significance through being seen in a new light. As Benjamin put it, facts become significant 'posthumously, as it were. . . . A historian who takes this as his [sic] point of departure stops telling the sequence of events like beads of a rosary. Instead he grasps the constellation which his own era has formed with a definite earlier one' (1973b, p.255).

Benjamin thus argued that the materials developed meaning only in the tension between their own framework of intelligibility and that brought by the researcher. In other words, each researcher at different periods, with different questions, and working in different intellectual and historical contexts, makes something different out of the same document or piece of information. Benjamin (1979) focused upon the way in which information moved through contexts and suggested that we can think of all our reading and work through this lens, so that even scholarly books, what we may think of as final products of research, are just a momentary pause in an endless flow. The books are just an in-between stage, produced from the author's collection of note files and waiting to be transformed into some future reader's collection of notes. As he put it:

The card index marks the conquest of three-dimensional writing, and so presents an astonishing counterpoint to the three-dimensionality of script in its original form as rune or knot notation. And today the book is already, as the present mode of scholarly production demonstrates, an outdated mediation between two different filing systems. For everything that matters is to be found in the card box of the researcher who wrote it, and the scholar studying it assimilates it into his own card index. (Benjamin, 1979, p.62)

Here, then, he highlights both the sense of continual translation and transformation of meaning, but also a sense of the multidirectional, **linear writing style** complex linkages that he felt were inhibited by a **linear writing style**. Benjamin pushed a writing practice that sought to engage with what he saw as a fragmented and objectified world by using material in the same style – through fragments and moments. What makes him interesting for us is that he saw this as necessitating a break from linear styles of configuring arguments. That linearity he saw as imposing a structure necessitated by the conventions of books on to material that was linked in more complex, multidirectional ways. Benjamin thus highlights a moment of tension in research felt by many of us when we have to try to push our ideas into a linear argument. His response was that instead of building a linear argument, he would work through images of juxtaposition and collage that would alter the meaning of each fragment and that this procedure would make new truths erupt, and, he hoped, disrupt the *status quo*, from the conjunctures and disjunctures between elements. Notably he refuses to prioritize either archive or interpreter: 'It isn't that the past casts its light on the present or that what is present casts its light on what is past; rather an image is that in which the Then and the Now come together in a constellation like a flash of lightning' (cited in Smith, 1989, p.50). Thus, for instance, he would present the latest shopping fad, next to what seemed a dowdy and obsolescent product to point out that both had made the same promise. It was a 'method [that] created "dialectical images" in which the old-fashioned, undesirable, suddenly appeared current, or the new, desired suddenly appeared as a repetition of the same' (Buck-Morss, 1986, p.100). The dialectical image sought to use contrast and comparison between things that were normally thought of as opposites (if put together at all) – the clashing and jarring of them would, he hoped, spark insights. Thus, Buck-Morss argues, he deploys historical material on prostitution alongside material on a rising consumer society to suggest how people are becoming commodified. As Benjamin himself described this practice:

Method of this project: literary montage. I needn't say anything. Merely show. I shall purloin no valuables, appropriate no ingenious formulations. But the rags, the refuse – these I will not inventory but allow, in the only way possible, to come into their own: by making use of them. (Benjamin, 1999, p.460, N1a, 8)

Given the period of the 1920s, Benjamin's scholarly thinking was linked to the then emergent aesthetic practice of surrealism and collage. We might think of the latter, where we have fragments of one material, from one context, taken and reused in another, with the effect of creating a new meaning, and Benjamin spent a lot of time exploring devices such as allegory as interpretative strategies. The task of analysing the city – Benjamin's project – becomes one of finding a way of putting together the material to express the urban reality.

Benjamin thus did not just think through a three-dimensional tangle of relationships, he also tried to perform it in his text. The method of collage was meant not just to discuss trends in the city, but to perform, exemplify and show the fragmented and disjunctural nature of that life, by not having theoretical approaches standing over, reflecting upon, the world but rather having ideas *emerge* from among and through the materials. Now this approach is not easy, nor is it always successful. Sometimes, it can become a surrender to the difficult and complex nature of our material, and sometimes it can be mistakenly taken as an abdication of the researcher's role in shaping the material. Benjamin, however, comes close to suggesting that shaping and juxtaposing is all the researcher really does. This is not without problems, since it means there is very little explication (as he said above: say nothing, only show), very little help for the reader who is meant to pick out the meaning for him/herself. Famously, Benjamin's friend, the critical theorist Theodor Adorno, accused his style of standing at the crossroads of positivism and mysticism, risking just reproducing empirical data in the hope of producing a revelation for the reader. But that was very much Benjamin's point – that the city did combine hard-edged capitalism along with almost mystical dreams and desires pushed by advertising. In this sense Benjamin is trying to find a mode of representation and analysis that fits his ontology – one that, as was noted in Chapter 5, allows the world to impact on our mode of analysis. The danger with Benjamin's method of piling up the *actualité* of experience and trying to get ideas to speak through the fragments is that it can come dangerously close to simply being an empirical assemblage. But it was Benjamin's answer to balancing theoretical clarity with empirical complexity, a dilemma with the twin dangers of surrendering to the '*mêlée*' or forcing things into too simple a framework. So, thinking through Benjamin is *not* to say 'anything goes'. Benjamin himself rather (un)helpfully pointed out that there is all the difference in the world between a confused presentation and the presentation of confusion.

So how does Benjamin help us think through research? Well, he offers a sense that the meaning of the materials we develop may burst out of pre-existing frameworks, that novelty may emerge through analysis, rather than it being about working out prior theories or prepared explanations. His analytical practice of using collage breaks down the divisions of concepts and materials to suggest that we create ideas from the juxta-position of very different types of materials, producing new interpretations between academic sources, observations, archives, documents and so on. He does not privilege either the 'empirical' or the 'theoretical' side of the material that is involved in analysis. In this sense he begins to suggest our analysis is crowded with materials, jostling together and he suggests we need to think about the multiple interrelationships of material, rather than seeing ideas emerging in some straightforward sequence from question, to field, to data, to written account.

Analysis as making narratives and coherent stories

Benjamin highlights the importance of how we order our concepts and ideas and the relationship of that ordering to our analysis. We have seen that he was unhappy with linear presentations, preferring instead a collage where elements related in multiple directions rather than just in sequence. One way of developing this notion of the importance of ordering to analysis, then, is to think of the 'fictive' quality of our work. Using this term about, say, history has been very provocative, since we normally set up 'factual', scientific or accurate accounts against 'works of fiction' which are implied to be imaginative, creative and simply not reflecting reality. Yet, we have seen in Chapter 1, and in this chapter, that there is not a 'mirror' on reality and that our analysis strives towards making a plausible account. So I am using the term to stress that all accounts are made, that fabrication is not a synonym for 'falsehood' but a process of constructing things. The best 'scientific' accounts involve imagination, artistry and creativity and all accounts involve the hard graft of tying elements together. What differs are the criteria by which differing audiences may judge an interpretation's success or validity – as we shall see in Chapter 9.

To give this some concrete substance, let us follow Michel de Certeau's (1986) study of the travel-writing of Jules Verne and his critique of 'those languages which deny their status as fictions in order to imply (or make one believe) that they speak of the real' (de Certeau, 1986, p.28). He argues that

doubled narrative

the effect of texts is to regulate and distribute places, through a **doubled narrative** – that is, they narrate narration – or, for our purposes, the story of our research frames the evidence we use. The notion of a doubled narrative needs some unpacking. Thus in Chapter 1 we saw our questions begin to pre-empt our data, or in this chapter, as Benjamin would have it, our way of finding information is perhaps as important as what is found. In other words, the events and elements of our analysis are framed by the structure, and made into interpretable instances in the light of the process, of research itself. He suggests that our materials function as evidence only because they are bound this way into a narrative. It is a doubled narrative since it gives meaning to the things it claims are evidence of its truthfulness. Applying this to the process of research, de Certeau argues that the structure that gives shape to the analysis is one of going out and into the

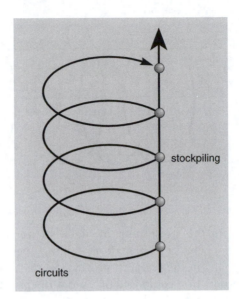

Figure 7.1

Source: de
Certeau, 1986,
p.146

stockpiling

circuits

world, then returning home with material that is transformed into data by
being brought home. This is illustrated in Figure 7.1.

In Figure 7.1 de Certeau shows a series of loops coming from a home
base and out into the field. He argues that interpretation is about turning
stockpile of   our travels to and from the field into a **stockpile of knowledge**, and he
knowledge   would suggest capitalizing on it, in terms of deriving status, authority and
academic qualifications from it. In other words, he sees analysis as, in part,
being about turning experience '*out there*' into knowledge '*back here*' that
brings with it some measure of power and prestige, echoing what in
Chapter 5 was called the 'squirrel–acorn' sense of collecting and hoarding
data. Indeed, de Certeau goes so far as to call it 'an accumulatory
economy' and sees the research 'narrative as the Occidental capitalization
of knowledge' (de Certeau, 1986). The accumulatory pattern of this is clear
in Figure 7.1, as each journey returns to the place of writing and re-
inscribes the centrality of the centre of calculation and inscription.

What this approach adds to the previous chapters is the suggestion
that when we separate finding knowledge and building upon it, this
separation is achieved by denying how analysis creates its own evidence
through denying the twofold narrative of analysis. So in his study of Jules
Verne's stories, he points out that they are punctuated by a structure of
setting out, having an adventure and returning to base to make sense of it
all. It is perhaps significant that the base is in the library of the fictional
Nautilus. That is, the economy is one of stockpiling and building at the
place where there is a cyclic return to the story's place of production. The
accumulation consists of building these disparate elements into a coherent
stock of knowledge. He sees this working by binding together the elements
to make a linear progressive line out of a series of circles (see Figure 7.2).

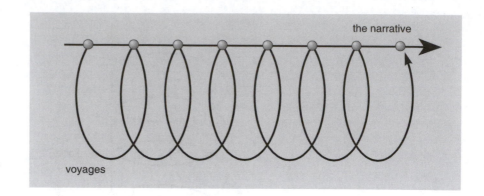

Figure 7.2
Source: de
Certeau, 1986,
p.146

Here the stockpiling of 'data' at home has to be transformed into an argument or explanation, linking together material derived at different points in the research process. So there is a tension between thinking and production composed of a series of episodic circuits and the need for a plot giving a forward moving account.

De Certeau argues that this structure of text and data is pervasive not just in 'fiction' but in how we accumulate and deploy evidence in general. But what he suggests we do is to look at the obverse of this, like looking at the photographic negative of this process, so that instead of seeing a solid accumulation de Certeau sees a series of gaps. Thus de Certeau asks the disarmingly simple questions: why is there more than one circuit? Why does the evidence in the first not prove the case? There is, he says, a moment at the end of each of these cycles where the account seems to come up short, to not really prove the case, where it says 'but that is not quite it' – and thus it commits to a new gathering of material. The issue he points us towards is whether any amount of data gathering can finally answer a question, or whether our research journey always stops short of such a final 'proof'. At a practical level this may well point to a simple truth that the number of circuits tends to reflect less an inherent logic of evidence and proof and more an arbitrary point where we have to stop – for a deadline set by timetables, funding, examiners, or even publishers. More philosophically, de Certeau suggests the text is not producing solid proof, piling arguments and evidence, but is what he terms a 'piling up of insufficiencies', putting together things that do not in themselves offer conclusive proof – or, we might say, stringing together a series of gaps or holes.

The structure of many academic texts is thus a repetitive going out and coming back, making the world into a story and accumulating intellectual capital all the while. To elaborate, we might note that de Certeau points out that Verne's books were based on the work of a researcher, called Marcel, hired by Verne, who worked in libraries building up material for the travel stories. He suggests this is a narrative capitalization of citation, where the process of interpretation conscripts past knowledge to the current project, meaning that:

> . . . the narrative displays a multiplication of trajectories, which unfurl an earlier writing in space, and of documents, which bury one past beneath displacements of location. But all of this occurs in the same place, in a book, or rather collection of books, each of which, due to its particular geography, is different from the preceding one, in other words stands *beside* the other, yet nevertheless repeats the same depth effect by placing itself *above* or *below* the other. (de Certeau, 1986, p.140, emphasis in original)

There is an unfurling sequence of writing and voyaging where both Marcel and Verne labour on texts only to bury them as 'foundational' strata in their own. It is this creation of foundations that de Certeau highlights and problematizes. An example is how we bring in previous stories through citations, leaning our work on someone else's. The implication is that since they said something we may take it as proven and as a simple building block, as foundations from which to argue. But he argues that none of them necessarily proves anything more than any other. Instead we might see these stories as alongside each, rather than with some relationship of verticality, or, after de Certeau, see them not as accumulating layers but as an accumulation of **fragments** or ruins from previous work – in other words, a piling up of incomplete parts – and it is the incompleteness that induces motion to the texts, as we strive to think what might add completeness. One implication of this is that a quest for a final answer inevitably fails. Our work may stop but there are always gaps and deficiencies. Not because we have failed to do things properly, but because the structure of interpretation is made up of gaps. We could always follow up one more reference in the back of a source, and in that we could find another, and another; one more field site might just add something to support an idea, but would also inevitably bring its own issues and conundrums that might be tested only by another site. In other words, our interpretation is always shifting, contestable and more or less provisional, so that the decision when it stops is more one of pragmatics than completeness. Inescapably one text leans on a previous one which in turn leans on a previous one, citation upon citation, ruins within ruins. De Certeau suggests some recognition of this fragility of interpretation. But he also cautions that interpretation has often been a 'violent' process where parts of the world are cajoled and reordered, made to speak to new purposes for our work. This reshaping is constructive, but it also tears apart previous orders. Or as de Certeau puts it:

fragments

> More exactly that speech [from the informant] only appears in the text in a fragmented, wounded state. It is present within it as a 'ruin'. In this undone speech, split apart by forgetting and interpretation, 'altered' in dialogic combat, is the precondition of the writing it in turn supports. (de Certeau, 1986, p.78)

The subjects of our work reappear as ghosts – haunting it – or as ruins and relics. They push us to write, they authorize our interpretation but the price is that they are inevitably altered – we interpret in their name but their voice is lost. De Certeau argues that our analysis does not make the field present, but rather fundamentally it is about dividing us off from it. This philosophical perspective thus outlines a scepticism that our concepts will ever match up to reality and suggests that a deep and inevitable rift exists between them. Logically, it also leads to scepticism about claims to interpretations being complete and self-sufficient, since it sees them composed of bits taken from elsewhere – be that the field, the archive or the library. It thus suggests interpretation is incapable of achieving '**closure**' or, as it is often put in the literature, it rejects '**totalization**', where an interpretation purports fully to explain events.

closure

totalization

De Certeau thus draws our attention to what he sees as a problematic creation of what he calls a '**logic of the same**', or a **monologic** account (that is, all in 'one voice' or from one perspective). He suggests our accounts are shot through with voices from absent others, producing **heterologic** accounts. Using his work we might look more critically at the place of knowledge as making certain things legible – at the expense of silencing others. As he put it, 'it would be wrong to think that these tools are neutral, or their gaze inert: nothing gives itself up, everything has to be seized, and the same interpretive violence can either create or destroy' (de Certeau, 1986, p.135). He is critical of the way in which, what he calls 'proper' places of knowledge, try to make the world transparent by fixing things in an analytic grid. He argues that actually the material always exceeds this grid. He also looks carefully at this 'place' as being one where we can accumulate knowledge by subjecting it all to the same interpretation. Instead he sees the process as more itinerant, with us, the researchers, thinking through different material in different places, in libraries, in the field, with a sort of textual and theoretical voyaging that complements empirical travels and travails. As he argues:

logic of the same;

monologic

heterologic

> . . . when someone departs the security of being there together . . . another time begins, made of other sorts of excursions – more secret, more abstract or 'intellectual' as one might say. These are the traces of things we learn to seek through rational and 'academic' paths, but in fact they cannot be separated from chance, from fortuitous encounters, from a kind of knowing astonishment. (de Certeau, cited in Terdiman, 1992, p.2)

De Certeau thus provides a critical eye upon interpretation in several ways. First, he points to the imposition of order as quite often a violent act through which the interpreter silences others. Secondly, he does this by linking notions of stockpiling knowledge with linear narratives. Instead he turns to narrative to undo these stockpiles, to suggest they are full of holes, and the larger the pile, the more holes. He is arguing that this claim in interpretation to produce evidence is actually an artefact of our accounts. The value placed on the evidence comes from the interpretation, and is not inherent in the data. More positively, he picks up on the notions of transformation to suggest we should think of our work not as a bringing together, not as placing knowledge in the cabinet but as displacing it, not accumulating but dispersing. It is this, he suggests, that opens our accounts to multiple logics and plurality.

Conclusion

Overall, then, the theme here has been to think about philosophical materials as part of an activity – as a doing among our research, not as reflections standing over and above it. The process of analysis I have tried to stress is thus an active and material one, one that involves making connections – and divisions – and where material is combined, recombined, decontextualized and recontextualized. The tension I have been focusing upon is how we see order emerging and being created. Both Benjamin and de Certeau caution as to the violence and constrictions of interpretative frames. Both ask us to think about analysis as a process of translation and transformation, and I have tried to illustrate this in terms of processing qualitative data and working with archival material. I have tried to show that what happens in the filing-cabinet can have impacts not just in terms of constraining and ordering but also disrupting interpretations. The sudden and surprising connections of material that Benjamin foregrounds come from seeing interpretation as flowing through the movement of information in and out of archives, collections, on to our desks, into our notes and into our texts. De Certeau, meanwhile, points to the limits of analyses, and suggests that trying to impose too much solidity on our analyses is to risk imposing an over-coherent view of the world. Instead he suggests opening our accounts to reinstate the silences and gaps as ways of engaging with the field, to see ourselves as journeying through, rather than standing over, our material.

All these accounts ask us to think about the politics and ethics of ordering our accounts, to see that this process is often, perhaps inevitably, one where we balance disciplining our material with allowing it to develop. The tension and dilemma is, then, often to work through how much the material is in our voice, or how much we are having others speak through it – be they informants, other writers or theorists. The chapter has also tried to suggest that our materials speak back to us; they may resist our analyses; they may push us in new directions. Interpretation is often a process where we are not wholly in control. On the plus side there can be serendipitous discoveries; on the negative side there are ill-fitting elements. The aim here has been to suggest that the work of analysis – and it is work – is bringing things together in new ways. I have also tried to show that this does not start when you 'return from the field', nor stop when you start writing a final report. Rather, it is a process of transformation and connection that flows through from initial questions and on to writing a final product, a process which the following chapters take up.

Further reading

An excellent account of Benjamin's work is provided in Susan Buck-Morss, *The Dialectics of Seeing: Walter Benjamin and the Arcades Project* (MIT Press, 1989). On interpreting the city, see Graeme Gilloch, *Myth and Metropolis: Walter Benjamin and the City* (Polity Press, 1996) or, for a more general discussion, Gilloch's *Walter Benjamin: Critical Constellations* (Polity Press, 2002). On Michel de Certeau, two good general guides with different takes on his work are Jeremy Ahearne, *Michel de Certeau: Interpretation and Its Other* (Polity Press, 1995) and Ian Buchanan, *Michel de Certeau: Cultural Theorist* (Sage, 2000). My own preferred outline of his approach is in the introductory essay by Wlad Godzich, 'The further possibilities of knowledge', in de Certeau's *Heterologies: Discourse on the Other* (Manchester University Press, 1986).

8
Writing reflexively

Nick Bingham

Introduction: write at the beginning

Over the last four chapters we have been exploring what is at stake in that period of the research process which stretches – as conventionally conceived – from the moment that you first 'enter the field' to when you 'analyse the data' which you collect there. Although we have been pressing you to do even more, this a period to which even in that conventional version you are expected to devote a great deal of thought. And not only thought but words, for it will be further expected that you will provide evidence of the care you have taken in choosing, justifying and perfecting your fieldwork and analytical methodologies as part of the final write-up of your research. But when it becomes time to produce that write-up, something very curious happens and you will find yourself back in a situation more like when the issue of how to produce a research question was presumed to be self-evident. In other words, when it comes to writing up, you are not really expected to think at all – you are expected to just do it.

Of course, this is not entirely true. Right from the start you already know that at some stage the movement – from an initial stance of facing the world, through playing with ideas, pushing limits, exploring, experimenting and encountering, right up to the (re)combination and (re)contextualization of the last chapter – which characterizes the research process (at least as we have been explicating it) has to be brought to something of a stop. Right from the start you already know that, without wanting to make it sound like too much of a Faustian pact, part of the deal which allows you to enjoy the literal and metaphorical travelling around what we have summarized as asking, investigating and interpreting in previous chapters, is that you will need to bring something back, to present something interesting or even original about your journey. Depending on whether that thought fills you with excitement or trepidation, you may experience this need either in the form of a desire or an obligation. Probably it will be a mixture of the two. Whichever, writing up will be at the back of your mind throughout the research process.

At the back of your mind, however, is where it is likely to stay. And this is precisely my point. It is all too rarely as social scientists that we are encouraged to bring writing up to the forefront of our thoughts in the same way as we are other parts of the research process. There is, I want to suggest, a very simple reason for this. And that is, as sociologist Laurel Richardson puts it, that 'in standard social science discourse, methods for accessing data are distinct from the writing of the research report, the latter assumed to be an unproblematic activity, a transparent record about the world studied' (Richardson, 2000, p.923).

What I will argue in this chapter is that this assumption that writing up is unproblematic and transparent in practice is a direct consequence of it being assumed to be unproblematic and transparent in theory. This assumption – that language gives us easy and direct access to the world we want to account for – is a big one. As we have already touched upon in this book during previous discussions of the word–world relationship, it both carries much philosophical baggage with it and has significant consequences for our ways of working as social scientists. By suggesting (after Richardson) that, on the contrary, writing up is far from unproblematic and transparent both in theory and in practice, and is every bit as much as a 'method of enquiry' (2000, p.923) as any of the other steps we have covered, I hope to convince you that it deserves as least as much 'thinking through'.

How successful I am in this will depend to a large extent on whether I can persuade you not to fall into the trap which is one of the first consequences of taking writing up to be unproblematic and transparent. And that is the temptation to leave it until the end. The point is well made by the sociologist Howard Becker in his classic guide to *Writing for Social Scientists* (1986). There he describes a series of graduate workshops during which he would force students to articulate their views of the process of writing up a research article, thesis or book. Most, he remarks, had the view that is:

> . . . embodied in the folk maxim that if you think clearly you will write clearly. They thought they had to work everything out before they wrote Word One, having first assembled all their impressions, ideas, and data and explicitly decided every important question of theory and fact. Otherwise they might get it wrong. They acted the belief out ritually by not beginning to write until they had every book and note they might possible need piled up on their desks. (Becker, 1986, p.18)

Becker recommends a rather different model to his students and readers: write early and write often. What I want to do in what follows is add to this simple but invaluable advice the suggestion that it might be equally as valuable to consider the *act of writing* itself early and often too.

Why? Because you have something to gain by thinking about writing up early and often. And that is opportunities. The opportunity, first, to reflect on why and how writing up makes a difference. We will turn to this in a moment, as I examine in the next section what is at stake in writing up and what are the other consequences (in addition to the temptation to leave it to the end) of how it is conventionally conceived. And the opportunity, secondly, to experiment with how and why writing up might be done differently. We will come to this in later sections of the chapter, where I explore how the work of the philosophers Jacques Derrida and Bruno Latour (to which you have already been introduced in this book) have served to expand what counts as writing up. I would argue strongly that taking these opportunities (and taking them seriously) will both make your encounter with the necessity of writing up more interesting and (not coincidentally) make the product of that encounter a better one.

Writing up conventionally

Even in this brief introduction to the chapter I have already asked a lot of you. Once again you are being expected to go along with the disruption of another of your, if not cherished, then at least familiar assumptions about the research process. By this stage in the book you have a right to pose a few questions of you own about precisely how much of a difference all this thinking through actually makes. Regarding our concerns here, you could reasonably ask, for example, why, if writing up is not actually unproblematic and transparent, is it represented as such? And even more to the point, if writing is not actually unproblematic and transparent, why does it *feel* like it is? Because, let's be honest, most of the time it does feel as if we can provide an account of the social that is 'measured, steady, as if all can be explained' to use the concise characterization of conventional social science writing style provided by Gillian Rose in Chapter 3. In fact, most of the time it feels natural to do so.

Such questions are both fair ones and good ones, and their answers are instructive in terms of our aims in this section to establish what is at stake in writing up and what the consequences are of how it is conventionally conceived. In order to move towards those answers, however, we need first to take a step back and revise a little history:

> Since the seventeenth century, the world of writing has been divided into two separate kinds: literary and scientific. Literature, from the seventeenth century onward was associated with fiction, rhetoric, and subjectivity, whereas science was associated with fact, 'plain language,' and objectivity (Clifford, 1986, p.5). Fiction was 'false' because it invented reality, unlike science which was 'true' because it purportedly 'reported' 'objective' reality in an unambiguous voice.
>
> During the eighteenth century, assaults upon literature intensified. John Locke cautioned adults to forgo figurative language lest the 'conduit' between 'things' and 'thought' be obstructed. David Hume depicted poets as professional liars. Jeremy Bentham proposed that the ideal language would be one without words, only unambiguous symbols. Samuel Johnson's dictionary sought to fix 'univocal meanings in

perpetuity, much like the univocal meanings of standard arithmetic terms' (Levine, 1985, p.4).

Into this linguistic world the Marquis de Condorcet introduced the term *social science*. He contended that 'knowledge of the truth' would be 'easy and error almost impossible' if one adopted precise language about moral and social issues (quoted in Levine, 1985, p.6). By the nineteenth century, literature and science stood as two separate domains. Literature was aligned with 'art' and 'culture'; it contained the values of 'taste, aesthetics, ethics, humanity, and morality' (Clifford, 1986, p.6) and the rights to metaphoric and ambiguous language. Given to science was the belief that its words were objective, precise, unambiguous, noncontextual, and nonmetaphoric.

But because literary writing was taking a second seat to science in importance, status, impact, and truth value, some literary writers attempted to make literature a part of science. By the late nineteenth century, 'realism' dominated both science and fiction writing. . . . Honoré de Balzac spearheaded the realism movement in literature. He viewed society as an 'historical organism' with 'social species' akin to 'zoological species.' Writers deserving of praise, he contended, must investigate 'the reasons or causes' of 'social effects' – the 'first principles' upon which society is based (Balzac, 1842/1965, pp.247–9). For Balzac, the novel was an 'instrument of scientific inquiry' (Crawford, 1951, p.7). Following Balzac's lead, Emile Zola argued for 'naturalism' in literature. In his famous essay 'The novel as social science,' he argued that the 'return to nature, the naturalistic evolution which marks the century, drives little by little all the manifestation of human intelligence into the same scientific path.' Literature is to be 'governed by science' (Zola, 1880/1965, p.271). (Richardson, 2000, pp.925–6)

realism

The social sciences, then, emerged at a time when belief in the powers of a certain '**realism**' was pervasive. The 'importance, status, impact, and truth value' that came from 'reporting' 'objective' reality (to paraphrase Richardson) was an aspiration in our field as across many others. Striving to position themselves as doing an equivalent job for the human world as scientists were doing for the physical world, early social scientists decided the best way to achieve this aspiration was to mimic the procedures of science in as many ways as possible. And that included a way of writing which was seen to be 'objective, precise, unambiguous, noncontextual, and nonmetaphoric' (to use Richardson's words again): to put it another way, unproblematic and transparent.

The consequences of adopting this way of writing in pursuit of an easy and error-free knowledge of the truth (as de Condorcet would have it), continue to be felt today, and will affect you when you come to write up as they do everyone else. For, over time, what we might think of as an envy of science on the part of those early social scientists has become sedimented in our ways of working to such extent that we could now call the unproblematic and transparent model the standard discourse of writing up in the social sciences. As you should remember from the discussion by John Allen in Chapter 1, discourses are what the philosopher Michel Foucault called groups of related ideas which govern the variety of ways in which it is possible to talk about something. By doing so (as you should also recall) they make it difficult, if not impossible, to think and act outside them. This is exactly what has happened with regards to writing up in the social sciences. Whether you are producing a report, a dissertation or a thesis, that is to say, it is unlikely (unless you think it through) that you will be aware of all the work that you are doing to keep up the chase for the ideals of science – objectivity, neutrality, truth – that, as we have seen, became the ideals of social science.

In fact, this is so true that it is easier to illustrate the sorts of exclusion and erasure that I am thinking about when I refer to this work by using examples from outside the social sciences. A good place to start is Bruno Latour's description of a trip into the field, as discussed by Doreen Massey and Sarah Whatmore in Chapters 4 and 5 respectively. You should recollect that one of his aims was to document in some detail just how many steps, transformations, and things were required for him (or anyone else for that matter) to be able to learn about the soils of Amazonia in a library in Paris. The other was to highlight that it is only if most of those steps, transformations, and things are deleted from the final report of the research as found in that library, that it is considered properly 'scientific'.

mediations

Now, what if I was to say that a similar effacement of most of the **mediations** that make possible – even constituted – your research is expected, if not demanded, in the conventional social science discourse of writing up (and analysis, as the latter chapter highlights). Just think about it. Although, as we noted earlier, you will likely be required to produce a description of your fieldwork and analysis as part of the final write-up of your research, what is wanted is the clean and tidy, *post hoc*, rational version that you will be familiar with from a thousand textbooks. What usually won't be welcomed is the messy, changing with events, pragmatic version that better describes the process as it inevitably actually happened. The version, that is, which would be the equivalent of the twists, turns and detours that Latour traced between Amazonia and the library.

By beginning in the sciences, then, we have been able to gain enough perspective to recognize the first exclusion or erasure that we make when writing up social science conventionally, and that is that we tend to delete many of the mediations on which all research depends. To get at the second erasure or exclusion that maintains as standard the social science discourse on writing up, I want to start in literature, the literature described by Richardson as 'realism' to be specific. As we saw in her quote 'governed by science' (like the social sciences), a whole lineage of French fiction-writers devoted themselves through the nineteenth century to producing novels and short stories that represented the truth of the social world. Despite the avowed purging from this work – in the quest for objectivity – of all traces of the personal and the use of distorting literary devices, as with science it turned out that getting at the real was not quite as straightforward as it seemed. The twentieth-century French theorist Roland Barthes, for example, argued with reference to literary realism that 'no mode of writing was ever more artificial than that which set out to give the most accurate description of Nature' (1967/1964, p.56). For him, the 'style of no style' was just as much a style as any other. And producing what he called 'the referential illusion' and the 'reality effect' (1986/1984) on which such realism depended for its success, required at least the same degree of artifice as do all other forms of literature.

My question is this: could the same accusation be levelled at social science as conventionally written up? Again, think about your own experience. When you write essays, reports, projects, dissertations and so on, do you consciously employ rhetorical devices such as metaphor, synecdoche and so on, or do you just think you are merely describing the 'way it is'. If the latter, then read what Barthes has to say:

> It is perhaps time to dispose of a certain fiction: the one maintaining that research is reported but not written: here the researcher is essentially a prospector of raw materials, and it is on this level that his [sic] problems are raised: once he has communicated his 'results,' everything is solved; 'formulation' is nothing more than a vague operation, rapidly performed according to a few techniques of 'expression' learned in secondary school and whose only constraint is submission to the code of the genre ('clarity', suppression of images, respect for the laws of argument). (Barthes, 1986/1984, p.70)

Maintaining the image of writing up in the social sciences requires not only deleting the mediations of research, it seems, but also repressing the literary features of our prose, keeping up the pretence that research is 'reported' and not 'written' in Barthes' terms. For, once again, it is only by denying that the forms of our texts are related to their meanings, that language in any sense constitutes reality, that our products can appear as unproblematic and transparent (see also Game and Metcalfe, 1996).

With these two exclusions and erasures in mind, I want to return to the questions with which this section began. I hope that you can now appreciate why I insisted that the history lesson was needed in order to answer them properly, for that history, whether you like it or not, is your inheritance in terms of writing up. Whether you like it or not, writing up conventionally feels natural because you have inherited a discourse in which it is natural. Whether you like it or not, writing up is represented as unproblematic and transparent because you have inherited a discourse in which it is unproblematic and transparent. And why? Because you have inherited a social science which continues to base its legitimacy on a certain version of science in which the world is presumed to be out there in ontological terms, knowable in epistemological terms, a world that, as a consequence, the (social) scientist potentially has authority to represent. And as with science, all the work that we unconsciously do to keep it seeming that our writing up is natural, unproblematic and transparent, and that the world is out there, knowable, goes unrecognized most of the time both by us and others.

We have established, then, that writing up as conventionally conceived in the social sciences is not as unproblematic and transparent as it purports to be. Does that mean we should dismiss it out of hand as a way of representing the world? I would suggest not, if for no other reason then that we cannot just reject it in any simple sense. As a discourse – and a very deeply rooted one at that – it enables what we do as social scientists as much as it restricts us. We would be fooling ourselves if we imagined we could discard it like a now unfashionable set of clothes. But on top of the impossibility of dismissing realism *tout court*, there is also the fact that it remains entirely appropriate for writing up some things, for some contexts, communities and audiences (for more on these, see the next chapter).

We are now a little more conscious of what is at stake in writing up conventionally and while the consequences of doing so should not lead you to disqualify this strategy entirely, it should however do two things. The first is to make you modest about what you claim when using this style – self-aware, to put it another way, of its effects and effectivity. Then, and secondly, it should make you ask the question of yourself: 'How can I write otherwise?' If you were still blindly trapped within the discourse of social science as you have inherited it, that question might sound like a cry of despair: 'Otherwise, how can I write?' Now that we have made at least a temporary escape, however, that same question can sound like the start of an exploration of how we can represent the world slightly differently: 'How can I write otherwise?' Or perhaps even: 'How can I write the world other-wise?' In other words, after we make the move of the first part of this chapter, writing up can no longer be a matter of innocence (as if it ever was) but another of those issues of judgement that permeate and percolate through your research process. Or as Barthes puts it, 'The multiplication of modes of writing is a modern phenomenon which forces a choice on the writer, making form a kind of behaviour and giving rise to an ethic of writing' (1967/1964, p.70). But choice requires alternatives and that takes us to the second half of the chapter.

A moment of reflection

At this point it is only fair that I answer another question which I feel you will have been asking for a little while now. That question is how, if the discourse that has shaped writing up as conventionally conceived in the social sciences is so powerful (as I have been suggesting), is it now all of a **writing otherwise**   sudden possible to talk about **writing otherwise** and choices? Again this is a question worth asking. Luckily the answer is worth giving in terms of my aims in this second half of the chapter, which is to provide you with the basis for experimenting with how and why writing up might be done differently.

The reason that I can start to talk about writing otherwise and choices has, of course, very little to do with me. Instead, it has everything to do with the fact that you are coming to writing up at a very interesting moment – a moment not just in the sense of a particular point in time, but perhaps also a moment in the sense of a turning point. For, as Avery Gordon explains in her wonderful book *Ghostly Matters* (1997), the context in which you will be doing your research is one in which a whole set of issues to do with the adequacy of conventional accounts of the social are very much up in the air:

> [O]ver the past ten or twenty years there has been a veritable assault on traditional ways of conceptualising, studying, and writing about the social world and the individuals and cultural artefacts that inhabit that world. Whether the post-1945 period is conceived as the loss of the West's eminent narratives of legitimation or as a series of signposts announcing the arrival of significant reconfigurations of our dominant Western organisational and theoretical frames – poststructuralism, post-colonialism, post-Marxism, postindustrialism, postmodernism, post-feminism – many scholars across various disciplinary fields are now grappling with the social, political, and epistemological confrontations that have increasingly come to characterise it. (Gordon, 1997, p.9)

And these scholars, I would argue, could and should include you. When you hear some of the phrases used to describe the 'assault' that Gordon describes, such as 'crisis of representation' or 'climate of prob-lematization', this may sound like quite an intimidating proposition. I want to reiterate from the introduction that, as long as you think about writing up early, such a situation need not be either a crisis or a problem for you, but instead an opportunity. In the remaining sections of the chapter I want to spend some time elaborating one very practical way in which you can

reflexivity   begin to take this opportunity, and that is to address the issue of **reflexivity**.

Though it has now gained considerable currency within the social sciences, reflexivity is a difficult notion to pin down (see Lynch (2000) for a review of at least six different senses in which it is used). For our purposes here, though, you can think about it as a way of interrogating the relationships between what you are writing about when you are writing up and the way that you write it (Woolgar, 1988; Ashmore, 1989). All

representations   **representations** (including the texts of social scientists) make (more or less obvious) reference to the world (the some-one(s) or some-thing(s) being represented). At the same time all representations make (more or less obvious) reference to themselves as representations. Being reflexive means taking this double sense of representation seriously. In this sense what I have been encouraging you to do in the first half of the chapter is to be reflexive about writing up as conventionally conceived in the social sciences. In the terms I used just now, we saw that the representations produced by that mode of writing up are assumed to relate to the social world that they are representing unproblematically and transparently. As such it is further assumed unnecessary to make any reference to these representations *qua* representations – they are supposed, after all, to tell things as they are. Thinking reflexively offers you the possibility of alternative modes of writing as well as critique, however; modes of writing which can operationalize the qualities of modesty, self-awareness and non-innocence that I was advocating you should take away from our discussion in the previous section. It is a taste of these alternatives and their philosophical underpinnings that I want to concentrate on for the rest of the chapter.

As I indicated in the introduction, I want to do this by making reference to the work of Jacques Derrida and Bruno Latour. My choice of these two figures is based on a number of considerations. The first is that you are already familiar with them to a certain extent after their introduction earlier in the book (Derrida particularly in Chapter 2, Latour particularly in Chapters 4 and 5). The second is that, because they take and enact very different positions on the issue of reflexivity, they usefully dramatize the debate about how to write otherwise. Thirdly, they are both authors who provide an exemplary consideration of our shared intellectual inheritance, recognizing that we cannot simply overturn what has become before. And finally, Derrida and Latour share a common approach to dealing with that inheritance of realism. They both wish, that is, to add back some of that work of the world in general and research in particular which, as you now know, is excluded or erased in conventional social science writing up.

Each takes a rather different approach to this final task. Derrida tends to follow and make visible the ways in which language works to provide our descriptions. Latour, on the other hand, is more inclined to trace and demonstrate the processes through which we are able to take things into account. They do, however, share an aversion to the emptied-out approach to writing up that realism offers. This is not to say that Derrida and Latour abandon the real. On the contrary, they both profess to be shocked when anything of the sort is suggested. Rather, they just want us to entertain the possibility that what seems like the most straightforward (unproblematic, transparent) way of getting at the world may not be the best way of doing it justice. And that, instead, other routes or detours may serve us better. In the next two sections you will get the chance to judge for yourself whether you agree.

Writing up with Derrida: deconstructive reflexivity

According to Derrida, the fantasy of an unproblematic and transparent mode of writing up in social science that you are now familiar with as

'realism' is only a minor manifestation – 'a modification' (Derrida, 1981b/
1972, p.64) – of a wider privileging of presence and immediacy (what he
terms logocentrism) within western thought. Throughout his career, but
especially in his earlier works of the late 1960s and early 1970s, Derrida
has sought to undermine and displace this privilege. In a series of detailed
readings of key texts by some of the most significant figures in that meta-
physical tradition, including the philosopher Plato, the writer Rousseau,
and the anthropologist Lévi-Strauss, he demonstrates that in each case their
work escaped their intentions or control in ways which they could not
admit. Central to this project has been a recasting of the notion of writing.
This involved radicalizing the structuralist account of language which is
based around the insight that words (and signs more generally) do not have
some necessary link to that to which refer, but mean only by virtue of their
difference from other words in the system (such that 'cat' does signify 'in
itself' but only by its difference from 'cap' or 'cad' or 'bat'). Having made
this move, 'writing' in Derrida's hands came to exceed its usual conno-
tations such that it now acts for him as a description of the conditions of
possibility of our knowledge or experience of the world in general.

At the risk of understatement, this is a significantly expanded version
of writing to that which you have been asked to engage with so far in this
chapter. The key to understanding it for our purposes here is the notion of
différance (a neologism coined by Derrida). In many ways, for Derrida,
différance is writing in his broad definition, at least in the sense that it is
the precondition for meaning of all sorts. The term can be thought of as
another way of getting at the movements of play and undecidability that
animate the world, as was described by Nigel Clark who also drew on
Derrida in Chapter 2. By exploiting the similarities between the French
words for 'differ' and 'defer', what it does specifically is draw our attention
to the fact that representation can never be the simple repetition of a pure
and present (unproblematic and transparent) origin. Instead, it must
always rely on the constitutive spatiality (difference as apartness and
separation) and temporality (difference as delay and postponement) of the
world.

This probably sounds formidably abstract. However, what I am trying
to do is reach a point where you can appreciate that what is particularly
interesting about Derrida in this context is that his questioning of logocentrism (and conventional writing up) does not merely influence the
content of his work, but also its form. In this sense his project is performative or perhaps better 'perverformative' (Derrida, 1987/1980, p.136).
In other words, when he writes, Derrida does not just theorize *about*
destabilizing the idea of an unproblematic and transparent relation to the
world, he actually *does it*. This is the way of writing that has become
known as 'deconstruction'. It is difficult to give you a sense in a chapter
like this just how different and sometimes disconcerting an experience
reading one of Derrida's perverformative or deconstructive texts can be,
especially compared to the unproblematic and transparent style with which

différance

deconstruction

you (and I) are probably more at home. Some of the quotes from Luce Irigaray's work used by Gillian Rose in Chapter 3 give a hint of the challenge, in that she too very self-consciously (reflexively) disrupts the connection between the represented and the representation. At the end of the day, without the space for lengthy extracts, my advice is simply to go and dip into one of his many books (*Dissemination* (1981b/1972) is as good a place to start as any).

For now, unless you have already done so, you will have to take my word for the (at least initial) strangeness of reading much of Derrida's output. This bemused reaction, however, is not elicited by accident but by design. As the literary theorist Barbara Johnson explains in her excellent translator's introduction to *Dissemination*:

> Because Derrida's text is constructed as a moving chain or network, it constantly frustrates the desire to 'get to the point'. . . . In accordance with its deconstruction of summary meaning, Derrida's writing mimes the movement of desire rather than its fulfilment, refusing to stop and totalize itself, or doing so only by feint. (Johnson, 1981, p.xvi)

How exactly does Derrida achieve this frustrating, moving chain quality to his writing though? According to Johnson, he employs a number of tactics or mechanisms. These include employing unusual '*syntax*'

> Derrida's grammar is often 'unspeakable' – i.e., it conforms to the laws of writing but not necessarily to the cadences of speech. Ambiguity is rampant. Parentheses go on for pages. . . . Punctuation arrests without necessarily clarifying

Or complicated '*allusions*'

> The pluralization of writing's references and voices often entails the mobilization of unnamed sources and addresses. All references to castration, lack, talking truth, and letters not reaching their destination, for example, are all part of Derrida's ongoing critique of [the French psychoanalyst] Jacques Lacan

Or texts that are characterized by '*fading in and out*':

> The beginning and endings of these essays are often the most mystifying parts. Sometimes, as in the description of Plato working after hours in his pharmacy, they are cryptically literary, almost lyrical. It is as though the borderlines of the text had to be made to bear the mark of the silence – and the pathos – that lie beyond its fringes, as if the text had first and last to more actively disconnect itself from the logos toward which it still aspires

Or levels of *'multiple coherences'*:

> The unit of coherence here is not necessarily the sentence, the word, the paragraph, or even the essay. Different threads of Dissemination are woven together through the bindings of grammar (the future perfect), 'theme' (stone, columns, folds, caves, beds, textiles, seeds, etc.), letters (or, d, i), anagrammatical plays (graft/graph, semen/semantics, lit/lire), etc.

And finally, the expression of *'Nonbinary logic'*:

> In its deconstruction of the either/or logic of noncontradiction that underlies Western metaphysics, Derrida's writing attempts to elaborate an 'other' logic. . . . Because Derrida's writing functions according to this type of 'other' logic, it is not surprising that it does not entirely conform to traditional binary notions of 'clarity'. (Johnson, 1981, pp.xvi–xviii)

Once again you might reasonably interject at this point and comment that this is all very well as far as elucidating *how* Derrida is able to write otherwise than unproblematically and transparently, but it does not really help or convince you *why*, as a relatively inexperienced social scientist, you would want to write like a superstar French philosopher. Why indeed? Certainly not for the sake of it (the worst reason of all). But perhaps because once you have got past the fiction that there is *one* right way of writing up social science, you can start to explore how different ways of writing – Derrida's included – are useful for getting at different things (just as they are not useful for getting as others).

Take, for example, the research done by the critical educationalist Patti Lather with her colleague Chris Smithies on the issue of women living with HIV/AIDS that was published in book form as *Troubling the Angels* (1997). Methodologically, the work was done in a quasi-ethnographic style, with the intention of producing a pretty conventional, 'straight-ahead' (Lather, 2001), popular academic story. When it was time to write up the research, Lather had second thoughts and decided to experiment with applying what she calls a little 'Derridean rigour' (Lather, 1993, also 2001) to the materials that she and Smithies had collected. The result was a book that combines short chapters based on interviews which give voice to the experiences of women living with the disease, 'inter texts' and illustrations which trace the resurgence of popular interest in angels and particularly their prevalence in AIDS discourses, a subtext commentary where Lather and Smithies tell their own stories of doing the research, some of the interviewees' own poems, letters, speeches and emails, and an epilogue that updates the reader on the progress of each woman interviewed and their reactions to a desktop-published version of the book (Lather, 2001).

Now while not only a Derridean text (she also notes the methodological and stylistic influence of Walter Benjamin which you will be familiar with from the last chapter), Lather is quite explicit about drawing on some of his principles and tactics that I have briefly sketched above. In 'putting deconstruction to work', as she put it, the aim was to 'ask hard questions about necessary complicities, inadequate categories, dispersing rather than capturing meanings, and producing bafflements rather than solutions' (Lather, 2001, pp.5–6), while still remaining accessible to a wide readership. In particular, she and Smithies wanted to break 'the realist frame' by including 'competing layers of the real', refuse 'mastery' by 'writing in a tentative authorial voice', use 'the loss of certainty and ethnographic certainty to explore new textual practices that enact such tensions in a way that stages the problem of representation', and trouble 'confessional writing and the romance voice' (all Lather, 2002).

The question you now might like to ask yourself in the context of the 'why?' issue is whether you think that these aims could have been achievable using the tools offered by writing up as conventionally conceived. If your answer (as mine would be) is 'no', then at least you have been convinced that thinking through and following through writing up otherwise has been worth while for someone. Whether there are specific lessons in Lather and Smithies' work for your own research is obviously for you to decide.

Writing up with Latour: reconstructive reflexivity

You will recall that we have already noted that Bruno Latour's rejection of an unproblematic and transparent realism shares certain affinities with that of Derrida. As he himself admits:

> It is true that viewed from above and afar they look alike since they both greatly diverge from the straight line that fundamentalists always dream to trace. Both insist on the inevitable tropism of mediations, on the power of all those intermediaries that make impossible any direct access to objectivity, truth, morality, divinities, or beauty. (Latour, 2002)

The next sentence – 'Resemblance stops there, however' – makes it very clear that, for Latour at least, this is as far as the similarities go. Indeed, it would be fair to say that he has been at pains to differentiate his approach to writing about the world otherwise from that of his illustrious compatriot. This effort became crystallized when Latour (1988) made an explicit distinction between two forms of reflexivity that he saw as possible within the social sciences, two forms (to repeat) of taking seriously the relationship between what you are writing about and how you are writing it. One, which he terms meta-reflexivity, Latour associates strongly with Derrida's influence and rejects wholesale. The other, which he calls infra-reflexivity, describes what he aspires to in his own work.

meta-reflexivity Latour characterizes **meta-reflexivity** in two ways: first, by its premise, which he describes as assuming the worst thing that can happen to any text is to be naively believed by those reading it, and, secondly, by the response to this premise by practitioners of reflexivity. The latter, he says, is to try to shift the attention of the reader from the world to the text. Latour, you will not be surprised to learn, disagrees with both the premise and the response. According to him, the challenge we face as social scientists is not to 'debunk' belief in our or others' accounts, but rather to 'slowly produce confidence again' (Latour, 2002). And as for the meta-reflexive version of writing up otherwise, Latour pulls no punches:

> The dire result of such a tack is visible in the prose of Derrida. . . . If the prose was just unreadable, not much harm would be done. But there is something worse in it; worse that is from their own reflexive point of view. Deconstructionists . . . consider that if enough methodological precautions are taken, then better texts (better, that is, in the sense of texts which solve the absence–presence quandary) can be written. Derrida really believes that by all his tricks, cunning, and entrapments, the texts he writes are more deconstructed that the column of a *New York Times* journalist writing about the latest plane crash. . . . Derrida believes that a text can escape from the fate of presence. (Latour, 1988, pp.166–8)

This is pretty scathing stuff, and you may judge it at least a little unfair from what you now know about Derrida. The point, though, is that it is against such an image of meta-reflexivity as well as against con-
infra-reflexivity ventional realism that Latour defines **infra-reflexivity**. He recommends following a number of 'principles' in order to attain this goal. You can usefully think of these (eight in the original, condensed for reasons of space down to three here) as offering an insight into the 'how?' of infra-reflexivity just as did Johnson's list of mechanisms in the case of deconstruction.

The first principle Latour recommends is spending some time and energy 'on the side of the known'. For him, meta-reflexivists spend too much of both on the side of the 'knowing' when what they should be doing is getting back to 'the world'. This is not the world of conventional realism, simply out there and easily knowable however, but the world to which all the steps, transformations, and especially non-humans that are deleted in that model have been added back. For Latour, it is one account that makes the world in this sense 'alive' that has more reflexivity than 'one hundred self-reference loops that return the boring thinking mind to the stage' (1988, p. 173).

The second principle of infra-reflexivity that Latour recommends is that we generate what he calls 'throw away explanations'. Instead of seeking to construct ever more powerful frameworks that can be applied to an ever wider number of situations (a pressure like so many others imported from the natural to the social sciences), he argues:

> Our way of being reflexive will be to render our texts unfit for the deadly proof race of who is right. The paradox is that we shall always look for weak explanations rather than for general stronger ones. Every time we deal with a new topic, with a new field, with a new object, the explanation should be wholly different. (Latour, 1988, p.174)

This is Latour's way, then, of guarding against that will to authority to which, as we have already noted, social science as conventionally written up can tend.

The final principle that Latour recommends that we follow in search of infra-reflexivity is 'replacing methodology by style'. According to Latour, the meta-reflexivists should accept that however devious they are in seeking to interrupt the relationship between representation and represented, they will always, like everyone else, be read in practice as saying something about something. Thus:

> . . . since no amount of reflexivity, methodology, deconstruction, seriousness, or statistics will turn our stories into non-stories, there is no reason for our field to imitate those few genres that have gained hegemony in recent time. To the few wooden tongues developed in academic journals, we should add the many genres and styles of narration invented by novelists, journalists, artists, cartoonists, scientists, and philosophers. The reflexive character of our domain will be recognised in the future by the multiplicity of genres, not by the tedious presence of 'reflexive loops'. (Latour, 1988, p.172–3)

In contrast to realism as conventionally conceived then, according to Latour, we should employ as many literary devices as possible in order to make stories 'lively, interesting, perceptive, and suggestive' (Latour, 1988, p.170).

If you are still with me, you should recognize that, having been introduced to something of the 'how?' of infra-reflexivity, now is the time to ask the 'why?', just as we did of Derrida. With Latour we have the chance to follow theory into practice even more directly, as he is at least as much a social scientist as he is a philosopher. Although, like Derrida, his output is prodigious, perhaps the fullest expression of what it means to

constructivism   write otherwise for Latour (what he calls '**constructivism**') is to be found in his case study of the automated train system known as Aramis. That study focused on why Aramis, having been trialled in Paris during the 1980s, had such a spectacular fall from grace and was eventually discarded. According to Latour, in writing up a lengthy period of research into book form he had three aims: first, to 'unravel the tortuous history of a state-of-the-art technology from beginning to end, as a lesson to the engineers, decision-makers and users whose daily lives, for better or for worse, depend on such technology', secondly, to 'make the human sciences capable of comprehending the machines they view as inhuman, and thus reconcile the educated public with bodies it deems to be foreign to the social realm', and finally, to 'turn a technological object into the central character of a narrative, restoring to literature the vast territories it should never have given up – namely science and technology' (all Latour, 1996, p.vii).

These are lofty ambitions, certainly more lofty than anything you should be attempting this early in your research career. That is not the point, however. The point is that, as with Lather, Smithies and deconstruction, for Latour the only way to meet these aims was to write otherwise than is conventional in the social sciences:

> What genre could I possibly choose to bring about this fusion of two so clearly separated universes, that of culture and that of technology, as well as the fusion of three entirely distinct literary genres – the novel, the bureaucratic dossier, and the sociological commentary? Science fiction is inadequate because such writing usually draws upon technology for setting rather than plot. Even fiction is superfluous, for the engineers who dreamed up unheard-of systems always go further, as we shall see, than the best woven plots. Realism would be misleading, for it would construct plausible settings for its narratives on the basis of specific states of science and technology, whereas what I want to show is how those states are generated. Everything in this book is true, but nothing in it will seem plausible, for the science and technology it relies upon remain controversial, open-ended. A journalistic approach might have sufficed, but journalism itself is split by the great divide, the one I'm seeking to eliminate, between popularising technology and denouncing its politics. Adopting the discourse of the human sciences as master discourse was not an option, clearly, for it would scarcely be fitting to call the hard sciences into question only to start taking the soft ones as dogma.
>
> Was I obliged to leave reality behind in order to inject a bit of emotion and poetry into austere subjects? On the contrary, I wanted to come close enough to reality so that scientific worlds could become once again what they had been: possible worlds in conflict that move and shape one another. Did I have to take certain liberties with reality? None whatsoever. But I had to restore freedom to all the realities involved before any of them could succeed in unifying the others. The hybrid genre I have devised for a hybrid task is what I call scientifiction. (Latour, 1996, pp.xiii–ix)

In practice what this means is that *Aramis* the book contains not only versions of different classic narratives, including at least the whodunit, the *Bildungsroman* (a story of a pupil learning from a teacher), and *Frankenstein*, but also a range of characters that includes a young engineer and his professor, who are given the task of establishing the reasons for the project's failure (who appear through dialogue reported by the former), the company executives and elected officials associated with Aramis (who appear through interview transcripts and other documents), an unnamed sociologist (who appears through a metacommentary on events), and last but not least Aramis itself (which appears to answer back to the constructions of everyone else). In short, from the very vivid presence of the world, through the one-off framework, to the mix of styles, *Aramis* the book is very consciously infra-reflexivity made flesh.

Once again, whether there is anything specific in this example that you might find useful in your own work must be for you to decide. By now, though, the general principle that I have been illustrating through the use of the work of first Derrida and now Latour should be clear. And that is simply that different ways of writing up can serve to draw attention to different aspects of the world. Although both our examples – *Troubling the Angels* and *Aramis* – might be described as polyphonic (or many-voiced) texts, the different sorts of reflexivity advocated by Derrida and Latour means that they are designed to do very different jobs. While in the former, the device of multiple points of view is employed to destabilize the notion that there can ever be a single univocal account of an event, in the latter, as you have just seen, it is intended to affirm the richness and work of the world. Which one better gets at the 'reality' of the situation is, of course, a philosophical question.

Conclusion: pleasurably write

This chapter has not been about how to write up any more than the other chapters have been about how to formulate a research question or do fieldwork. Heaven forbid if you feel that you now have to produce texts like Derrida's or Latour's. Rather, it has been about how (and why) to think about writing up (and what we might learn about that from Derrida, Latour and others). We have come a long way now from our starting point of the assumption (even if it was only mine) of the process as unproblematic and transparent, to a place where I hope you feel that there are other ways of writing up than those which we have inherited that are both possible and legitimate. If that makes you want to go away and learn more about generating these alternatives all well and good, but if it just means that you are a little more sensitive to the workings of the realism which we perhaps inevitably inhabit most of the time, then that is fine too. I would not want to end without making one final, important point, however. And this is that, while I have been urging you throughout the chapter to take writing seriously, I would not want you to go away thinking you have to take it too seriously. For all their differences, one of the qualities that Derrida and Latour share is their obvious enjoyment of the craft of writing and their quick eye for the productive pun or the judicious joke. If nothing else, then, they stand as excellent examples of the fact that taking pleasure in your texts (to paraphrase Barthes, 1975/1973) need not be an obstacle to good social science but may be the best way of achieving it.

Further reading

Passionate Sociology by Anne Game and Andy Metcalfe (Sage, 1996) is an accessible and very enjoyable read about many of the issues covered in this chapter (and in Chapters 7 and 9). The writing is, as the title suggests, impassioned and, though written from within sociology, has far wider applicability. To follow through debates about writing strategies, it is worth seeking out two excellent texts: Laurel Richardson's *Writing Strategies: Reaching Diverse Audiences* (Sage, 1990) and E. St Pierre and W. Pillow *Working the Ruins: Feminist Poststructural Theory and Methods in Education* (Routledge, 2000).

9
Situated audiences
Michael Pryke

Introduction

Earlier chapters in this part have taken you through some of the philosophical quandaries of analysis and techniques of writing. This chapter sets out to raise a number of issues and questions surrounding writing your research 'into the world' as it moves from the specific confines of the university.

The chapter begins by reflecting on the academic context in which much research is carried out. And so the next section takes us into one of the main spaces of academic writing – the university. It is in such a context that you will set about the task, the activity and thus the practice of writing. As the last chapter has highlighted, writing your research is not just a case of 'writing up'. And if we reflect on this very particular environment in which much research writing is done, it becomes clearer that what you write, indeed how you write, is strongly shaped by the qualities – the conventions and the expectations – of the spaces of the university. To make sense of how this works we can draw upon the ideas of the late Pierre Bourdieu, whose insights into what he calls 'habitus' caution us about how the academy fashions research, researcher and writing alike.

We then go on to consider how you think about and write for your audience. Because of all the work that you have put into your research, you will have definite views about what you want a reader to take from it. As this implies, you may think the audience is 'just there', ready made, as it were, and that the interpretation of what you write is just a matter of fact. However, as this section suggests, the processes involved are not so straightforward. In part, this is because of the existence of what Stanley Fish, a leading literary critic, calls 'interpretive communities'. This notion takes further what Bourdieu has told us about the characteristics and some of the practices of academic habitus. If we follow Fish, then the existence of such communities impacts not only upon what you write and for whom, but also the interpretation of what you write.

The 'context of practices' of academic writing, of conventions and of interpretation, is developed further in the following section. Here we return to Edward Said (from Chapter 1) and work with what he has to say about particular aspects of interpretation. Through Said we introduce into the inner workings of the academic habitus and interpretive communities wider authoritative webs of power, be they cultural or political. These webs, he feels, shape the possibilities of certain types of interpretation. What Said cautions us against is the desire to demonstrate 'mastery' of your field or the desire to achieve the status of 'expert' as you write your research into existence, and how you conceive your relationship with your audience.

The last section provides another angle on the researcher–audience relationship as we set about the task of writing. Here we continue with Said to consider another aspect of this relationship. This time the focus is on how the movement of ideas creates audiences. In the latter part of the section we take up Gayatri Spivak's suggestion to think of your audience as 'co-investigator' and use this idea to re-work relationships and responsibilities that run between researcher and audiences.

In sum, the chapter offers work drawn from a number of philosophers and writers within the humanities and social sciences. In their own, complementary, ways each helps you to reflect on the transit of your research as it nears reception and potentially travels among a range of audiences. While Bourdieu, Fish, Said and Spivak offer different readings of reception and they place different emphases on what they feel to be its key moments, there is a common thread to be found in the way each of them highlights the importance of reflecting on the contexts of writing research, cautions you about the characteristics of the communities you write into, and notes some of the responsibilities you owe to your audiences.

Contexts and academic authorship

This brief section outlines the significance of certain contexts to writing research. The context of the university is going to be our starting point, as to begin here allows us to reflect on how strategies, conventions and expectations of writing your research into the world are established, almost from the outset. Yet how best are we to engage the workings of such spaces, how might they shape the writing, the *authoring*, of research as we 'redirect energy from "the world" to the page' (Said, 1978, p.24)? Authoring is italicized simply to underscore the importance of this activity. Its importance arises because it involves producing or crafting into existence something that you are responsible for. The responsibilities begin to emerge if you think for a moment about what is entailed in bringing your research into the world. To take a few examples, and as the previous two chapters have signalled, in writing you are 'versioning' the work of others, adapting ideas, pulling in quotes from canonical texts and perhaps interviews, too. To be an author thus furnishes you with the potential to acquire and exercise authority, that is, the power to authorize: for example, to control – whose ideas make it to the page – or to silence –

certain interviewees, rather than others. These are all significant respon-sibilities and should affect how you think about readers, communities and audiences, as will become clearer as the chapter develops. But maybe this is taking us too far, too quickly. We still have to get a better feel for how such potential authority is shaped, at least initially.

So, let's see where the ideas of the French social theorist, the late Pierre Bourdieu, might lead us. In his book *Homo Academicus*, published in 1984 (English translation 1988), he focused on the 'social space in which academic practice is accomplished' and although his research attended to the practices of the French academy, what he highlights in the organization of this space has wider applicability and is of interest to us. The approach adopted in *Homo Academicus* was influenced by his earlier work published in 1980 (English translation 1990) under the title *The Logic of Practice*. It was in this book that he developed the concept of habitus.

habitus   What is central to **habitus** is the idea of a system of 'structuring dispositions' (Bourdieu, 1990/1980, p.52). This is not exactly a user-friendly term but, as we shall see, it is key to his argument. Its significance begins to unfold once we learn that dispositions are made, 'constituted' is Bourdieu's preferred word, through practices – the ways we set about accomplishing certain tasks. A word of caution is needed, for while Bourdieu uses the term 'structuring structures', this is not to imply that the habitus is full of clunky regulations that work mechanically to organize practices. For Bourdieu, quite the opposite holds: in his words, the habitus is 'Objectively "regu-lated" and "regular" without being in any way the product of obedience to rules'; it is a space that 'can be collectively orchestrated *without* being the product of the *organizing action of the conductor*' (1990/1980, p.53, emphasis added). In our words, what goes on in such spaces seems natural if not necessary; you simply find yourself conforming, going with the flow. And it is in just this way – through the passive absorption of seemingly natural procedures – that, for us, the significance of habitus emerges.

We now begin to have a feel for what impact the academic habitus might have on what is deemed acceptable research procedure and what is not. Bourdieu is suggesting that it is possible to view the space of the university, the site of much research, not as a context in which all thoughts might be entertained – the presumed autonomy of academia – but as an arrangement of practices that work to limit such discursive freedom. The closing down of such freedom is the result of the way habitus generates 'thoughts, perceptions, expressions and actions' (1990/1980, p.55): in other words, the academic's '"common sense" behaviours'.

This gives some flavour of the academic habitus in action. Yet, how does the idea of habitus apply in the 'concrete' situation of writing your research? Maybe in writing a dissertation, for example, you have become aware of how certain requirements are mediated by particular authoritative figures and that a degree of 'self-censorship' and an 'obliga-tory reverence towards masters' (1988/1984, p.95) have already crept into your research methods. If this is so, then the academic habitus is working its magic. And if we follow Bourdieu's line of thought further, then what we can take from habitus is the reminder that the writing of research is an activity that takes place within an atmosphere where practices and conventions pressure us towards 'confirming and reinforcing' rather than 'transforming'. We are reminded of all of these points as Bourdieu unmasks the 'cult of brilliance':

> The cult of 'brilliance', through the facilities which it procures, the false boldness which it encourages, is less opposed than it might seem to the prudence of academica mediocritas, to its epistemology of suspicion and resentment, to its hatred of intellectual liberty and risk; and colludes with appeals to 'reliability' (*le sérieux*) and its prudent investments and small profits, to spoil or discourage any thought liable to disturb an order founded on resistance to intellectual liberty or even on a special form of anti-intellectualism. The secret resistance to innovation and to intellectual creativity, the aversion to ideas and to a free and critical spirit, which so often orientate academic judgements, as much as the viva of a doctoral thesis or in critical book reviews as in well-balanced lectures setting off neatly against each other the latest avant-gardes, are no doubt the effect of the recognition granted to an institutionalized thought only on those who implicitly accept the limits assigned by the institution. (Bourdieu, 1988/1984, pp.94–5)

In many ways this quote condenses much of what this section has had as its focus. Our aim has been to establish the importance of reflecting on the context of research writing, the fabric of the academic habitus. It should be stressed, however, that what we have outlined is not that the specifics of one academic habitus, such as the Sorbonne (the site of Bourdieu's work), may be applied universally. Our understanding of the workings, the practices, of the habitus, 'as embodied history, internalized as second nature' (1988/1984, p.56) is portable, yes, but to appreciate its full effects requires knowledge of how the habitus is embedded (Chun, 2000, p.60). What is generated in the academic habitus, its products – ideas, research agendas, and so on – is mediated through historically specific cultural and political conditions. You might like to reflect on your own experience in the university system *simply to appreciate better how such mediation of, say, conventions and certain practices works*. The impact of such embeddedness, how the habitus is formed more fully through exposure to wider networks of influence – how the university and business collude, for example – does have very real consequences, as we will discover in the next two sections.

Interpretive communities

This section now moves from the consideration of one very particular community, the academy, to the very real possibility that there may be a range of communities for your research. It is concerned with the idea of different audiences, the different interpretations each may place on your research and how figuratively you stand in relation to them. There is, no doubt, a number of ways to think about such relationships. One is captured by Stanley Fish's notion of '**interpretive communities**'. Fish came up with this term in response to the question: 'what is the source of interpretive authority: the text or the reader?' This question emerged in the circles of literary studies. While this specific context and the debates that surround Fish's response, first aired in his book *Is There a Text in this Class?* (1980), need not concern us here, the relationship between interpretive communities and forms of authority is something worth exploring. Although this is a theme shared with Bourdieu, we are not running over the same ground in the same way. For what Fish provides us with is another approach to the workings of habitus and how the norms and expectations of any one of them affect the reception of research. Fish's 'anti-formalist' or 'anti-foundationalist' approach achieves this, although not without problems, as we will see shortly, through the manner in which he highlights not simply the existence of interpretive communities, but how the interests and beliefs held by any community affect how a text is read, interpreted, let into the fold, as it were. More of this in a short while.

margin note: interpretive communities

A useful way into this notion of interpretive communities, and one that frees us from the risk of exposure to the history of fierce debates within literary studies that surround this term, is to begin by understanding such communities as **contexts of practice**, another phrase employed by Fish to deliver the same message. This draws attention to how interpretive communities become constructed as contexts where certain practices and beliefs gain authority and can thus be employed to influence interpretation. This again, as you will recognize, contains echoes of Bourdieu and his talk of habitus, and reminds us of the consequences not just of engaging in research, but of the impact of specific contexts in which that research is written and how it is written for certain audiences. By using the term contexts of practice, however, Fish draws our attention to how 'the self', you or me as a researcher, is always constrained. And as he argues in another text, *Doing What Comes Naturally*, such constraints are not to be picked up or thrown off at will – the self free from restraints, he stresses, is a myth – simply because they are 'constitutive of the self and of its possible actions' (1989, p.27). What this means is that constraints will always be in place; to be without them is unthinkable.

margin note: contexts of practice

Yet for Fish these constraints are not fixed and the reason for this is that they are interpretive. They are interpretive practices 'forever being altered by the actions they make possible' (1989, p.27). Central to such practices is the claim that we live in a rhetorical world, a claim to which Fish and others subscribe. This position, he wishes to argue, 'is inevitable once one removes literal meaning as a constraint on interpretation' (1989, p.25). A number of implications follow from this approach, several of which speak directly to how we wish to employ the idea of interpretive communities in thinking about the relationship between researcher and her/his audience, and it these to which we will now turn. The first is that intention, what you intend for your research and how you wish it to be made sense of, is not a straightforward process. Intention must be interpretively established and this is something, Fish insists, that can only be achieved through persuasion. Secondly, the ability to persuade is something that is always contingent; dependent, that is, on the context of practices informing the realization of intention. Thirdly, and this is in many ways where we came into this discussion of interpretive communities, preparing the reception of your philosophically informed research is a practice which is already constrained by the character of the community in which you have conducted your work. This community has shaped you and given you direction, Fish would argue.

To take us back for a moment to the issue of one's position in relation to an interpretive community, Fish argues that 'understanding is always possible, but not from the outside'. To be inside a community facilitates an important degree of intelligibility. With echoes of earlier discussions of Latour, he reaffirms this point in addressing one of his critics, Meyer Abrams, an academic from the world of literary studies:

> The reason that I can speak and presume to be understood by someone like Abrams is that I speak to him *from within* a set of interests and concerns, and it is in relation to those interests and concerns that I assume that he will hear my words. If what follows is communication or understanding, it will not be because he and I share a language, in the sense of knowing the meanings of individual words and the rules for combining them, but because a way of thinking, a form of life, shapes us, and implicates us in a world of already-in-place objects, purposes, goals and procedures, values, and so on; and it is to the features of that world that any words we utter will be heard as necessarily referring. (Fish, 1989, p.41, emphasis in original)

In the way he highlights 'ways of thinking', 'purposes', 'goals' and 'procedures', Fish reminds us, as researchers, of the need to reflect on how we perform research within the specific habitus of the academy, what such a performance entails and the consequences. And it is not too difficult to turn this argument further towards our concerns and to address some of the issues that Fish's position raises for us as we consider writing research into the world. To engage in academic debate, for example, about the significance of a particular research 'finding' (say, the changing gender composition of unemployment or the influence of industrialized farming in the latest outbreak of BSE), to put forward your arguments, to offer counter-arguments to the criticisms of other academics, to argue over what counts as suitable evidence, can be done, Fish would say, only because there is an agreed discourse shared by the researcher and the research community. And, as we have already learnt from the discussion of

Foucault in Chapter 1, the existence of such a discourse allows these and other actions in the performance of academic research to proceed, and proceed only because they are 'already assumed'.

If we accept Fish's thesis, then it raises the problem of how research written for one community is translated, made available, to another. One obvious suggestion might be to provide (seemingly) clear definitions; guidelines on how to make sense of the research. But the provision of such definitions, to 'someone on the outside' of an interpretive community, as Fish argues, does not help either. Why? Well 'because in order to grasp the meaning of an individual term, you must already have grasped the general activity [a particular area of academic research] in relation to which it could be thought to be meaningful; a system of intelligibility cannot be reduced to a list of the things it renders intelligible' (Fish, 1989, p.41). It is here that the importance of being in or out of particular communities has a significant effect for Fish. To 'grasp the general activity' it is necessary, he argues, to be within a context of practices. Understanding is determined, he says, within the confines of a community. What is more, 'it is only in situations – with their interested specifications as to what counts as a fact, what it is possible to say, what will be heard as argument – that one is called on to understand' (1989, p.41). And, for this reason, understanding is in a sense locked into situations, particular contexts, and cannot be expected to move unproblematically across interpretive communities: different communities hold different beliefs which contextualize the process of understanding.

There are, as his critics have pointed out, a number of problems with the way Fish understands the workings of beliefs, how these become situated in, and indeed are separable into, particular communities (Graff, 1999; Michael, 2000, pp.81–3). For Fish, interpretive communities and the beliefs held by each have a definite inside and outside. As one critic has pointed out, this leads to a position where understanding – how understanding is pulled from a text, as it were – is 'always specific to particular systems of intelligibility' (Graff, 1999, p.39). Each situation produces practices of interpretation that are context-dependent. But this does depend on knowing exactly where one community, system of intelligibility or situation ends and another begins. The task of recognizing where the limits of a purely academic community lie is possibly eased by the existence of some fairly explicit coda; after all, the academic haunt contains very particular, if not peculiar, practices associated with a certain kind of knowledge production, as Bourdieu has reminded us.

What does this mean for the doing and writing of research and where might it lead us? As we have begun to broaden our focus from the isolated academic habitus, so we have had to take in the webs and flows that entangle any simple notion of writing up. If you consider the arguments that underpin the notion of interpretive communities as an extension of Bourdieu's concept of habitus, then the two combined help you to reflect on what might be involved should you wish to write your research into a number of communities, not just an academic one. You may wish to think for a moment what this implies for your work. Fish's arguments, for all their faults, lead us – if not force us – to take the issue of interpretation a step further. More immediately, we now move on to consider your responsibilities to audiences, and your relationship to them. These are the issues to which we now turn.

Interpretation: from mystical to open communities

By now you should have a sense of the contexts in which you write and how these contexts work to create you as a researcher. We now take our discussion of the influences of 'conventions, habits and traditions' shaped in the academic habitus, a stage further. Here our focus broadens. In this section we ask how the specific context of the academic habitus and the inner workings of interpretive communities may be influenced by wider flows of power, be these cultural or political, and how, as a consequence, the researcher's relationship to wider audiences may be altered.

politics of
interpretation

To do this, we consider the work of Edward Said, introduced in Chapter 1. His approach to understanding what he refers to as the '**politics of interpretation**' helps us to develop a fuller view of the processes at play as your research gets written into wider communities and to grasp how wider communities may affect the interpretation of what has been written. Said follows Fish's argument about the importance of interpretive communities and how this notion rightly shifts the focus to the moment of impact where the text meets the reader. What is more, Said notes, in accordance with Fish, this moment of interaction should not be seen as a private affair. For if understood in this way, the encounter simply inflates 'the role of solitary decoding at the expense of its just as important *social context*' (Said, 1982a, p.8, emphasis added). Indeed the use of words such as 'audience' or 'community' reminds us, Said notes, that no one writes simply for themselves. There is always 'an Other' and this turns writing into a social activity which has 'unforeseen consequences, audiences, constituencies' (1982a, p.3). Said pushes what Fish has to say about 'interpretation being the only game in town', a little further. He does this by asking why it is that some interpretations or persuasions, to follow Fish more exactly, are more powerful than others. And this is why Said emphasizes the politics of interpretation. For both Fish and Said (and with

persuasion

echoes of Rorty from Chapter 1) **persuasion** is key. It is on this rhetorical act, rather than, say, scientific demonstration, that (much of) the social sciences and humanities depend. The researcher is always writing to persuade. Yet what influences act on the process of persuasion and how do they get to limit some writing and promote others? Said offers some clues.

He commences his essay on interpretation with three short but exacting questions: 'Who writes? For whom is the writing being done? In what circumstances?' (1982a, p.1). While these are questions worth carrying with you as you reflect on much that has been noted in this section, we want to pursue some answers to them here. Said uses these questions and the issues they raise to gain a better understanding of the 'ingredients', as he terms it, of making interpretation. In doing this he draws our attention to the wider context into which, and the 'cultural moment' through which, the writing of research takes place. Said helps us to develop an appreciation of the influences active in the shaping of research as it moves from the academic habitus into wider audiences. He reminds us of the bridge that has to be negotiated as your research – and think here of your research performing the role of emissary – moves between 'the world of ideas and scholarship' and 'the world of brute politics, corporate and state power' (1982a, p.2). Such a reminder has real purchase in today's world, as an example from the USA illustrates (with a referential nod to Bourdieu and our earlier discussions):

> The kind of institutional setting that has fostered symbiotic relationships with business in a US context of corporate restructuring differs from that found elsewhere. In essence, these a priori conditions have a direct influence on the production, management, and circulation of knowledge not only because they shape at an unconscious level the relevance of certain kinds of acceptable knowledge but also because they regulate the norms, rites and strategies through which academic 'subjects' construct knowledge and maintain the system. (Chun, 2000, p.53)

Now, from our standpoint – one almost wholly preoccupied by the anxieties of reception within the confines of the academy – all this just might seem quite dramatic and of little purchase to what we have to say through our research. Nevertheless, Said pulls at our attention by high-lighting two important ingredients of interpretation: first, what he calls 'affiliations' that ease the transit between worlds; and, secondly, the 'culture of the moment' which is an ingredient, he argues, that helps to mask the collaborations involved.

What Said is driving at is something that he and others feel to be at the centre of the 'constitution of modern knowledge' and this is the role of 'social convention'. This is a process that affects both writing and inter-pretation of what is written. Conventions, uniformity, he argues, following Foucault in *The Archaeology of Knowledge* (1972/1969) congeal into disciplines, fields or territories (see Chapter 1). It is these techniques that shape the character of a discipline. These 'protect' the field and its 'adher-ents', Said says, by offering coherence, integrity and social identity. What this means for you as you prepare to write – and this is simply a continuation of the affects of procedure you have been working through within the institution of the university – is that your writing must in many senses conform to the practices, or ways of going about such a task, that dominate your field. As Said comments:

> You cannot simply choose to be a sociologist or a psychoanalyst; you cannot simply make statements that have the status of knowledge in anthropology; you cannot merely suppose that what you say as a historian (however well it may have been researched) enters historical discourse. (Said, 1982a, p.7)

How you write your statements, how you lay out your research, has, then, to conform to certain disciplinary techniques. Indeed, as this implies, what you write about has already been affected by the disciplinary field you occupy within the academic habitus, and in turn has limited the ways in which you view your research object. Moreover, as this suggests, Said here speaks directly to and reinforces our earlier discussions of the impact of the habitus of the university. He flags again the power and authority that make the context of research and writing:

> You have to pass through certain rules of accreditation, you must learn the rules, you must speak the language, you must master the idioms, and you must accept the authorities of the field – determined in many of the same ways – to which you wish to contribute. (Said, 1982a, pp.7–8)

This may well lead to a situation whereby the interpretive community becomes ever more rarefied, its language impenetrable to outsiders, and ensures that 'stability and orthodoxy' prevail and remain unassailable. Said's particular example helps to illustrate this. It is the growth of what he calls the 'cult of the expert', the producer of 'specialist knowledge'. Such specialists, whose knowledge becomes privileged, Said suggests, have been encouraged because of their closeness to corporate and state powers (1982a; 1982b, pp.21–2; 1994). Yet it is worth pointing out, a similar outcome – as you are no doubt aware – may just as easily be produced by self-made avante-garde cliques, those academics wickedly satirized by Frederick Crews (2002) as 'tribalizing proponents' of deconstructionism, post-structuralist Marxism, to give just two examples.

This is a slightly romantic view of the university-based intellectual. We live, after all, in societies dominated by the 'ethos of professionalism', where to be a 'credentialled expert' in your field is rapidly becoming the only way to be heard (Michael, 2000, p.10). Nevertheless, the point Said wishes to draw to our attention is how, through a cumulative effect, intellectual landscapes may be altered completely with the result that only certain notions and concepts may be legitimated. Our concern, however, is less with shifts in whole landscapes. It is rather with what makes expertise and what acquiring it means for your relationship to audiences, and how we might wish to rethink the **researcher–audience relationship** at the expense of disciplinary codes. This line of argument suggests that there is a danger – the danger of losing any glimmer of 'humanistic obligation' (Bové, 1986, p.185) – in thinking only of your academic audience, of

researcher–
audience
relationship

caring about little else, desiring only 'abstract correctness' at the expense of communicating with other audiences.

The question then, for us, becomes: what does a researcher do if he/ she wishes to write in a way that acknowledges a wider interpretive context? This should not be read to imply that a straightforward answer exists; that a set number of steps can be followed which lead beyond a situation where the research is read by the discipline alone 'to everyone else's unconcern', to use Said's phrase. Perhaps, instead, it is a case of becoming aware of the existence and effect of practices that work hard to ensure that research remains within a 'fiefdom forbidden to the uninitiated' (Said, 1982a, p.9) and a recognition of the need to reflect on how such practices work and how, bit by bit, they might be eroded, however gradually: in sum, a context of practices – the adoption of certain accepted techniques of writing and analysis, for instance. So let us run with Said a little further and consider what he has to say about the possibility of a more open community of interpretation, one less bound by the religiosity of the academy. One way in which such an opening might be thought about brings us back to Said's three questions and to the issue of persuasion.

Said reaches for Gramsci and through him reminds us of the constructed nature of reality, in particular that as

> [a]ll ideas, philosophies, views, and texts *aspire to the consent* of their consumers, . . . there is a set of characteristics unique to civil society in which texts – embodying ideas, philosophies and so forth – *acquire power* through what Gramsci describes as *diffusion, dissemination* into and hegemony over the world of 'common sense'. (Said, 1982a, p.11, emphasis added)

What does this all mean? Well, to begin with it suggests strongly that texts do not automatically have authority, granted from on high, as it were. Your piece of research does not, simply by virtue of being 'your research', have seniority over other accounts. On its own it is only so many typed pages. Something more is required if it is to gain legitimacy within and beyond the academic habitus. Said gives us a clue as to how authority is operationalized. Intellectual authority, for him, is made through a 'web of filiations and affiliations' (1982a, p.2). This idea certainly offers the possibility not only to help us to understand something more of the operation of academic authority, but also to take us outside the confines of Fish's interpretive communities. Interpretation, when viewed along these lines, should be thought of as taking place through a criss-crossing of efforts, as Said puts it; we should be open to a heterogeneity of interpretive skills and techniques. For Said, then, it is not possible to think of one authority, no single centre of interpretation and thus no one explanation. This already asks us to think outside the 'rigid structure' of specialist fields where 'licensed members' revere words like expert: 'To acquire a position of authority within the field is, however, to be involved internally in the formation of a canon, which usually turns out to be a blocking device for methodological and disciplinary self-questioning' (1982a, p.16). Said's emphasis on expertise and the way that communities create the 'cult of the expert' is a reminder of just how 'institutional affiliations with power . . . assumed unquestioningly' (1982a, p.18) enable the emergence, the possibility of, expertise in the first place. To retreat into academic interpretive communities, rarefied constituencies, is to close off the possibility of open interpretive contexts and thus limit the way you can think about writing about the objects of research. How might interpretive communities, then, be opened?

For more secular interpretive communities to be created 'requires a more open sense of community as something to be won and of audiences as human beings to be addressed' (Said, 1982a, p.19). Said holds strong views on this. A politics of interpretation, he states, demands a replacement of non-interference and specialization with '*interference*, a crossing of borders and obstacles' (1982a, p.24, emphasis in original). Where this leaves us is not with any firm answer but maybe a first step in rethinking your relationship as a responsible researcher and communicator of research with not just one, but many audiences. In Said's words:

> . . . we need to think about breaking out of the disciplinary . . . to reopen the blocked social processes ceding objective representation (hence power) of the world to a small coterie of experts and their clients, to consider that the audience . . . is not a closed circle of . . . professional critics but the community of human beings living in society, and to regard social reality in a secular rather than a mystical mode, despite all the protestations about realism and objectivity. (Said, 1982a, p.25)

This shift from the enclosed, mystical community to the open and secular is one of the responsibilities of intellectuals, Said argues (again with the support of Gramsci), those who produce research agendas. The next section takes us further into this sense of re-attuning oneself to one's audience.

Ideas–movement–audiences

Ideas move. They travel. And as they move, so they constitute new audiences. The aim is to consider how, in their movement, the ideas that you have shaped in the processes of research have contributed to the making of an audience. This is our main concern. In exploring it, however, we need
affiliations   to consider the associations or '**affiliations**' we have become involved in during the research and how these influence the types of audience we make and how we address each as we write research to a conclusion. This will serve as a reminder that even at this point in the research, at its reception,

responsibilities we still cannot escape 'intellectual' **responsibilities** – the responsibilities of being read, responsibilities owed to communities and to audiences alike – and consequences that follow (Said, 1994).

Let us take one step back. Think for a moment about how you have got to this stage of writing. You have crafted and re-crafted a research question; you have engaged in work in the field; you have begun your analysis; and you are thinking through your writing. All the time there has been movement; you have been exposed to and been enabled by ideas that have travelled. You have taken ideas written in one context, read them and applied them in another, and are now set to write them into yet another location cum audience. Put slightly differently, in undertaking your research you have transported ideas, you have put them to work to suit your research needs (and maybe added some new ones, too!), and, in writing, you are due to set them off on further travels. Yet they are not the same ideas; they have been inflected to meet your needs, reworked to fit with your disciplined research techniques, and now they are set to be released. And because of these diversions and concerns, some explicitly disciplinary, another audience has been in the making. The general point is that, in researching and writing, you are participating in the movement of ideas and that this movement transforms ideas and thereby helps to make new audiences.

All this begins to suggest that there are a number of things we need to think about in the transition 'ideas–movement–audience'. One is to attend to what such travels say of ideas – their 'limits, possibilities and inherent problems', to borrow from Said (1983, p.230). If ideas are moved and put to work in ways and in circumstances often far removed from the context in which they were conceived, what should we be mindful of at this stage of research, as it is written into new travels, as it is taken up by a variety of audiences?

There are, no doubt, several ways to think about such travels, such movements of ideas. Yet we need a way of thinking that keeps in focus the relationship between ideas and audiences, and one that does not lose sight of the researcher/writer. One way is to remind ourselves of the stages Said sees as common to the movement of any idea (and here you may well note similarities with Doreen Massey's discussion of the spatialities of knowledge in Chapter 4). There is a 'set of initial circumstances in which the idea . . . entered discourse'. A second stage is the distance traversed. Here he is referring, in his words, to 'a passage through the pressure of various contexts as the idea moves from an earlier point to another time and place where it will come into new prominence' (emphasis added). The third stage is the conditions of acceptance or resistance that greet the moved idea. The last stage is where the partly or wholly 'transformed' idea arises from its 'new position in a new time and place' (Said, 1983, all quotes from p.227). We need not linger on each of these stages. For our purposes what is particularly interesting is what Said has to say about the second and third stage, the contexts through which ideas move and settle, and how such movement is conditional in part on their acceptance in a new environment. One of the risks of such movement is that of misreading and misinterpretation, both on the part of the researcher and the reader of the research written with the travelled ideas. We will simply note this now for, as Said remarks, to understand movement of ideas simply in terms of possibilities of misreading and misinterpretation is to overlook a central influence that is of interest to us at this stage of thinking through research. And that is the influence of situation (Said's preferred word for context). Situations or contexts have important parts to play (Said would insist that their role is in fact the determining one) in changing ideas and thus helping to constitute audiences.

As you may have already sensed, the issues that Said raises here are not far removed from those raised in our earlier discussions of habitus, contexts and communities. A significant if underlying emphasis in what Said notes is precisely the way situations, places that is, wider than those identifiable with, say, the institutional practices and conventions of the university, 'condition', 'limit' and 'apply pressures' to which each researcher–writer, to use another of Said's words, responds. It is tempting to say that situations help to produce ideas through a controlled process of refraction. This is something that we should be aware of as we write through influences and try to persuade under altered circumstances.

Said makes his position clear in his acclaimed book, *The World, the Text and the Critic* (1983), where he states that texts are what he terms 'worldly'; they are 'events'. For him, a text is of the social world – it is secular – and hence located in historical moments of human life (1983, p.4). He secures and illustrates this point by drawing attention to the circumstances in which Erich Auerbach's *Mimesis* (1953) was written. This was a book written by a German author exiled to Istanbul at the time of the Nazi regime. To write in exile is to risk losing 'the web of culture', as Said phrases it. Culture here, for Said, is 'symbolized materially by libraries, other scholars, books, and research institutes'. These and other forces embed an author in a very particular process and environment or habitus. And culture – 'possessing possession' is one of Said's translations – works in an authoritative manner through the ways it 'authorizes limits' to what may be written. The power of this form of culture lies, then, in what is permitted in fields of knowledge, in research, in writing, and so on. Arbiters, those in 'elevated or superior positions', thereby possess the authority to 'legitimate, demote, interdict, and validate' (1983, p.9), to dominate, in other words, knowledge production. Both Auerbach and Said refer to how, in their workings, these cultural processes work on the researcher/writer like a grid of techniques, almost ensuring as a result that canons of scholarship surround and 'saturate' the research/writing process.

Said draws our attention to how some of these cultural influences are acquired not by birth or nationality, for example, in which case the writer/researcher is bound to them filiatively, but are worked at affiliatively. Such affiliative relationships, associations struck up during the research, for example, might be the product of deliberate political or social convictions or the circumstances of your research in the field. In other words, some of our actions that as researchers we wish to address, those whom we wish to make our audience, are decisions we make; they are down to us. Both filiative and affiliative relationships impose pressures on us. We may choose which affiliations we wish to work ourselves into and respond to: the research that is conducted and the text that gets written are both worldly, remember. Like the texts, we too are part of the social/natural world. And responsibilities and consequences are very much part of that world. Said is simply reminding us of the responsibilities to audiences we have as researchers/writers. It is another prompt to reflect on the relationship that may exist, and which we may wish to alter, between researcher, in the cloistered academic world, and the 'world of events and societies'. This is also a conscious reminder that what we are engaging in is always situated. We need to be mindful of the 'political, social and human values entailed in the reading, production, and transmission of every text' (1983, p.26).

Again the emphasis is on responsibilities and the encouragement is to look beyond the immediate habitus of writing and to think about consequences of preparing research for reception. Here Said is moving Fish's interpretive communities into a more worldly and critical environment. For what Said is saying is that we need to be mindful of the historical, political, and social 'configurations' that enable interpretive communities to emerge and exist. This echoes Said's position in *Beginnings*, as you will recall, where he argues that we always make a start in the 'in the 'always-already' begun realm of continuously human effort' (1983, p.26), as he puts it. Writing then is not something that takes place in isolation, on blank sheets of papers, and without consequences: 'any text . . . is a network of often colliding forces . . . a text in its actually *being* a text is a being in the world; it therefore addresses anyone who reads it' (1983, p.33, emphasis in original). What Said writes can be read as a plea to think about the type of space into which you are writing and the types of space, audience, that you may wish to contribute to creating as you move, and are moved by, ideas.

Audiences as co-investigators

If Said offers a way of developing Fish's notion of interpretive communities not as closed, semi-religious gatherings but as 'open, secular, affairs', then maybe we can take this one step further. Another writer, Gayatri Spivak, offers an opportunity to broaden what we have discussed so far. In an interview in the journal *differences*, Spivak provides us with another strand to help think through the researcher–audience relationship, and thus ways of negotiating the transit between communities – between researcher and audiences.

Some of the anxieties noted earlier, such as how you might write in accessible, inclusive ways, might be approached differently (but not necessarily eased!) by reflecting on the researcher–audience relationship. One step may be to take up Spivak's suggestion that, among other things, the **co-investigator** audience is invited to become, as she names it, a **co-investigator**. In the interview she was asked to reflect on the 'question of the audience' and how she has come to think about her relationship to it, or perhaps more fully, to them. Her comments are informed by her theoretical position, one influenced by the contemporary French philosopher, Derrida (see Chapters 2 and 8), and her desire to 'build for difference'. The quotes, although long, are worth sticking with as they contain her own way of talking/ thinking about writing alongside philosophical influences:

> . . . one thing that I will say is that when one takes the representative position – the homeopathic deconstruction of identity by identity – one is aware that outside of that representation of oneself in terms of a stream, there are areas completely inaccessible to one. Of course, that's a given. In the same way, it seems to me, that when I said 'building for difference,' the sense of audience is already assuming that the future is simply a future present. So, to an extent, the most radical challenge of deconstruction is that notion of thought being a blank part of the text given over to a future that is not just a future present, you know. So in that sense, the audience is not an essence, the audience is a blank. When I was speaking of building for difference, I was thinking of the fact that an audience can be constituted by people I cannot even imagine, affected by this little unimportant trivial piece of work, which is not just direct teaching and writing. That business displaces the question of audience as essence or fragmented or exclusivist or anything. Derrida calls this a responsibility to the trace of the other, I think, and that I find is a very . . . It's something that one must remind oneself of all the time. That is why what I cannot imagine stands guard over everything that I must/can do, think, live, etcetera. (Spivak, 1989, p.152)

There's a lot going on in this quote, much of which is rooted in her movement of ideas. Yet what's telling about it is that clearly she has not left behind – in the research 'proper', it's almost tempting to say – the philosophies and philosophers with whom she has worked in her research. In fact her talking and contemplating philosophically about her audience provokes and perpetuates for her a big question of where the research stops and further confuses the issue of the researcher's identity shaped alongside the research. As she goes on to say:

> . . . when an audience is responsible, responding, invited, in other words, to co-investigate, then positionality is shared with it. Audience and investigator: it's not just a binary opposition when an audience really is an audience. That's why, I mean I hadn't thought this through, but many of the changes I've made in my position are because the audience has become a co-investigator and I've realized what it is to have an audience.

You know what I'm saying? An audience is part of one. An audience shows us something. Well, that is the transaction, you know, it's a responsibility to the other, giving it faces. (Spivak, 1989, p.153)

And an important element in this responsibility is to reflect on the whole process of communication. This in part provokes consideration of what it means to be read. As Spivak, herself a bit of an academic superstar, dwells on her relationship to her audience, she begins to suggest a way of writing that seems to ask 'what is the purpose of my writing?' This for her becomes a method:

> . . . where one begins to imagine the audience responding, responsible and invited to be co-investigator, one starts owning the right to have one's invitation accepted, given that the invitation is, like all letters, open letters intercepted and that people turn up in other places for other occasions with that invitation, so that we begin to deconstruct that binary opposition bit by bit. I don't see that particularly as de-essentializing. It's something else . . . (Spivak, 1989, p.153)

A number of words and phrases that Spivak employs strike me as worth reflecting upon. For instance, her phrase the 'audience as co-investigator' is a gesture to us to adopt other styles of 'writing' – writing 'otherwise' as it was put in Chapter 8 – and to rethink the relationships and connections, and the various inequalities they contain and maintain, actively made through research. To view, like her, your research as an 'invitation' to an audience, encourages you to work away at the divide that separates the researcher and the audience. As the audience is imagined as 'responding', so 'responsibilities' begin to emerge and in many ways, as we have learnt from Said, have to be pre-empted, anticipated and written into the account of your research.

Yet perhaps this imagining comes too easily and needs to be thought through with more caution. For instance, we should not forget that our identities – importantly here taking the guise of researcher – are very much active in the act of responding. When we engage in research, just as with every other aspect of our lives, we are 'performing identities' that are 'both raced and sexed' (and classed) and through them we 'enact affectively embodied realities that are necessarily purblind to the extent of the [highly unequal] risks [we] run, the exclusions [we] perpetuate – in order to exist at all' (Dhairyam, 1994, p.43). To 'deconstruct the binary opposition' between researcher and audience, to promote co-investigation, as Spivak does, is admirable but requires a degree of reflexivity as we remember the unequal powers and visibilities – not everyone, for example, has the same ability or authority to 'turn up in other places', literally or metaphorically – that make both sides of the divide. These issues, and the many other responsibilities noted in this chapter, are significant; others, too, will no doubt emerge as you mull over the contexts, communities and audiences entangled in your research. They all call for responses.

Conclusion

We started this chapter with a reasonably simple proposal: that the context within which academic research is practised impacts upon what gets done, as research, and what gets written, as research. We explored this with the help of Pierre Bourdieu's idea of the habitus and thought about how this might be applied to the academy. This helped us to appreciate why preparing the reception of research is not a straightforward affair. Why this is so was developed as the discussion moved on to reflect on the influence that not just disciplinary but wider communities might have on the interpretation of what you write as research. By working with Stanley Fish's notion of 'interpretive communities' we were able to see something of how such groupings affect not only what you write but how what you write is interpreted.

One advantage of thinking about interpretive communities in this way is that the act of writing is seen as part of wider, influential webs and flows that lie beyond the academic habitus. This idea was taken further as the chapter unfolded. Edward Said reminded us of the authoritative webs of cultural and political power that inform the politics of interpretation and restrain the possibilities of particular kinds of reception. The latter part of the chapter developed this theme of the researcher–audience relationship by considering Said's notion of the interplay between researcher and audience achieved through the movement of ideas. The chapter concluded by working Spivak's suggestion to think of the audience as 'co-investigators' into our concern to contemplate the contexts, communities and responsibilities entangled in the reception of research.

Further reading

Anxious Intellects: Academic Professionals, Public Intellectuals and Enlightenment Values by John Michael (Duke University Press, 2000) provides an instructive engagement with many of the themes of this chapter: Chapter 3 provides an engaging critique of Stanley Fish (and Richard Rorty). Edward Said's *Reith Lectures* (*Representations of the Intellectual*) (Viking, 1994) will take you through many of his chief concerns and reflections of the role and responsibilities of intellectuals. Said's *Beginnings* (The Johns Hopkins University Press, 1978) is well worth a read as it establishes much of the terrain he explores in his later texts, some of which are cited in this chapter. In *The Spivak Reader* (Routledge, 1996) the editors, Donna Landry and Gerald Maclean, provide a useful collection of Gayatri Spivak's writings, together with an interview during which she reviews her work over recent years.

CONCLUSION TO PART III

The aim of Part III has been to invite reflection on the assumptions that have been worked into accepted approaches to analysis and writing. As you will have realized, the focus has not lingered on the practicalities of writing and of making sense of fieldwork, but has rested rather with the issues surrounding what is at stake in writing and analysis. And what is at stake are ideas and their place in this stage of the research process. Just because research is coming to end, with the fruits of empirical work sitting in front of you, does not mean that 'thinking' is over and done with. The chapters have shown that this is far from the case. With echoes of earlier chapters, thinking is to be *extended* through acts such as sifting through and recombining your data (to follow Chapter 7), while, in the spirit of Chapter 8, in the act of writing the task of forming and shaping ideas is to be exercised and stretched still further; the responsibilities that attach to writing for different audiences and that arise from the movement of ideas, for example, also need to be philosophically reflected upon (Chapter 9). Put slightly differently, and with a mind to the consequences of thinking approaches, what the chapters have tried to do is to show how the outcome of the research process bears the hallmark of particular assumptions about the world.

For, as we have seen from earlier chapters, philosophies are, in a sense, incriminated in research from the start and research always bears the hallmark of particular persuasive rhetoric. Hence to work with and use a certain set of ideas, is to analyse and write into existence, as it were, one philosophically laden outcome rather than another. To adopt an alternative set of thinking tools may well lead to a different outcome, although the data, the same empirical starting point, may be shared by both approaches (as we saw in Chapter 7). This may be a simple point but in itself it has significant implications. Its importance grows if we recall what it means (to use some of the language of Chapter 7) to recombine our thoughts about analysis and writing in such a way as to allow other philosophical influences to work with us as we work away at the materials gathered in the previous stage of research. The dialogue with other approaches has, we hope, allowed us to be exposed to 'new' ideas, to be provoked by alternative moves. In Chapter 8, for example, 'traditional' thoughts about writing up were asked to justify their assumptions about just what is involved in this stage of the research process. This was explored further in Chapter 9 where the contexts of writing, the movement of ideas and researcher–audience relationships led to the possibility of reflecting on how the reception of research might be reworked. Similarly, in Chapter 7, the task of making sense of materials was rethought in terms of what analysis might involve if the vocabulary coined in one philosophical school, such as 'certainty' and 'completeness', was replaced by another, one that began to sketch analysis in terms of recontextualization, translation and transformation.

All of this, as the Introduction to Part III noted, is about taking time to think through what effect the differences in philosophical assumptions make to the conduct and outcome of the research process. And here perhaps it is important to note that we are not suggesting, in our encouragement to play with ideas, to ruminate with the help of a range of philosophical materials, that in the place of the demands of, say, rigour, precision and accuracy, we offer approaches that say 'anything goes'. For, as we have already seen at various stages of the book, these other philosophical lines establish their own procedures that are just as demanding in terms of what they imply for the conduct and consequences of research. In Part III the words of caution relate to the responsibilities and practices of analysis and of writing. In the case of Chapter 7, to take one example, we saw how Benjamin's idea of literary montage offered a form of analysis where prepared explanations were replaced with a call to see what might come of the juxtaposition of different types of material, where neither the empirical nor the theoretical is to be privileged, yet where – and this is a significant reminder of what this approach entails – a 'confused presentation' is a world apart from Benjamin's sought-after 'presentation of confusion'. The difference, both in research practice and outcome, is what the philosophical line demands from the outset.

In both Part III and in the book as a whole we hope to have encouraged you to adopt a variety of thinking crafts and skills so that you will feel confident enough not always to want to hug the shore of the familiar, and to know why you may wish to think philosophies through the research process ahead.

Bibliography

Ahearne, J. (1995) *Michel de Certeau: Interpretation and Its Other*, Cambridge, Polity Press.

Amdur, R.J. and Bankert, E. (2002) *Institutional Review Boards*, New York, Jones and Bartlett.

Ashmore, M. (1989) *The Reflexive Thesis*, London, University of Chicago Press.

Atkinson, T. and Claxton, G. (eds) (2000) *The Intuitive Practitioner*, Buckingham, Open University Press.

Auerbach, E. (1953) *Mimesis: Representation of Reality in Western Literature*, written in Istanbul between May 1942 and April 1945 (trans. from the German by W.R. Trask), Princeton, NJ, Princeton University Press. (First published in Germany in 1946.)

Balibar, E. (1998) *Spinoza and Politics*, London, Verso.

Balzac, H. de (1965) Preface to *The Human Comedy* from *At the sign of the Cat and Packet* (C. Bell, Trans, 1987) in R. Ellman and C. Feidelson, Jr (eds) *The Modern Tradition: Backgrounds of Modern Literature*, New York, Oxford University Press, pp.246–54. (First published in 1842.)

Barry, A. (2002) 'The anti-political economy', *Economy and Society*, vol.31, no.2, pp.268–84.

Barthes, R. (1967) *Writing Degree Zero & Elements of Semiology*, London, Jonathan Cape. (First published in 1964.)

Barthes, R. (1975) *The Pleasure of the Text*, New York, Hill and Wang. (First published in 1973.)

Barthes, R. (1986) *The Rustle of Language*, Oxford, Blackwell. (First published in 1984.)

Bastick, T. (1982) *Intuition: How We Think and Act*, Chichester, John Wiley & Sons.

Becker, H. (1986) *Writing for Social Scientists*, Chicago, IL, University of Chicago Press.

Benjamin, W. (1973a) 'The image of Proust' in *Illuminations* (ed. and with an introduction by Hannah Arendt; trans. H. Zohn), London, Fontana, pp.196–210.

Benjamin, W. (1973b) 'Theses on the philosophy of history' in *Illuminations* (ed. and with an introduction by Hannah Arendt; trans. H. Zohn), London, Fontana, pp.245–55.

Benjamin, W. (1979) *One Way Street and Other Writings* (trans. E. Jephcott and K. Shorter), London, New Left Books.

Benjamin, W. (1999) *The Arcades Project* (trans. H. Eiland and K. McLaughlin), prepared on the basis of the German volume edited by R. Tiedemann, Cambridge, MA, Harvard University Press.

Bernstein, R. (1991) *The New Constellation*, Cambridge, Polity Press.

Bourdieu, P. (1988) *Homo Academicus* (trans. P. Collier), Cambridge, Polity Press. (First published in France in 1984.)

Bourdieu, P. (1990) *The Logic of Practice* (trans. R. Nice), Cambridge, Polity Press. (First published in France in 1980.)

Bové, P.A. (1986) *Intellectuals in Power: Genealogy of Critical Humanism*, New York, Columbia University Press.

Brown, S.D. and Stenner, P. (2001) 'Being affected: Spinoza and the psychology of emotion', *International Journal of Group Tensions*, vol.30, pp.81–105.

Buchanan, I. (2000) *Michel de Certeau: Cultural Theorist*, London, Sage.

Buck-Morss, S. (1986) 'The flâneur, the sandwichman and the whore: the politics of loitering', *New German Critique*, vol.39, pp.99–139.

Buck-Morss, S. (1989) *The Dialectics of Seeing: Walter Benjamin and the Arcades Project*, Cambridge, MA, MIT Press.

Burke, C., Schor, N. and Whitford, M. (eds) (1994) *Engaging with Irigaray: Feminist Philosophy and Modern European Thought*, New York, Columbia University Press.

Butler, J. (1990) *Gender Trouble: Feminism and the Subversion of Identity*, London, Routledge.

Butler, J. (1993) *Bodies That Matter: On the Discursive Limits of Sex*, London, Routledge.

Butler, J. and Cornell, D. (1998) 'The future of sexual difference: an interview with Judith Butler and Drucilla Cornell', *Diacritics*, vol.28, pp.19–42.

Callon, M. (1986) 'The sociology of an actor-network: the case of the electric vehicle' in Callon, M., Law, J. and Rip, A. (eds) *Mapping the Dynamics of Science and Technology*, London, Macmillan, pp.19–34.

Callon, M. (1998) 'An essay on framing and overflowing: economic externalities revisited by sociology' in Callon, M. (ed.) *The Laws of Markets*, Oxford, Blackwell, pp.244–69.

Callon, M., Meadel, C. and Rabeharisoa, V. (2002) 'The economy of qualities', *Economy and Society*, vol.31, no.2, pp.194–217.

Campbell, D. and Shapiro, M.J. (eds) (1999) *Moral Spaces*, Minneapolis, MN, University of Minnesota Press.

Caputo, J.D. (1993) *Against Ethics*, Bloomington and Indianapolis, IN, Indiana University Press.

Caputo, J.D. (1997) *Deconstruction in a Nutshell: A Conversation with Jacques Derrida*, New York, Fordham University Press.

de Certeau, M. (1984) *The Practice of Everyday Life*, Berkeley, CA, The University of California Press.

de Certeau, M. (1986) *Heterologies: Discourses on the Other*, Manchester, Manchester University Press.

Chanter, T. (1995) *The Ethics of Eros*, London, Routledge.

Cheah, P. (1996) 'Mattering', *Diacritics*, vol.26, pp.108–39.

Cheah, P. and Grosz, E. (1998) 'Of being-two: introduction', *Diacritics*, vol.28, pp.3–18.

Chun, A. (2000) 'The institutional unconscious; or, the prison house of academia', *Boundary 2*, vol.27, no.1, pp.51–74.

Clifford, J. (1986) 'Introduction: Partial truths' in J. Clifford and G.E. Marcus (eds) *Writing Culture: The Poetics and Politics of Ethnography*, Berkeley, University of California Press, pp.1–26.

Clifford, J. (1990) 'Notes on (field) notes' in Sanjek, R. (ed.) *The Makings of Anthropology*, Ithaca, NY, Cornell University Press.

Colebrook, C. (2000) 'From radical representations to corporeal becomings: the feminist philosophy of Lloyd, Grosz and Gatens', *Hypatia: A Journal of Feminist Philosophy*, vol.15, pp.76–93.

Cook, I. and Crang, M. (1995) 'Doing ethnographies', *Concepts and Techniques in Modern Geography* (CATMOG), no.58.

Coomber, R. (2002) 'Signing your life away? Why Research Ethics Committees (REC) shouldn't always require written confirmation that participants in research have been informed of the aims of the study and their rights – the case of criminal populations', *Sociological Research Online*, vol.7, no.1, available at http://www.socresonline.org.uk/7/1/coomber.html [accessed February 2003].

Crang, M. (1997) 'Analyzing qualitative materials' in Flowerdew, R. and Martin, D. (eds) *Methods in Human Geography: A Guide for Students Doing a Research Project*, London, Longman, pp.183–96.

Crang, M. (2001) 'Filed work: making sense of group interviews' in Limb, M. and Dwyer, C. (eds) *Qualitative Methods for Geographers*, London, Arnold, pp.215–33.

Crawford, M.A. (1952) *Introduction to* Old Goriot, New York, Penguin.

Crews, F. (2002) *Postmodern Pooh*, London, Profile Books.

Deleuze, G. (1983) *Nietzsche and Philosophy*, London, Athlone Press. (First published in 1962.)

Deleuze, G. (1988a) *Spinoza: Practical Philosophy* (trans. R Hurley), San Francisco, CA, City Lights Books. (First published in 1970.)

Deleuze, G. (1988b) *Bergsonism*, New York, Zone. (First published in 1966.)

Deleuze, G. (1994) *Difference and Repetition*, London, Athlone Press. (First published in 1968.)

Deleuze, G. (1995) *Negotiations*, New York, Columbia University Press.

Deleuze, G. (2001/1981) *Spinoza* (2 CDs), Paris, Gallimard.

Deleuze, G. and Guattari, F. (1987) *A Thousand Plateaus: Capitalism and Schizophrenia*, Minneapolis, MN, University of Minnesota Press. (First published in 1980; also London, Athlone, 1988.)

Deleuze, G. and Guattari, F. (1994) *What is Philosophy?*, London, Verso. (First published in 1991.)

Derrida, J. (1976) *Of Grammatology*, Baltimore, MD, The Johns Hopkins University Press. (First published in 1967.)

Derrida, J. (1978) *Writing and Difference*, London, Routledge. (First published in 1968.)

Derrida, J. (1981a) *Positions*, Chicago, IL, University of Chicago Press. (First published in France in 1972.)

Derrida, J. (1981b) *Dissemination*, London, Athlone. (First published in France in 1972.)

Derrida, J. (1987) *The Post Card*, Chicago, IL, University of Chicago Press. (First published in France in 1980.)

Derrida, J. (1988) *Limited Inc.*, Evanston, IL, Northwestern University Press.

Derrida, J. (1995) *Points . . . Interviews, 1974–1994*, Stanford, CA, Stanford University Press.

Derrida, J. (1997) *The Politics of Friendship*, London, Verso.

Derrida, J. (1999) 'Word processing', *Oxford Literary Review*, vol.21, pp.3–17.

Derrida, J. (2001) *On Cosmopolitanism and Forgiveness*, London, Routledge. (First published in 1997.)

Dezalay, Y. and Garth, B.G. (1996) *Dealing in Virtue*, Chicago, IL, University of Chicago Press.

Dezalay, Y. and Garth, B.G. (1998) 'Droits de l'homme et philanthropie hégémonique', *Actes de la Recherche en Sciences Sociales*, no.121–122.

Dhairyam, S. (1994) 'Racing the lesbian, dodging white critics' in Doan, L. (ed.) *The Lesbian Postmodern*, New York, Columbia University Press, pp.25–46.

Dick, P.K. (1993) *Do Androids Dream of Electric Sheep?*, London, HarperCollins. (First published in 1968 by Doubleday, New York.)

Driver, F. (2000) 'Field-work in geography', *Transactions of the Institute of British Geographers*, vol.25, pp.267–8.

Driver, F. (2001) *Geography Militant: Cultures of Exploration and Empire*, Oxford, Blackwell.

Duneier, M. (1999) *Sidewalk*, New York, Farrar Strauss Giroux.

Fabian, J. (1983) *Time and the Other: How Anthropology Makes its Object*, New York, Columbia University Press.

Fish, S. (1980) *Is There a Text in this Class? The Authority of Interpretive Communities*, Cambridge, MA, Harvard University Press.

Fish, S. (1989) *Doing What Comes Naturally: Change, Rhetoric, and the Practice of Theory in Literary and Legal Studies*, Oxford, Clarendon Press.

Foucault, M. (1970) *The Order of Things: An Archaeology of the Human Sciences*, London, Tavistock Publications. (First published in France in 1966.)

Foucault, M. (1972) *The Archaeology of Knowledge* (trans. A.M. Sheridan), London, Tavistock Publications. (First published in France in 1969.)

Foucault, M. (1977) *Language, Counter-Memory, Practice* (ed. D.F. Bouchard), Ithaca, NY, Cornell University Press.

Foucault, M. (1981) 'The order of discourse' in *Untying the Text: A Poststructuralist Reader* (ed. R. Young), Boston, MA, London and Henley, Routledge and Kegan Paul. (First published in France in 1970.)

Fox-Keller, E. (1983) *A Feeling for the Organism: The Life and Work of Barbara McClintock*, San Francisco, CA, W.H. Freeman.

Franklin, W. (1979) *Discoverers, Explorers, Settlers: Diligent Writers of Early America*, Chicago, IL, University of Chicago Press.

Franklin, W. (2001) 'Language and event in new world history' in Robertson, S.L. (ed.) *Defining Travel: Diverse Visions*, Jackson, MI, University Press of Mississippi, pp.117–31.

Game, A. and Metcalfe, A. (1996) *Passionate Sociology*, London, Sage.

Garrett, D. (ed.) (1996) *The Cambridge Companion to Spinoza*, Cambridge, Cambridge University Press.

Gatens, M. (1996) *Imaginary Bodies*, London, Routledge.

Gatens, M. and Lloyd, G. (1999) *Collective Imaginings*, London, Routledge.

Gilligan, C. (1990) *In a Different Voice*, Cambridge, MA, Harvard University Press.

Gilligan, C., Ward, J.V. and Taylor, J.M. (eds) (1990) *Mapping the Moral Domain*, Cambridge, MA, Harvard University Press.

Gilloch, G. (1996) *Myth and Metropolis: Walter Benjamin and the City*, Cambridge, Polity Press.

Gilloch, G. (2002) *Walter Benjamin: Critical Constellations*, Malden, MA, and Cambridge, Polity Press.

Godrich, W. (1986) 'The further possibilities of knowledge' in de Certeau, M., *Heterologies: Discourses on the Other*, Manchester, Manchester University Press.

Gordon, A. (1997) *Ghostly Matters*, Minneapolis, MN, University of Minnesota Press.

Graff, G. (1999) 'Headnote' in Veeser, H.A. (ed.) *The Stanley Fish Reader*, Oxford, Blackwell, pp.38–9.

Gross, P. and Levitt, N. (1994) *Higher Superstition: The Academic Left and its Quarrels with Science*, Baltimore, MD, The Johns Hopkins University Press.

Grosz, E. (1994) *Volatile Bodies: Towards a Corporeal Feminism*, Bloomington, IN, Indiana University Press.

Grosz, E. (1999a) 'Darwin and feminism: preliminary investigations for a possible alliance', *Australian Feminist Studies*, vol.14, pp.31–47.

Grosz, E. (ed.) (1999b) *Becomings*, Ithaca, NY, Cornell University Press.

Guattari, F. (1995) *Chaosmosis*, Sydney, NSW, Power Publications.

Gullan-Whur, M. (1998) *Within Reason: A Life of Spinoza*, London, Jonathan Cape.

Hacking, I. (1999) *The Social Construction of What?*, Cambridge, MA, Harvard University Press.

Hardt, M. and Negri, A. (2001) *Empire*, Cambridge, MA, Harvard University Press.

Hass, M. (2000) 'The style of the speaking subject: Irigaray's empirical studies of language production', *Hypatia: A Journal of Feminist Philosophy*, vol.15, pp.64–89.

Holstein, J. and Gubrium, J. (1997) 'Active interviewing' in Silverman, D. (ed.) *Qualitative Research: Theory, Method and Practice*, London, Sage.

Hyndman, J. (1995) 'Solo feminist geography: a lesson in space', *Antipode*, vol.22, no.2, pp.197–208.

Irigaray, L. (1985) *This Sex Which is Not One* (trans. C. Porter), Ithaca, NY, Cornell University Press. (First published in 1977.)

Irigaray, L. (1993a) *An Ethics of Sexual Difference* (trans. C. Burke and G.C. Gill), London, Athlone Press.

Irigaray, L. (1993b) *Je, Tu, Nous: Toward a Culture of Difference* (trans. A. Martin), London, Routledge.

Irigaray, L. (1993c) *Sexes and Genealogies* (trans. G.C. Gill), New York, Columbia University Press.

Irigaray, L. (1996) *I Love To You: Sketch of a Possible Felicity in History* (trans. A. Martin), London, Routledge.

Irigaray, L. (2000) *To Speak is Never Neuter*, London, Athlone Press.

Irigaray, L. (2002) *Between East and West: From Singularity to Community* (trans. S. Pluhacek), New York, Columbia University Press.

Johnson, B. (1981) 'Translator's introduction' in Derrida, J. (1981b).

Johnson, C. (1993) *System and Writing in the Philosophy of Jacques Derrida*, Cambridge, Cambridge University Press.

Kancelbaum, B. (2002) 'Social scientists and institutional review boards', *Social Science Research Council Items and Issues*, Spring, pp.1–5.

Kaplan, A. (1990) 'Working in the archives', *Yale French Studies*, vol.77, pp.103–16.

Kaplan, G.T. and Rogers, L.J. (1990) 'The definition of male and female: biological reductionism and the sanctions of normality' in Gunew, S. (ed.) *Feminist Knowledge: Critique and Construct*, London, Routledge, pp.205–28.

Katz, C. (1994) 'Playing the field: questions of fieldwork in geography', *Professional Geographer*, vol.46, no.1, pp.67–72.

Kerin, J. (1999) 'The matter at hand: Butler, ontology and the natural sciences', *Australian Feminist Studies*, vol.14, pp.91–105.

Killen, M. and Hart, D. (eds) (1995) *Morality in Everyday Life*, Cambridge, Cambridge University Press.

Kirby, V. (1997) *Telling Flesh*, London, Routledge.

Kirby, V. (2001) 'Quantum anthropologies' in Simmons, L. and Worth, H. (eds) *Derrida Downunder*, Palmerston North, Dunmore Press.

Landry, D. and Maclean, G. (eds) (1996) *The Spivak Reader*, London, Routledge.

Lather, P. (1993) 'Fertile obsession: validity after poststructuralism', *The Sociological Quarterly*, vol.34, no.4, pp.673–93.

Lather, P. (2001) 'Applied Derrida: (mis)reading the work of mourning in educational research', available at: http://www.coe.ohio-state.edu/plather/papers/trifonas%20doc.pdf [accessed February 2003].

Lather, P. (2002) 'Qu(e)er(y)ing research/policy/practice', available at: http://www.coe.ohio-state.edu/plather/foucault.pdf [accessed February 2003] (forthcoming in Baker, B. and Heyning, K. (eds) *Dangerous Coagulations? The Uses of Foucault in the Study of Education*, New York, Peter Lang).

Lather, P. and Smithies, C. (1997) *Troubling the Angels: Women Living With HIV/ AIDS*, Boulder, CO, Westview Press.

Latour, B. (1988) 'The politics of explanation: an alternative' in Woolgar, S. (ed.) (1988), pp.155–76.

Latour, B. (1996) *Aramis: Or the Love of Technology*, Cambridge, MA, Harvard University Press.

Latour, B. (1997) 'Stengers's shibboleth. Foreword to Stengers I', *Power and Invention*, Minneapolis, MN, Minnesota University Press, pp.vii–xx.

Latour, B. (1999) *Pandora's Hope: Essays on the Reality of Science Studies*, Cambridge, MA, and London, Harvard University Press (Chapter 2: 'Circulating reference', pp.24–79).

Latour, B. (2002) 'The promises of constructivism', available at: http://www.ensmp.fr/~latour/articles/article/087.html [accessed February 2003] (forthcoming in Ihde, D. (ed.) *Chasing Technoscience: The Matrix of Materiality*, Bloomington, IN, Indiana University Press).

Law, J. and Hassard, J. (eds) (1999) *Actor Network Theory and After*, Oxford, Blackwell.

Levine, D.N. (1985) *The Flight from Ambiguity: Essays in Social and Cultural Theory*, Chicago, University of Chicago Press.

Limb, M. and Dwyer, C. (eds) (2001) *Qualitative Methodologies for Geographers: Issues and Debates*, London, Arnold.

Livingstone, D.N. (1990) 'Geography, tradition, and the scientific revolution: an interpretative essay', *Transactions NS*, vol.15, pp.359–73.

Lloyd, G. (1984) *Man of Reason: 'Male' and 'Female' in Western Philosophy*, London, Methuen.

Lloyd, G. (1996) *Routledge Philosophy Guide to Spinoza and the 'Ethics'*, London, Routledge.

Lorraine, T. (1999) *Irigaray and Deleuze: Experiments in Visceral Philosophy*, Ithaca, NY, Cornell University Press.

Lynch, M. (2000) 'Against reflexivity as a source of academic virtue and source of privileged knowledge', *Theory, Culture and Society*, vol.17, no.3, pp.26–54.

Marcus, G. (1995) 'Ethnography in/of the world system: the emergence of multisited ethnography', *Annual Review of Anthropology*, vol.24, pp.95–117.

Massumi, B. (ed.) (2002) *A Shock to Thought*, London, Routledge.

Metcalf, P. (2002) *They Lie, We Lie*, London, Routledge.

Michael, J. (2000) *Anxious Intellects: Academic Professionals, Public Intellectuals and Enlightenment Values*, Durham, NC, and London, Duke University Press.

Moreau, P. (1996) 'Spinoza's reception and influence' in Garrett, D. (ed.) *The Cambridge Companion to Spinoza*, Cambridge, Cambridge University Press, pp.408–34.

Morris, M. (1992) 'Great moments in social climbing: King Kong and the human fly' in Colomina, B. (ed.) *Sexuality and Space*, Princeton Papers on Architecture, Princeton, NJ, Princeton Architectural Press, pp.1–51.

Naess, A. (1975) *Freedom, Emotion and Self-Subsistence*, Oslo, Universitets-vorlaget.

Naess, A. (1977) 'Spinoza and ecology' in Hessing, S. (ed.) *Speculum Spinozanum 1677–1977*, London, Routledge.

Newman, F. and Holzman, L. (1997) *The End of Knowing*, London, Routledge.

Nicholson, L.J. (ed.) (1990) *Feminism/Postmodernism*, London, Routledge.

Nunberg, G. (1997) 'Farewell to the information age', *The Future of the Book*, Berkeley, CA, University of California Press, pp.103–38.

Office for Human Research Protection (1993) *Protecting Human Subjects* (prepared by R.L. Penslar), Washington, DC, US Department of Health and Human Services (latest edn 2001), available at http://ohrp.osophs.dhhs.gov/irb/irb_guidebook.htm [accessed February 2003].

Outram, D. (1996) 'New spaces in natural history' in Jardine, N., Secord, J. and Spary, E. (eds) *Cultures of Natural History*, Cambridge, Cambridge University Press, pp.249–65.

Paulson, W. (2001) 'For a cosmopolitical philology: lessons from science studies', *Substance # 96*, vol.30, no.3, pp.101–19.

Pellegram, A. (1998) 'The message in paper' in Miller, D. (ed.) *Material Cultures: Why Some Things Matter*, London, UCL Press, pp.103–20.

Pink, S. (2000) *Doing Visual Ethnography*, London, Sage.

Power, M. (1998) *The Audit Society*, Oxford, Oxford University Press.

Prigogine, I. and Stengers, I. (1982) 'Postface: Dynamics from Leibniz to Lucretius', *Hermes: Literature, Science, Philosophy*, Baltimore, MD, The Johns Hopkins University Press, pp.137–55.

Prigogine, I. and Stengers, I. (1984) *Order Out of Chaos: Man's New Dialogue with Nature*, New York, Bantam (reissued 1989).

Rabinow, P. (1977) *Reflections on Fieldwork in Morocco*, Berkeley, CA, The University of California Press.

Rich, A. (1987) *Blood, Bread and Poetry: Selected Prose 1979–1985*, London, Virago.

Richardson, L. (1990) *Writing Strategies: Reaching Diverse Audiences*, London, Sage.

Richardson, L. (2000) 'Writing: a method of inquiry' in Denzin, N. and Lincoln, Y. (eds) *Handbook of Qualitative Research*, London, Sage, pp.923–48.

Rorty, R. (1980) *Philosophy and the Mirror of Nature*, Oxford, Basil Blackwell.

Rorty, R. (1982) *Consequences of Pragmatism*, Brighton, The Harvester Press.

Rorty, R. (1989) *Contingency, Irony and Solidarity*, Cambridge, Cambridge University Press.

Rorty, R. (1991a) *Objectivity, Relativism, and Truth: Philosophical Papers Vol. 1*, Cambridge, Cambridge University Press.

Rorty, R. (1991b) *Essays on Heidegger and Others: Philosophical Papers Vol. 2*, Cambridge, Cambridge University Press.

Rorty, R. (1999) *Philosophy and Social Hope*, Harmondsworth, Penguin.

Rose, G. (2000) 'Practising photography: an archive, a study, some photographs and a researcher', *Journal of Historical Geography*, vol.26, no.4, pp.555–71.

Rothman, D.J. (1991) *Strangers at the Bedside*, New York, Basic Books.

Rothman, D.J. (1997) *Beginnings Count*, New York, Oxford University Press.

Said, E. (1978) *Beginnings: Intention and Method*, Baltimore, MD, and London, The Johns Hopkins University Press.

Said, E. (1982a) 'Opponents, audiences, constituencies, and community', *Critical Inquiry*, vol.9, no.1, pp.1–26.

Said, E. (1982b) 'Reflections on recent American "left" literary criticism' in Spanos,

W.V., Bove, P.A. and O'Hara, D. (eds) *The Question of Textuality: Strategies of Reading in Contemporary American Criticism*, Bloomington, IN, Indiana University Press, pp.11–30.

Said, E. (1983) *The World, the Text and the Critic*, Cambridge, MA, Harvard University Press.

Said, E. (1994) *Representations of the Intellectual: The 1993 Reith Lectures*, London, Viking.

Seale, C. (ed.) (1998) *Researching Society and Culture*, London, Sage.

Shea, C. (2000) 'Don't talk to humans', *Lingua Franca*, September, pp.26–32.

Smith, G. (1989) *Benjamin: Philosophy, Aesthetics and History* (trans. R. Sieburth and L.H. Afreu), Chicago, IL, Chicago University Press.

Sparke, M. (1996) 'Displacing the field in fieldwork' in Duncan, N. (ed.) *BodySpace: Destabilising Geographies of Gender and Sexuality*, London, Routledge, pp.212–33.

Spinoza, B. de (1677 [1996]) *Ethics (Part III On the Origin and Nature of the Emotions)*. Translated by Edwin Curley. London, Penguin.

Spivak, G.C. (1976) 'Preface' in Derrida, J. (1976).

Spivak, G.C. (1989) 'In a Word. Interview' (with Ellen Rooney), *differences: A Journal of Feminist Cultural Studies*, vol.1, no.2, pp.124–56.

St Pierre, E. and Pillow, W. (2000) *Working the Ruins: Feminist Poststructural Theory and Methods in Education*, New York, Routledge.

Stassart, P. and Whatmore, S. (2003) 'Metabolising risk: food scares and the un/re-making of Belgian beef', *Environment and Planning A*, vol.35, no.3, pp.449–62.

Stengers, I. (1994) *L'effet Whitehead*, Paris, Vrins.

Stengers, I. (1996) *Cosmopolitiques*, 5 vols, Paris, La Découverte and Les Empêcheurs de Penser en Rond.

Stengers, I. (1997) *Power and Invention: Situating Science* (trans. P. Bains), Minneapolis, MN, University of Minnesota Press.

Stengers, I. (2000) *The Invention of Modern Science* (trans. D.W. Smith), Minneapolis, MN, University of Minnesota Press.

Strathern, M. (ed.) (2000) *Audit Cultures*, London, Routledge.

Strauss, A. (1987) *Qualitative Analysis for Social Scientists*, Cambridge, Cambridge University Press.

Strauss, A.L. and Glaser, B.G. (1967) *Discovery of Grounded Theory: Strategy for Qualitative Research*, New York, Aldine de Gruyter.

Terdiman, R. (1992) 'The response of the other', *Diacritics*, vol.22, no.2, pp.2–10.

Thrift, N.J. (2000) 'Afterwords', *Environment and Planning D: Society and Space*, vol.18, pp.213–55.

Thrift, N. (2001) 'Still life in nearly present time: the object of nature' in Macnaghten, P. and Urry, J. (eds) *Bodies of Nature*, London, Sage.

Thrift, N. (2002) 'Summoning life' in Cloke, P., Crang, P. and Goodwin, M. (eds) *Envisioning Geography*, London, Arnold.

Thrift, N.J. (2003) 'A geography of unknown lands' in Duncan, J. and Johnson, N. (eds) *Companion to Cultural Geography*, Oxford, Blackwell.

Ulmer, G. (1994) *Heuretics: The Logic of Invention*, Baltimore, MD, The Johns Hopkins University Press.

Varela, F.J. (1999) *Ethical Know-how: Action, Wisdom and Cognitive*, Stanford, CA, Stanford University Press.

Wark, M. (1994) *Virtual Geography: Living with Global Media Events*, Bloomington, IN, Indiana University Press.

Weed, E. (1994) 'The question of style' in Burke, C., Schor N. and Whitford, M. (eds) (1994), pp.79–110.

Whitehead, A.N. (1978) (1929) *Process and Reality*, New York, The Free Press.

Whitford, M. (1991) *Luce Irigaray: Philosophy in the Feminine*, London, Routledge.

Whitford, M. (1994) 'Irigaray, utopia and the death drive' in Burke, C., Schor, N. and Whitford, M. (eds) (1994), pp.379–400.

Wilson, E.A. (1999) 'Somatic compliance: feminism, biology and science', *Australian Feminist Studies*, vol.14, pp.7–19.

Woolgar, S. (ed.) (1988) *Knowledge and Reflexivity*, London, Sage.

Zola, E. (1965) 'The novel as social science' in R. Ellman and C. Fiedelson, Jr (eds) *The Modern Tradition: Backgrounds of Modern Literature*, New York, Oxford University Press, pp.270–89. (First published 1880.)

Index